IMAGES
of America

MARITIME CECIL COUNTY

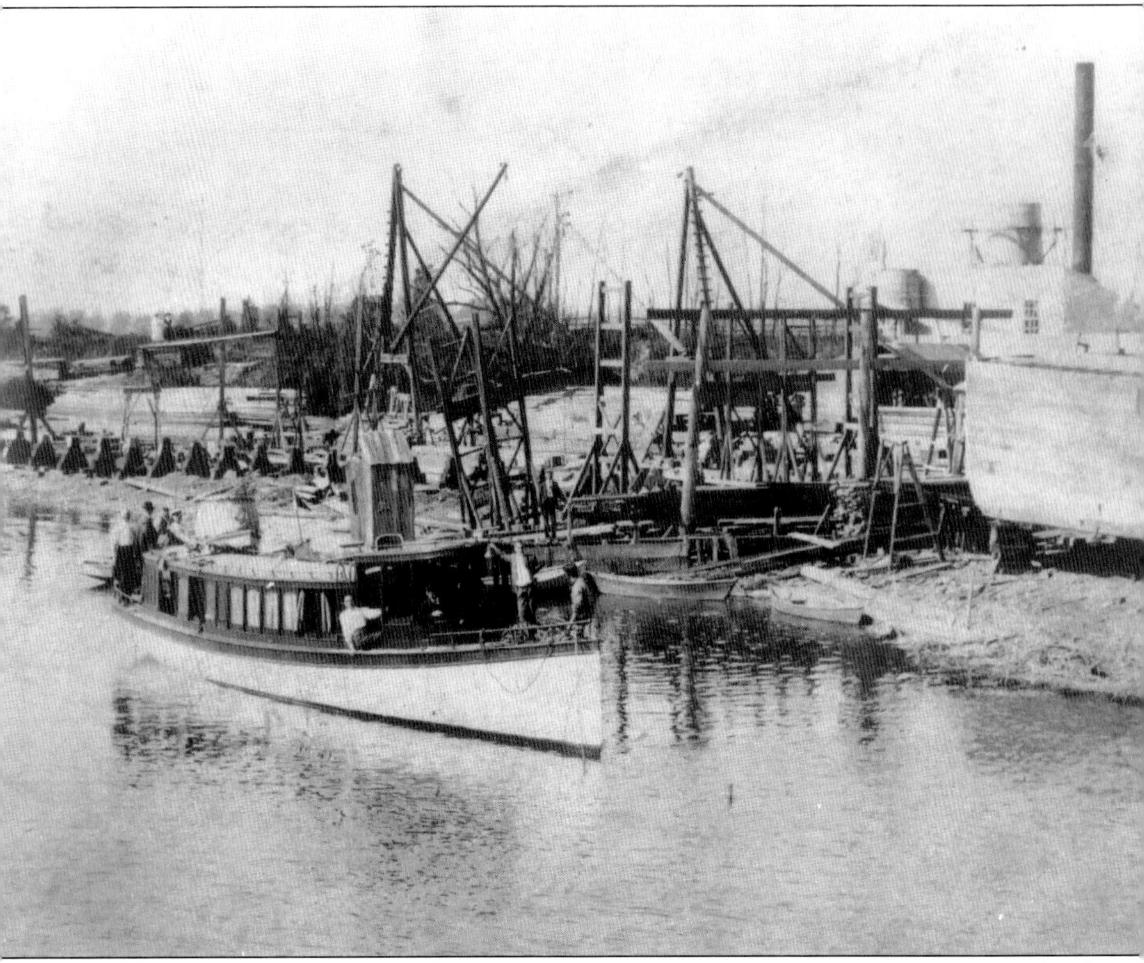

A cabin steam-powered passenger cruiser travels past the Deibert Brothers boatyard on Little Elk Creek at Elk Landing in the early 1900s. (Courtesy of Jack Manning.)

On the Cover: A c. 1900 photograph by Alonzo Barry, who owned a photographic gallery in Port Deposit, promotes sailing for tourists staying at the Falls Hotel. (Courtesy of the Port Deposit Heritage Corporation.)

IMAGES
of America

MARITIME CECIL COUNTY

Christopher Knauss

ARCADIA
PUBLISHING

ISBN 978-0-7385-4446-5

Published by Arcadia Publishing
Charleston, South Carolina

Printed in the United States of America

Library of Congress Catalog Card Number: 2007920919

For all general information contact Arcadia Publishing at:
Telephone 843-853-2070
Fax 843-853-0044
E-mail sales@arcadiapublishing.com
For customer service and orders:
Toll-Free 1-888-313-2665

Visit us on the Internet at www.arcadiapublishing.com

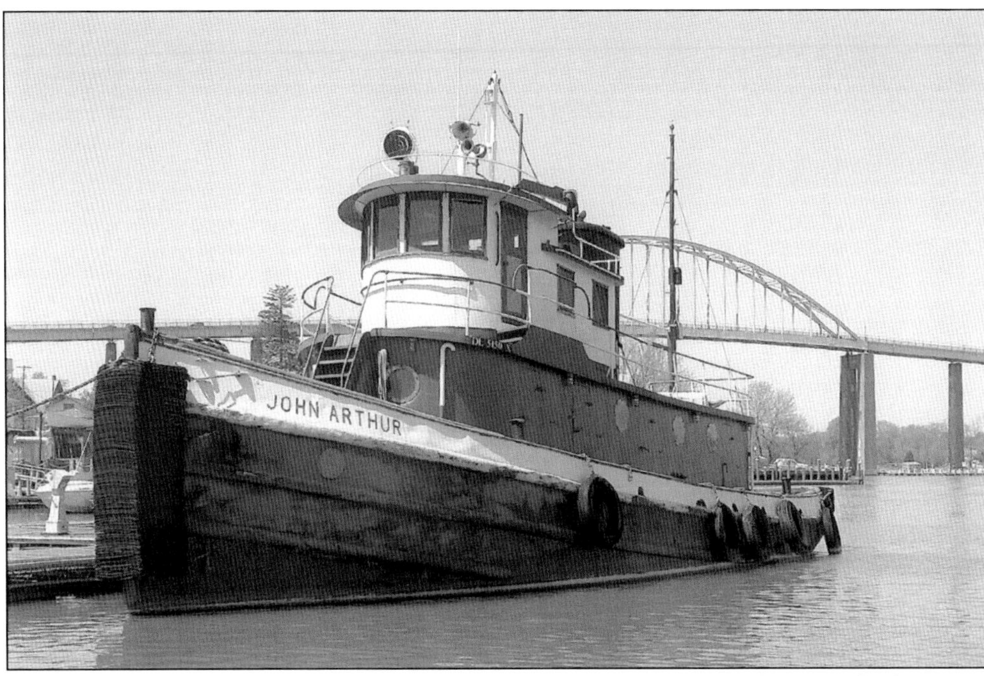

Cecil Countian George Coates went looking for an engine and found one in the bayous of Louisiana, attached to a 1942 tugboat named *John Arthur*. He bought the engine and the boat and piloted it all the way home to Chesapeake City in the spring of 2004. Coates now conducts tours on the *John Arthur* and opens it to the public during special occasions. (Photograph by Christopher Knauss.)

Contents

ACKNOWLEDGMENTS

This book was made possible by the Historical Society of Cecil County and the many people who have contributed their time and photographs to the society over the years. Many of the society's pictures appear in this pictorial history. Thanks to Mike Dixon, president of the society; to Eric Jodlbauer, collections manager; and to Milt Diggins, the society's journal editor, who greeted me enthusiastically when I first entered the building on Main Street and patiently answered my numerous questions throughout compiling this book. I would also like to thank Barbara MacKenzie for her scanning efforts and Billie Todd, who helped me with some computer problems.

Jack Manning, of North East, also contributed many photographs as well as his extensive knowledge of waterfowling history. Others contributing, for which I am grateful, include Barbara Brown, Perryville Town Commissioner; Erika Quesenbery, curator of the Paw Paw Museum; Richard LeGates; Larry Ortt; Lee Collins; Jim Tomlin, project manager of the U.S. Army Corps of Engineers, Chesapeake City; David Hawley, Chesapeake and Delaware Canal engineer; the Port Deposit Heritage Corporation; the Chesapeake Bay Maritime Museum, the Mariner's Museum; the U.S. Naval Academy Museum; the Upper Bay Museum; the Cecil County Public Library; William Betts, curator of Tolchester Beach Revisited Museum; Kim Righi of Mount Harmon Plantation; *Fishing in Maryland* magazine; the many folks at the National Archives, the Maryland State Archives, and the Library of Congress; and Chesapeake Publishing and *Mariner* magazine.

Special thanks go to my family for their support and encouragement: my wife, Janice; my children, Claire and Lukas; my parents, Don and Joe Ann; my brothers, Jim, Lee, and Steve; and my sister, Anne. This book is dedicated to them.

Introduction

Spaniards entered the Chesapeake Bay a century or more before the settlement of Maryland. In 1588, the Spanish mariner Vincente Gonzales explored all the way to the head of the Chesapeake, but the first documented accounts of the bay's shores are those prepared by an Englishman, Capt. John Smith. In 1608, Smith left Jamestown, Virginia, twice on expeditions of discovery in a small sailboat called a shallop. These ventures included the mapping of the Chesapeake Bay. The second undertaking led Smith and his crew to the head of the Chesapeake and into Cecil County.

Smith wrote about four branches of water in the county: the Sassafras, Elk, Northeast, and Susquehanna Rivers. The Native Americans at that time used canoes for traveling and for trading. Smith noted that the Susquehannocks possessed iron hatchets that they purchased from Northern tribes. The northern Native Americans probably acquired them from French fur traders, making that the first record of foreign trading goods reaching the Chesapeake.

European civilization of the bay had begun, and settlers sailed into the region looking to capitalize on new trade and undiscovered riches. Water travel was the easiest and most economical method of transportation, and trading posts and small towns developed along strategic geographic points. With their emigration, Europeans brought new tools and techniques for cultivating the land. Agriculture and the means of delivery progressed, and the region was transformed into a booming rural economy.

Located within the major north-south transportation corridor of the United States, with 241 miles of shoreline alongside the massive Chesapeake Bay, Cecil County and its history are defined by waterfront life. This pictorial history attempts to present an entertaining general history of the county's waterways and the culture that flourishes upon its shores.

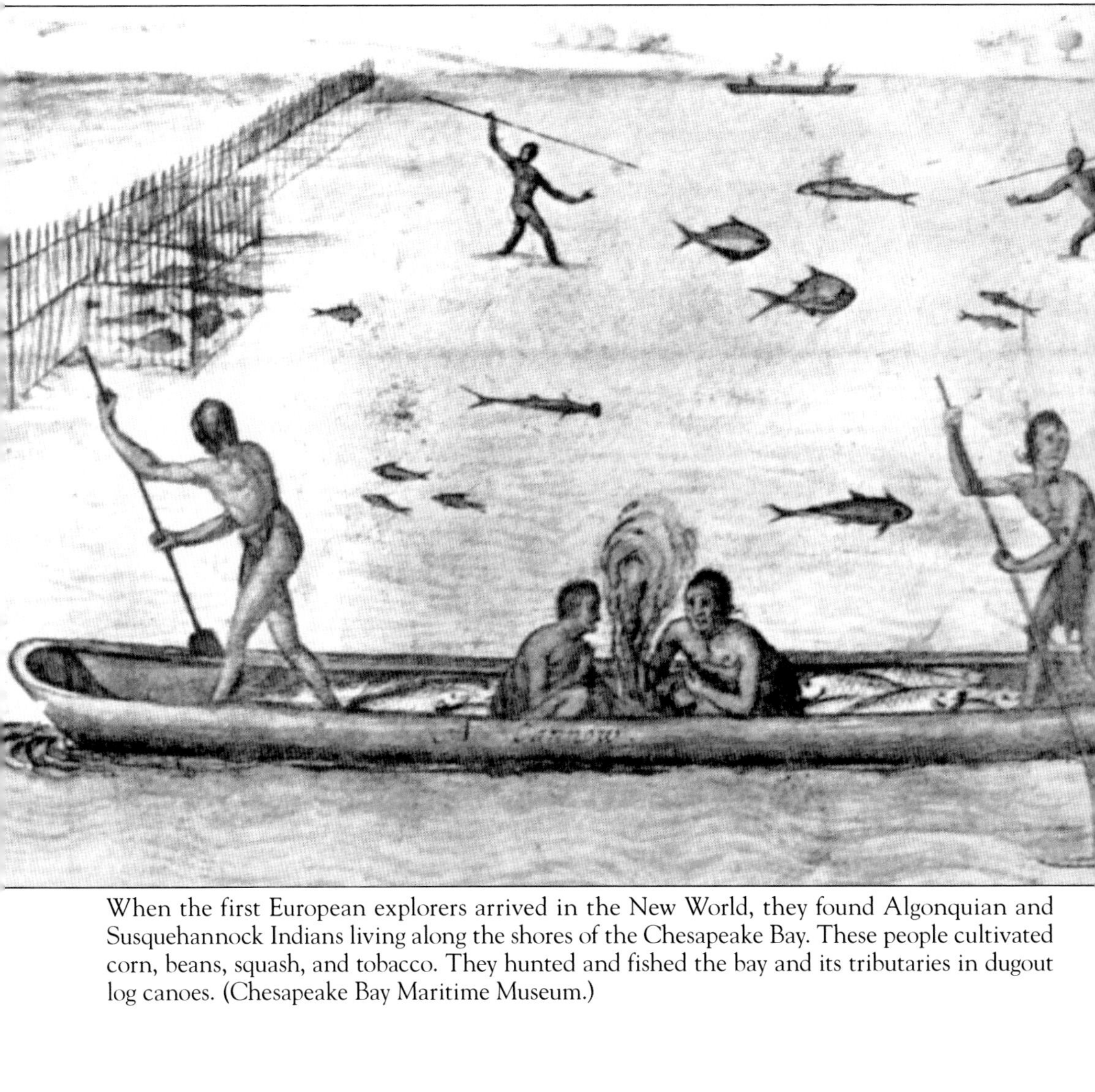

When the first European explorers arrived in the New World, they found Algonquian and Susquehannock Indians living along the shores of the Chesapeake Bay. These people cultivated corn, beans, squash, and tobacco. They hunted and fished the bay and its tributaries in dugout log canoes. (Chesapeake Bay Maritime Museum.)

One

Trading Posts

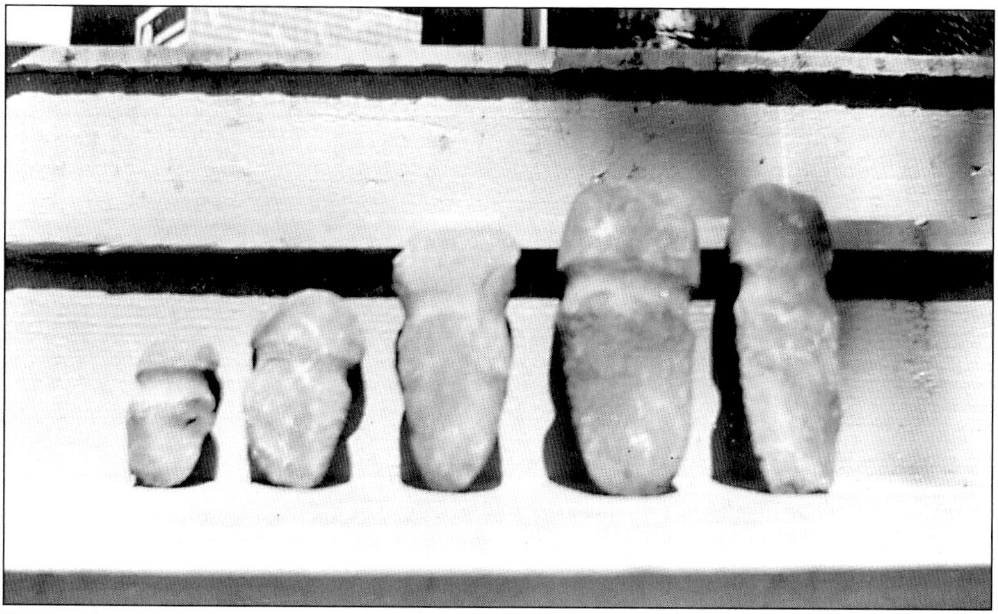

During the initial settlement of Cecil County and through much of the Colonial era, land travel was difficult, and most journeys were made by water. The county developed like much of the Chesapeake Bay region because of water accessibility and the ability to grow sought-after tobacco on level land. People used the waterways because they offered easier, speedier transportation of trade goods. Trading posts opened along Cecil County's five major rivers. The native Susquehannock Indians traded furs with the Dutch, the French, and the English, including William Claiborne, who established one of Maryland's first settlements on Cecil's Garrett Island, then known as Palmer's Island. Tobacco soon became the staple commodity of Maryland. In the 1720s, 30,000 to 35,000 hogsheads crammed with tobacco were yearly exported to Great Britain. Native American tool relics found along the rivers in Cecil County include arrowheads and implements of warfare. The Native Americans traded skins and furs with the "white men" in exchange for knives, cloth, mirrors, and other objects. Not all of the Native Americans were friendly, and white settlers built a fort on Palmer's Island, for security. (Courtesy of the Historical Society of Cecil County.)

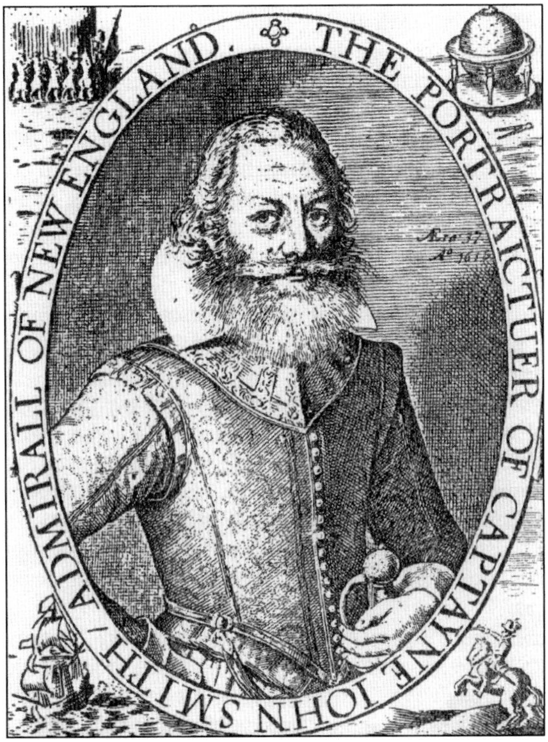

Capt. John Andrew Smith (1580–1631) was an English soldier, sailor, and author. Between the spring of 1607 and the fall of 1609, Captain Smith and a dozen crewmen explored the Chesapeake Bay and its tributaries, sailing and rowing over 3,000 miles in an open boat called the *Discovery Barge*. Smith was the first white man to explore and document the region now called Cecil County. Through his written accounts, we know about the Native Americans who inhabited the area and what their life was like during that time. He explored the Northeast, Elk, Sassafras, and Susquehanna Rivers. (Capt. John Smith's *General History*.)

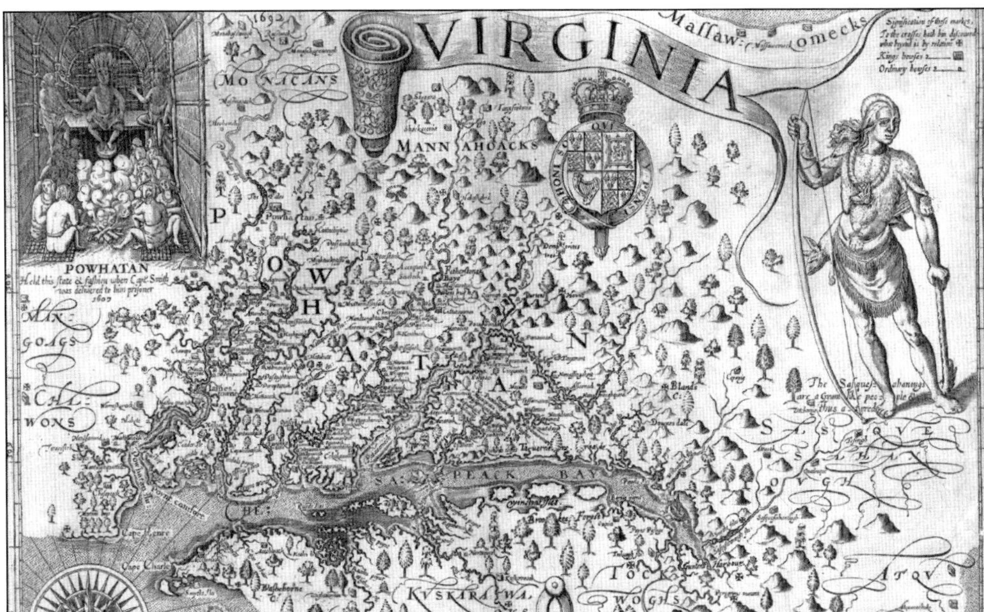

Captain Smith's expedition had three goals: to search for silver and gold, trade with the native people and assess their strength, and find the fabled Northwest Passage to India. Smith and his crew succeeded only in their second objective, but they also created the first detailed historical record of the Chesapeake. Smith mapped the bay in the process and published his map in England in 1612. Throughout the 17th century, that map served as the primary guide for bay settlers, who formed the foundation for what would become the United States. (Capt. John Smith's map of 1612.)

In April 1607, a trio of English ships—the *Susan Constant*, the *Godspeed*, and the *Discovery*—arrived at the mouth of the Chesapeake Bay. On board was a courageous captain named John Smith whose explorations of the vast estuary would open up a new continent. Today replicas of the *Susan Constant*, left, and *Godspeed* (shown here) and the *Discovery* are moored at Jamestown Settlement's pier for visitors to explore. (Courtesy of the Jamestown-Yorktown Foundation.)

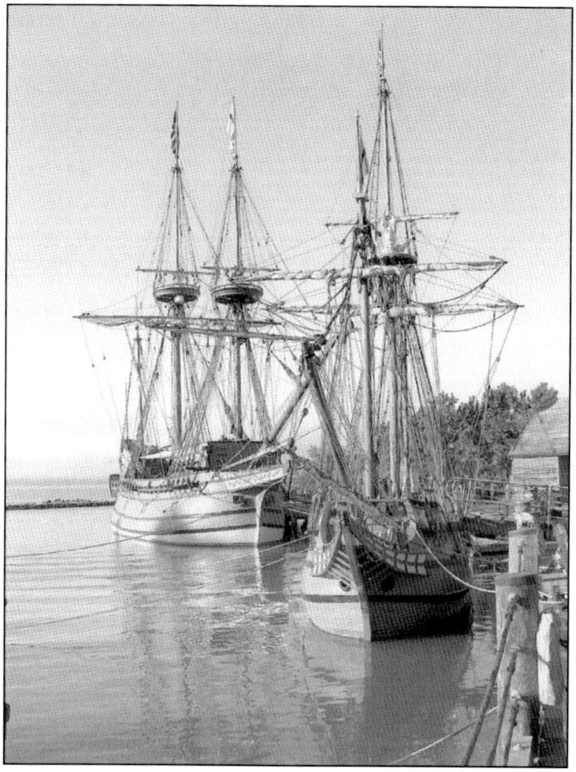

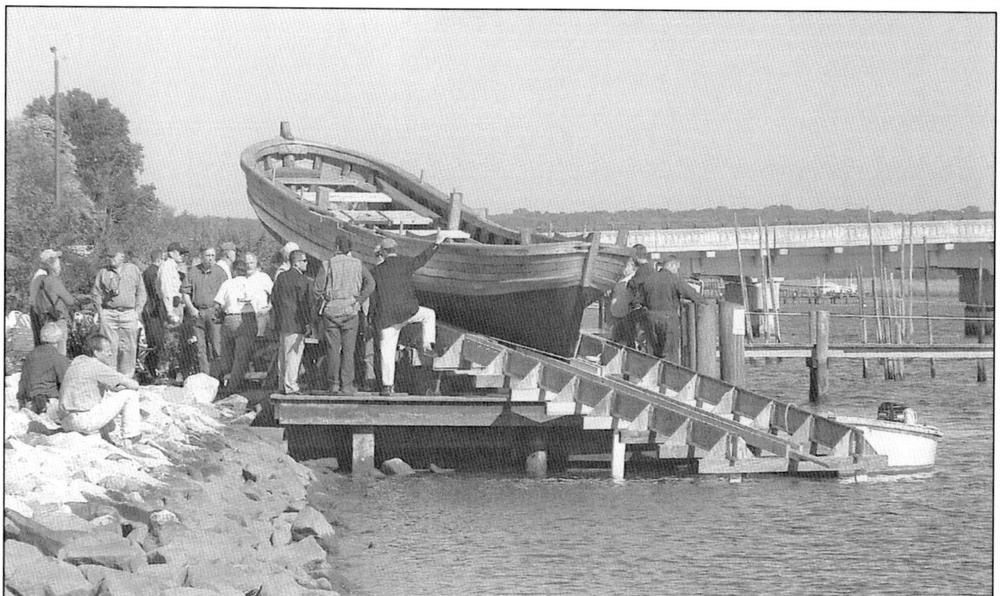

A replica of Capt. John Smith's *Discovery Barge* shallop, built in Chestertown, awaits its launch into the Chester River on Friday, November 4, 2005. Smith used the shallop to make his exploration of the Chesapeake Bay in 1608. Most likely, the vessel was built in England and transported to North America in the hold of the *Susan Constant*, the flagship of the Jamestown fleet. (Photograph by Christopher Knauss.)

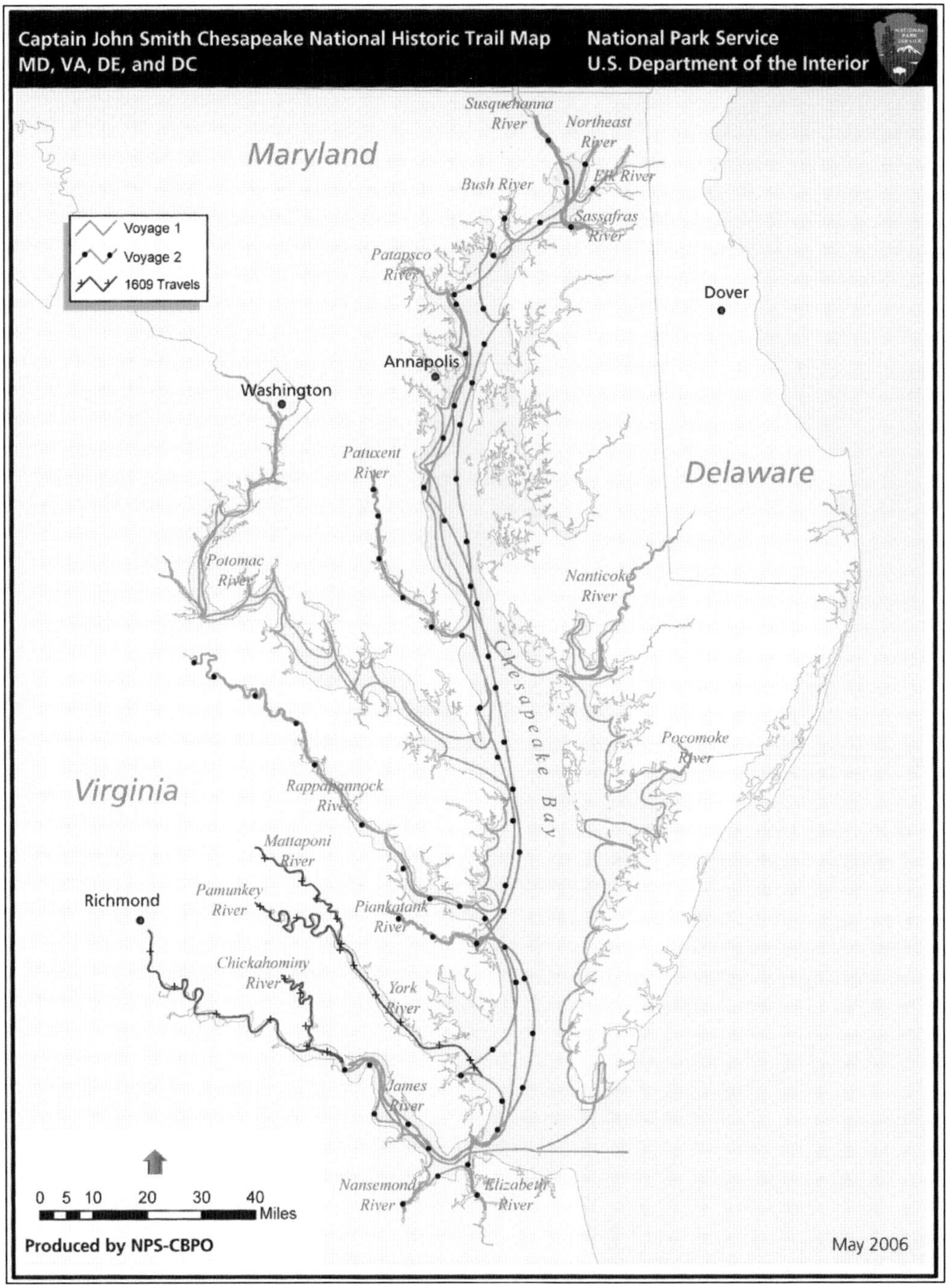

Legislation authorizing the Capt. John Smith Chesapeake National Historic Trail passed Congress in December 2006. Smith and his compatriots covered thousands of miles along the Chesapeake Bay and its tributaries in multiple voyages from Jamestown in the first decade of the 1600s. The Smith Trail is the 17th National Historic Trail that Congress has established and the first completely aquatic trail. (Courtesy of the National Park Service.)

A group of Susquehannock Indians who lived on the Susquehanna River visited Capt. John Smith on the Tockwogh (Sassafras) River in the summer of 1608. Smith wrote, "Sixtie of those gyant-like people came downe, with presents of Venison, Tobacco-pipes three feet in length, Baskets, Targets, Bowes and Arrowes." Among the Susquehannocks visiting was the chief, whose physical appearance astonished Smith: "The calfe of whose leg was three quarters of a yard about, and all the rest of his limbes so answerable to that proportion, that he seemed the goodliest man we ever beheld." (Capt. John Smith's map of 1612.)

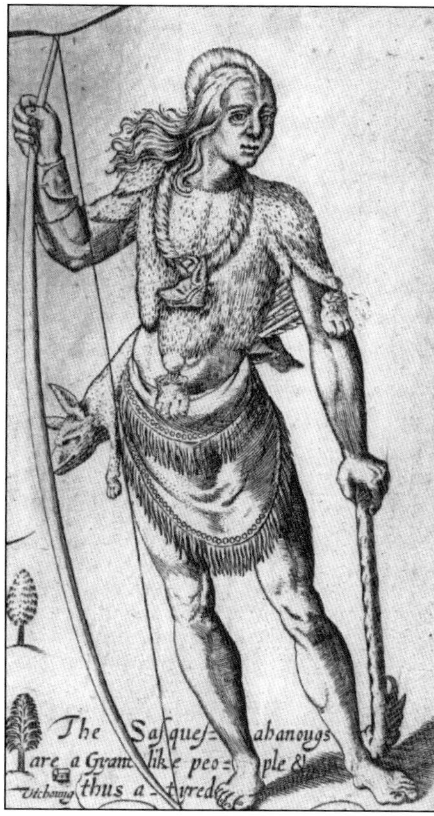

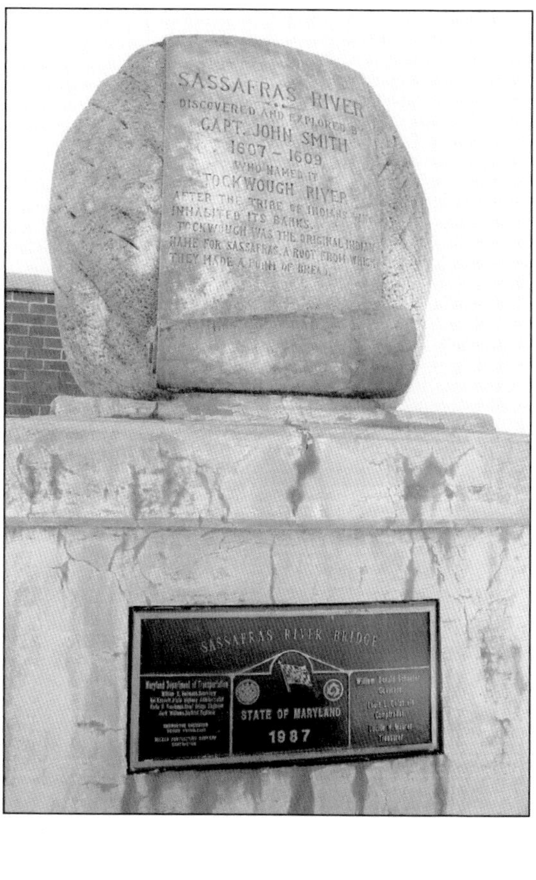

Motorists traveling over the Sassafras River Bridge may wonder what the round structure is at the top of the bridge monument. The round piece depicts a loaf of Native American bread. The Tockwogh Indians ground the root of the tockwogh (arrow arum) plant to make meal for the bread. (Photograph by Christopher Knauss.)

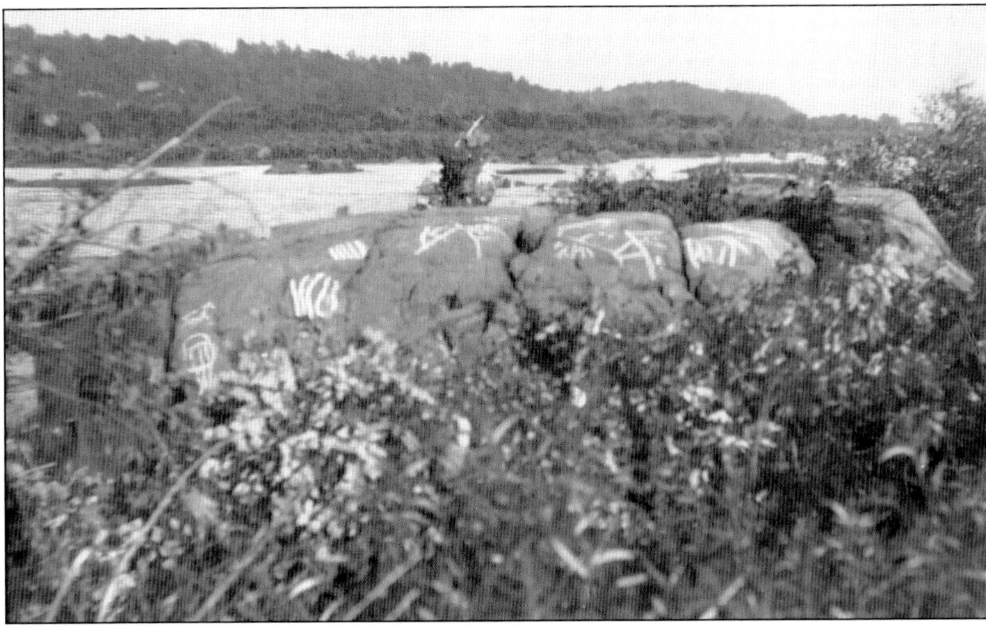

Native American petroglyphs, prehistoric rock carvings, were photographed at several locations along the Susquehanna River, including these at Bald Friar. The pictures carved included items like fish, turkeys, the sun, crabs, and trees. When William Penn asked about them, the Native Americans at the time said they had been there before the time of their grandfathers' grandfathers. Some of the rock carvings were preserved before the area was flooded over by the building of the Conowingo Dam. (Courtesy of the Historical Society of Cecil County).

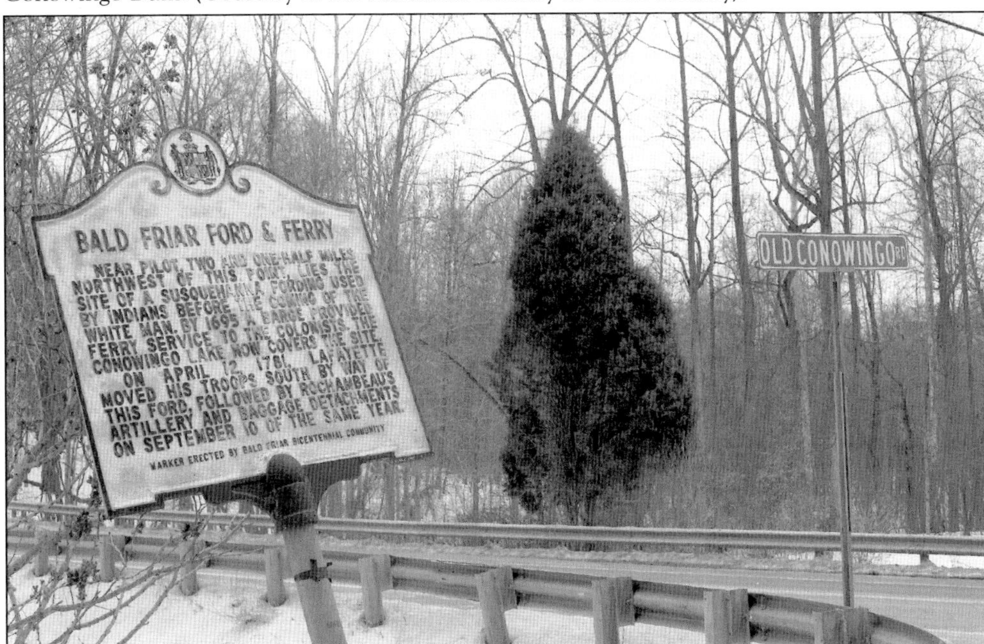

This weather-beaten historical signage in upper northwest Cecil County is near the location of much Native American and Colonial activity. A barge providing ferry service across the Susquehanna was known to exist in the area as early as 1695. (Photograph by Christopher Knauss.)

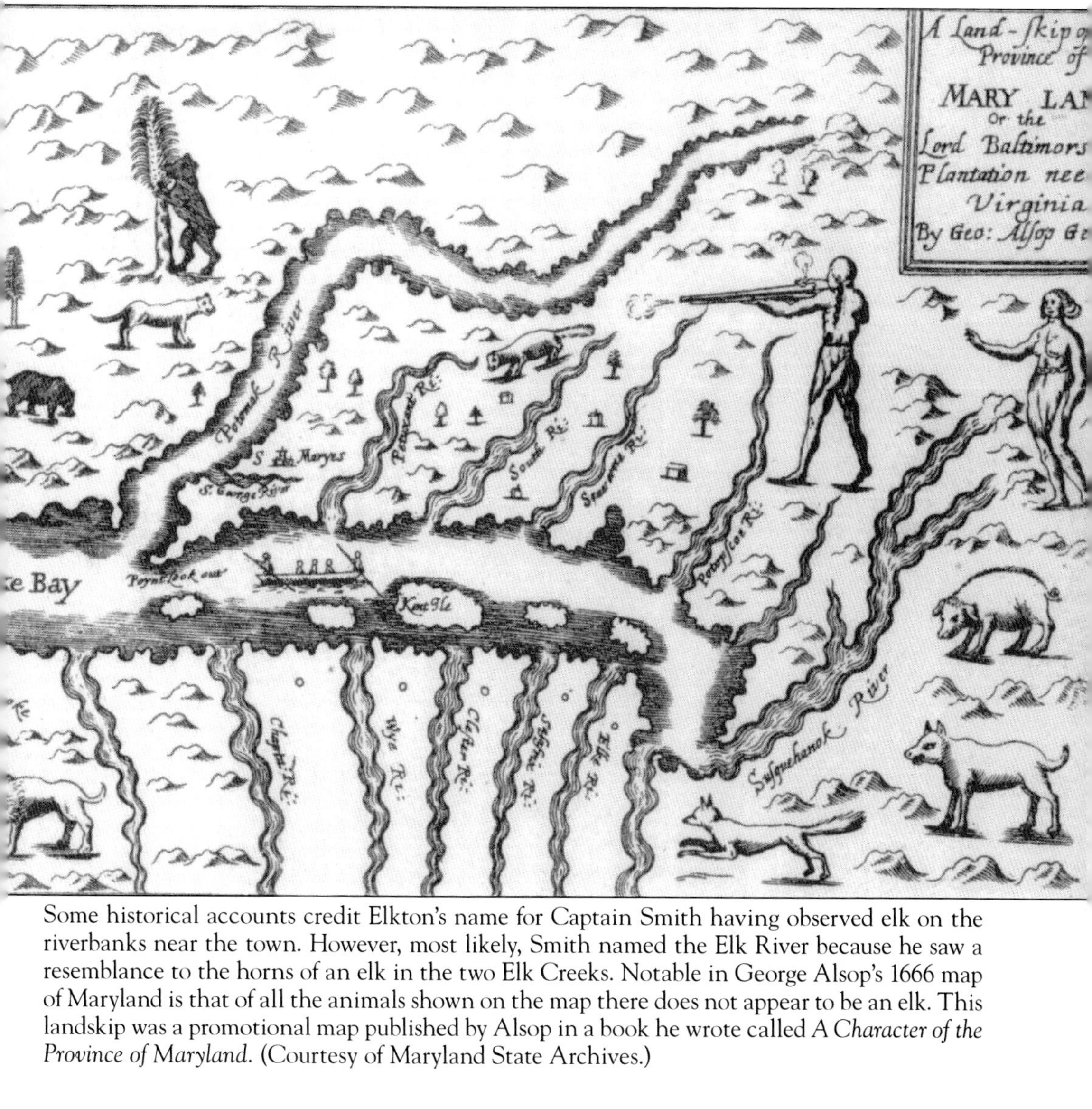

Some historical accounts credit Elkton's name for Captain Smith having observed elk on the riverbanks near the town. However, most likely, Smith named the Elk River because he saw a resemblance to the horns of an elk in the two Elk Creeks. Notable in George Alsop's 1666 map of Maryland is that of all the animals shown on the map there does not appear to be an elk. This landskip was a promotional map published by Alsop in a book he wrote called *A Character of the Province of Maryland.* (Courtesy of Maryland State Archives.)

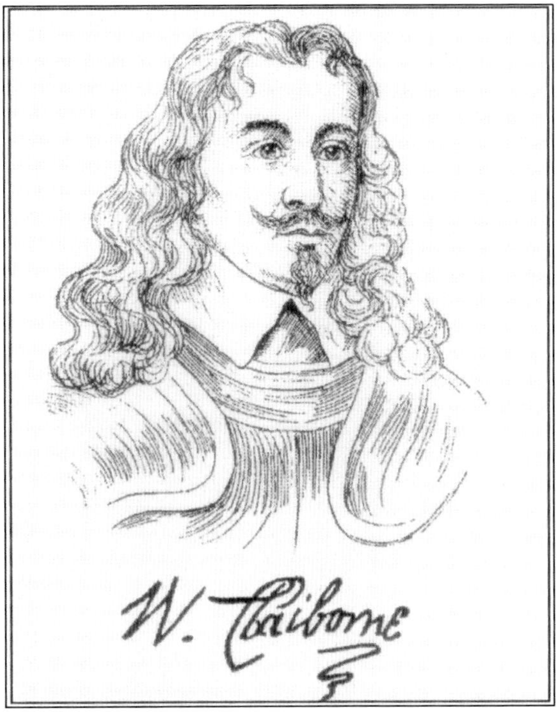

In 1627, William Claiborne, an Englishman, obtained a license that permitted him to trade with the Native Americans in the Chesapeake Bay region, and he became active in the fur trade. His trading activities took him throughout the Bay region, and he ultimately established two trading posts, one on Kent Island and another on Palmer's Island at the mouth of the Susquehanna River, what is now considered Cecil County. Claiborne is credited with building the first large boat in Maryland, the pinnace *Long Tayle*, built to defend his trading posts against enemies. (Courtesy of Chesapeake Publishing.)

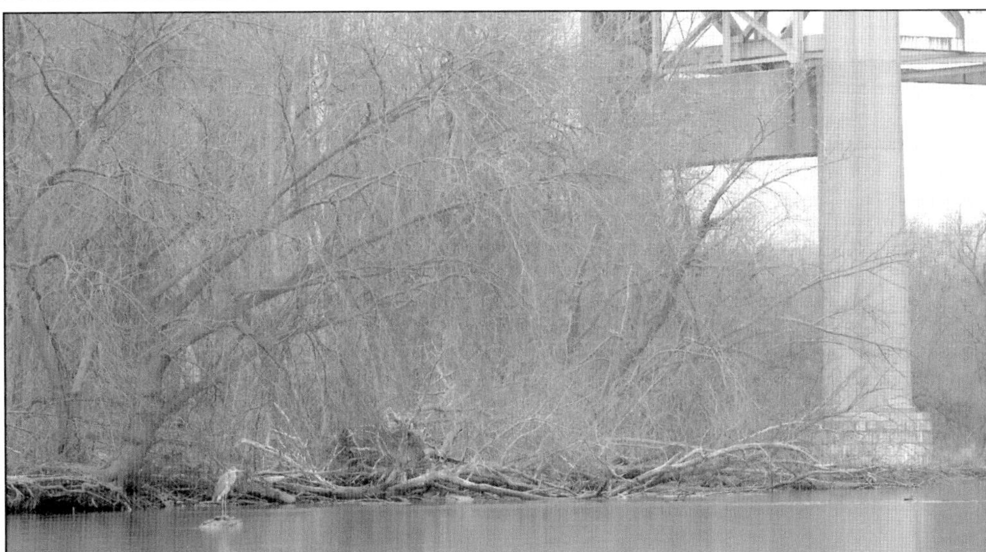

Though Cecil County was not established by Lord Baltimore and his colonists until 1674, a small settlement came prior to that time. In 1622, Edward Palmer received a land grant for Palmer's Island, now known as Garrett Island, on the lower Susquehanna River. He intended to found a university but was not successful. In 1633, William Claiborne opened a trading post on Palmer's Island in what was then called Virginia. He traded for beaver fur with the Susquehannocks. A small settlement and a plantation surrounded the post. The British built Fort Conquest there in 1637 after evicting Claiborne and his Virginia traders. The U.S. Fish and Wildlife Service purchased Garrett Island in June 2005, and the island is now protected as a national wildlife refuge. (Photograph by Christopher Knauss.)

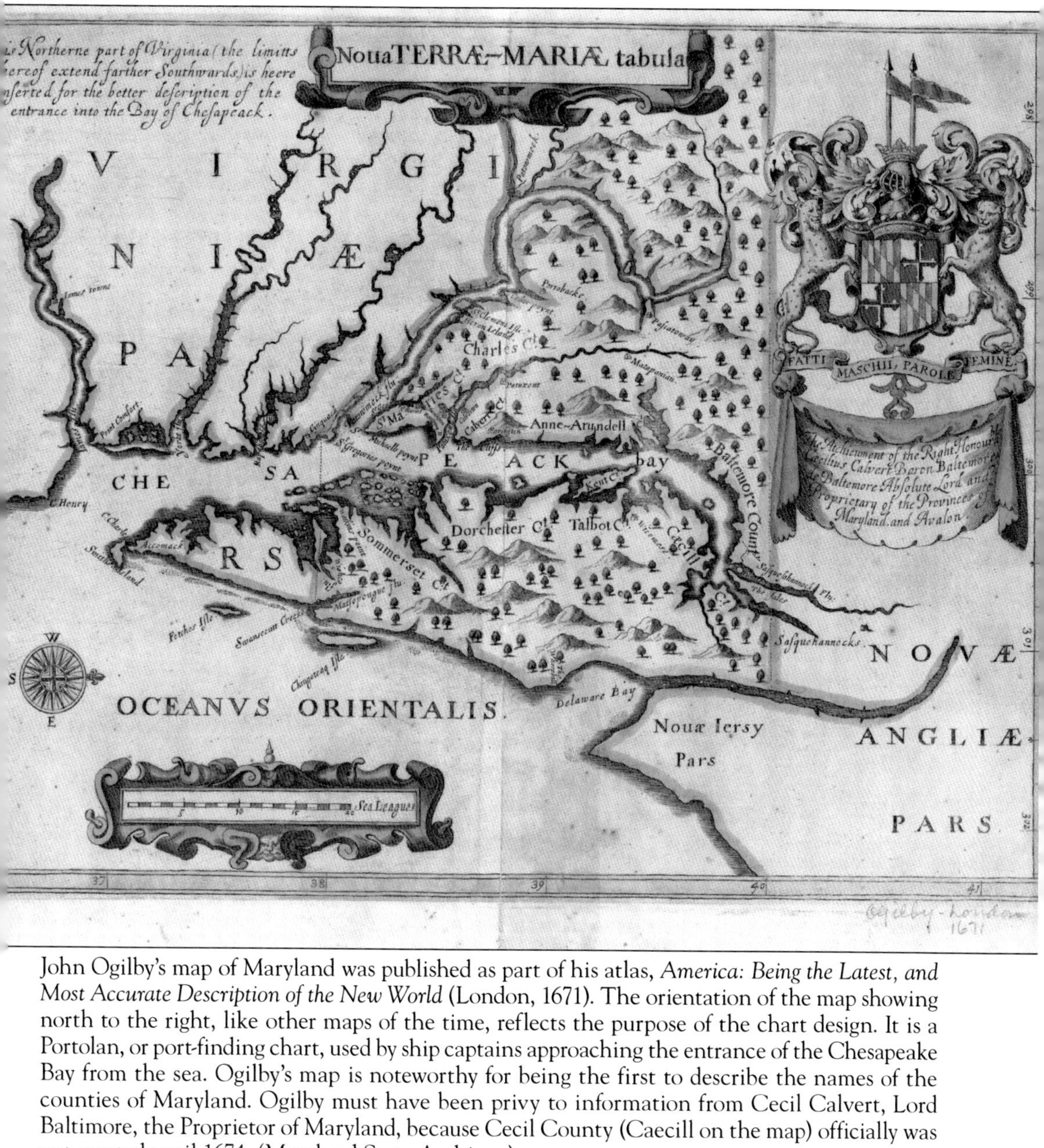

John Ogilby's map of Maryland was published as part of his atlas, *America: Being the Latest, and Most Accurate Description of the New World* (London, 1671). The orientation of the map showing north to the right, like other maps of the time, reflects the purpose of the chart design. It is a Portolan, or port-finding chart, used by ship captains approaching the entrance of the Chesapeake Bay from the sea. Ogilby's map is noteworthy for being the first to describe the names of the counties of Maryland. Ogilby must have been privy to information from Cecil Calvert, Lord Baltimore, the Proprietor of Maryland, because Cecil County (Caecill on the map) officially was not created until 1674. (Maryland State Archives.)

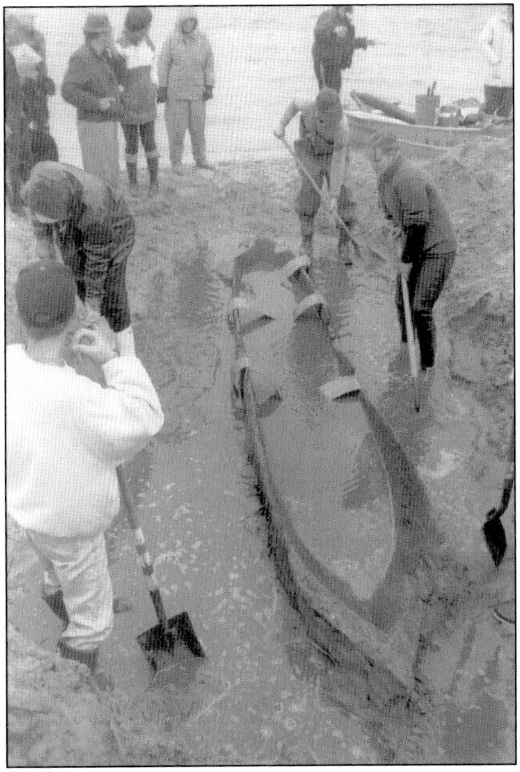

Archeologists uncover a dugout canoe found in October 1993 at the confluence of the Choptank River and La Trappe Creek in Talbot County, Maryland. The canoe was believed to be a mix of European and Native American craftsmanship dating back to the 1600s or 1700s. Using mostly tulip poplar trees, Native Americans throughout the Chesapeake region made the canoes by using controlled burning and scraping out the charred remains with oyster shells and crude tools. (Photograph by Roxanne Doster Watts; courtesy of the *Star Democrat.*)

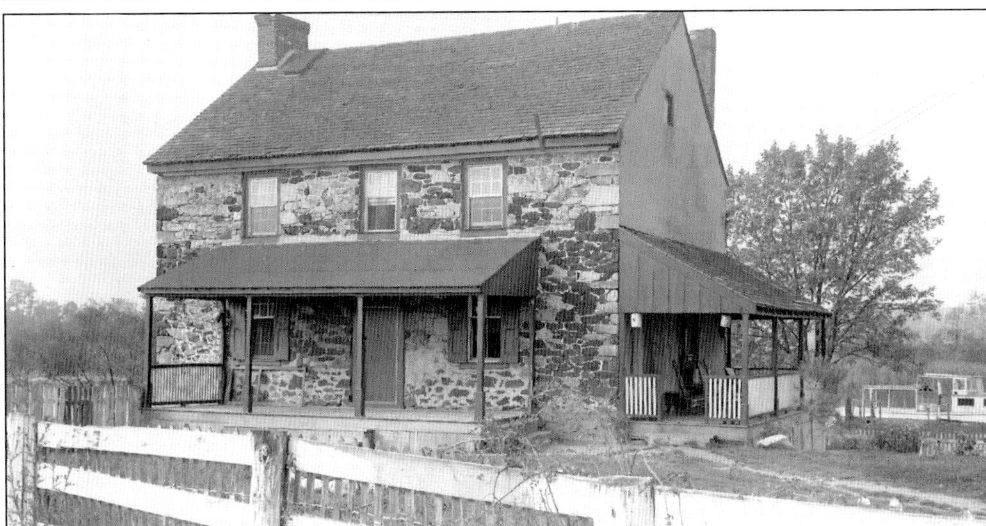

One of Cecil County's most historic tracts of land is situated at the confluence of the Little Elk and Big Elk Creeks. The site was one the area's earliest transportation corridors. In 1655, Minquas (Susquehannock) Indians presented Gov. John Claudius Rising of New Sweden with the land called Sahakitko in exchange for the promise the Swedes would establish a trading post. Zebulon Hollingsworth, in the early part of the 18th century, acquired two parcels of land at the site, now known as Elk Landing. This stone building at Elk Landing, shown in 1936, was originally constructed as a dwelling and later became a tavern. Note the boat on the water to the right near the building. (Library of Congress.)

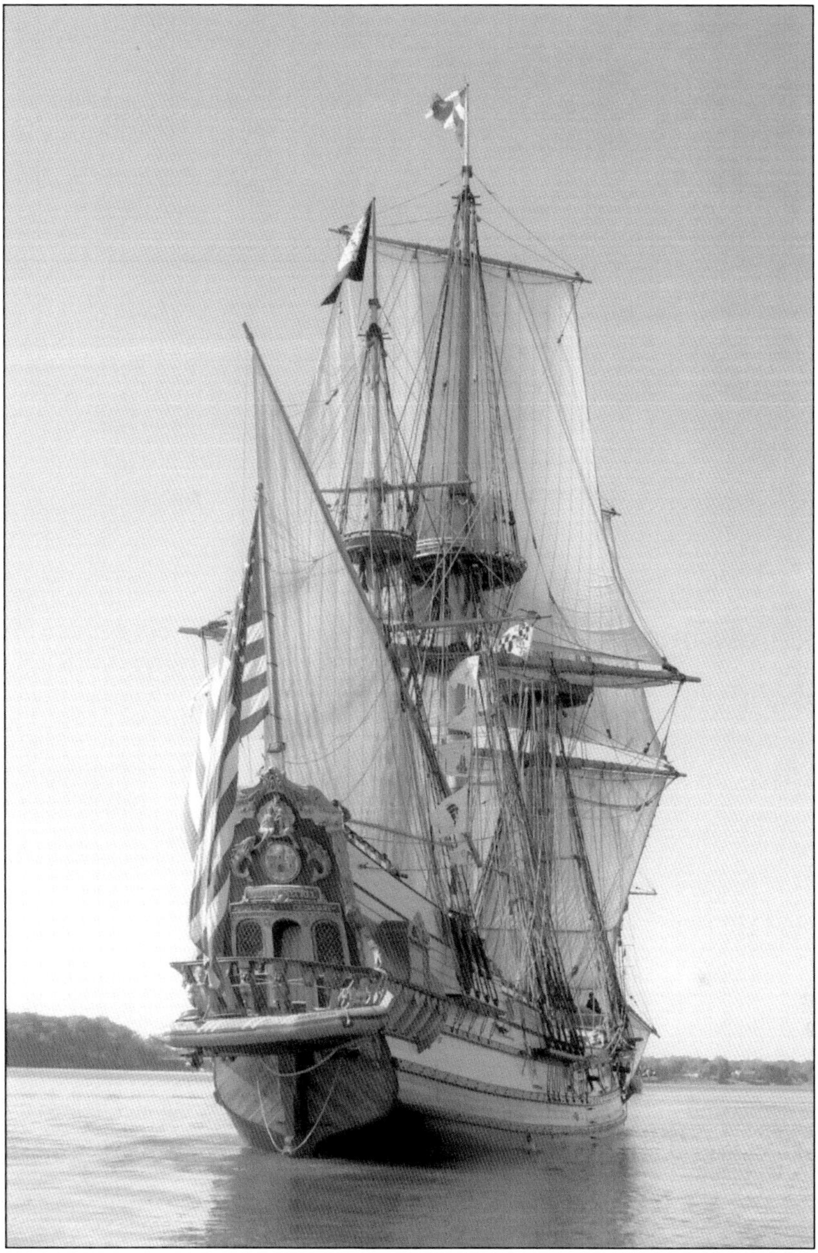

About 1690, Jon Hanson Steelman, a Swede, built a wooden structure at Elk Landing and established a trading post with the Native Americans. The original *Kalmar Nyckel* sailed from Sweden to the New World in 1638 to establish the first permanent European settlement in the Delaware Valley, the colony of New Sweden in present-day Wilmington, Delaware. She made a total of four round-trip crossings of the Atlantic—more than any other ship of the era. Many of Cecil County's early settlers came from Delaware and as far north as Philadelphia. By the terms of its charter, Maryland extended to the Delaware Bay, the Delaware River, and to the mouth of the Schuylkill River in Pennsylvania. This modern-day reproduction of the *Kalmar Nyckel* was photographed while it participated in the schooner *Sultana*'s annual Downrigging Weekend on the Chester River in Chestertown, Maryland. (Photograph by Christopher Knauss.)

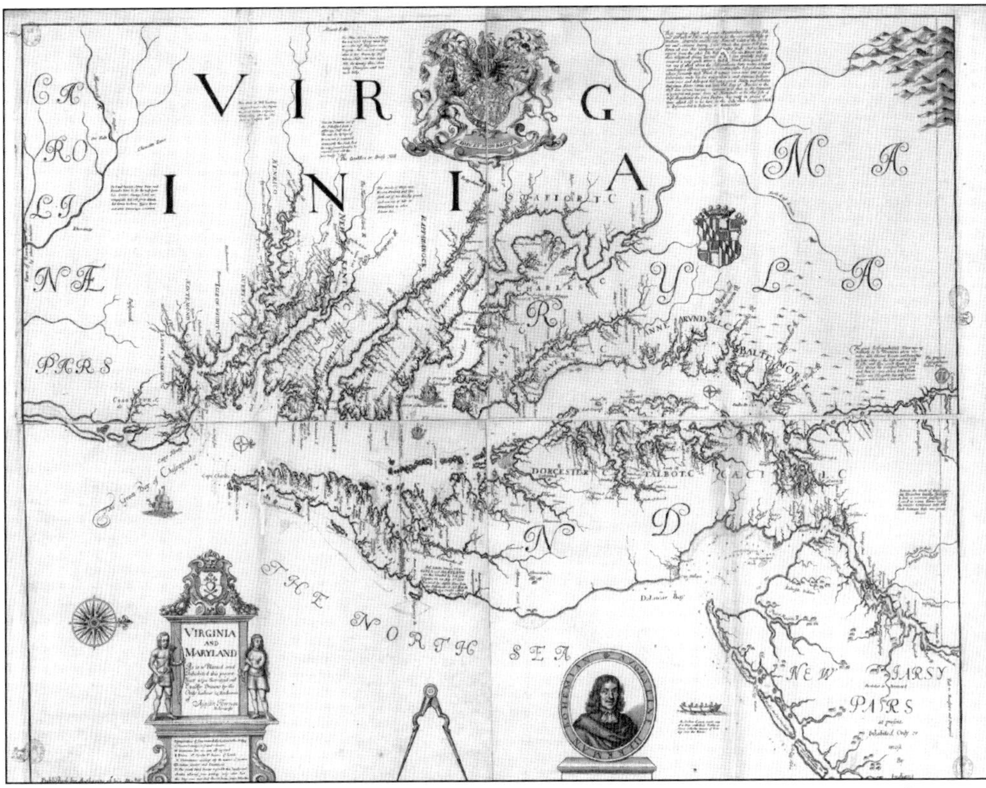

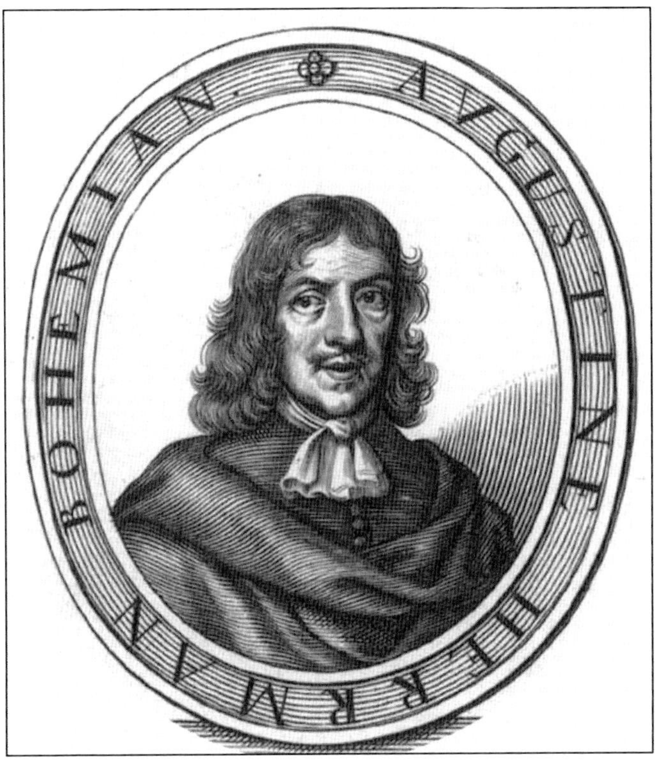

Augustine Herrman first traveled to Cecil County in the mid-1600s on a mission from New Amsterdam (New York) governor Peter Stuyvesant. Herrman was an expert mapmaker and brokered a deal with Lord Baltimore to make a map of Maryland in exchange for extensive Cecil County land holdings. Herrman was also the force behind the naming of "Cecill County," which was previously part of Baltimore County. The county was named for Caecilius Calvert, second Baron Baltimore (1605–1675), who was the first proprietary governor of the colony of Maryland from 1632 until his death in 1675. (Augustine Herrman's 1670 Map of Virginia and Maryland, Maryland State Archives.)

In 1680, land consisting of most of Port Deposit and Perryville was given by Lord Baltimore to his cousin Col. George Talbot under the name Susquehanna Manor. It was hoped that Talbot would extend the rule of Lord Baltimore to Delaware Bay. But in 1684, Talbot killed the king's tax collector, Christopher Rousby, during an argument. In the cold of winter, January 1685, he escaped custody in Virginia with the help of his wife and two Irish friends on a shallop navigated by Roger Skreen. Legend says that Talbot then hid in a cave at Port Deposit on Mount Ararat, where he was fed by falcons. Later in 1685, he surrendered and was convicted in Virginia. But he was pardoned through the influence of Lord Baltimore and then disappeared from Maryland history. (Courtesy of the Port Deposit Heritage Corporation.)

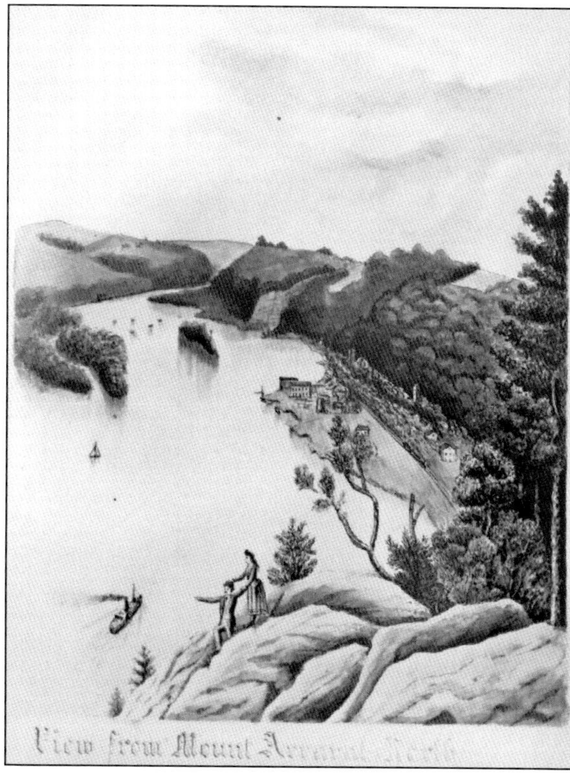

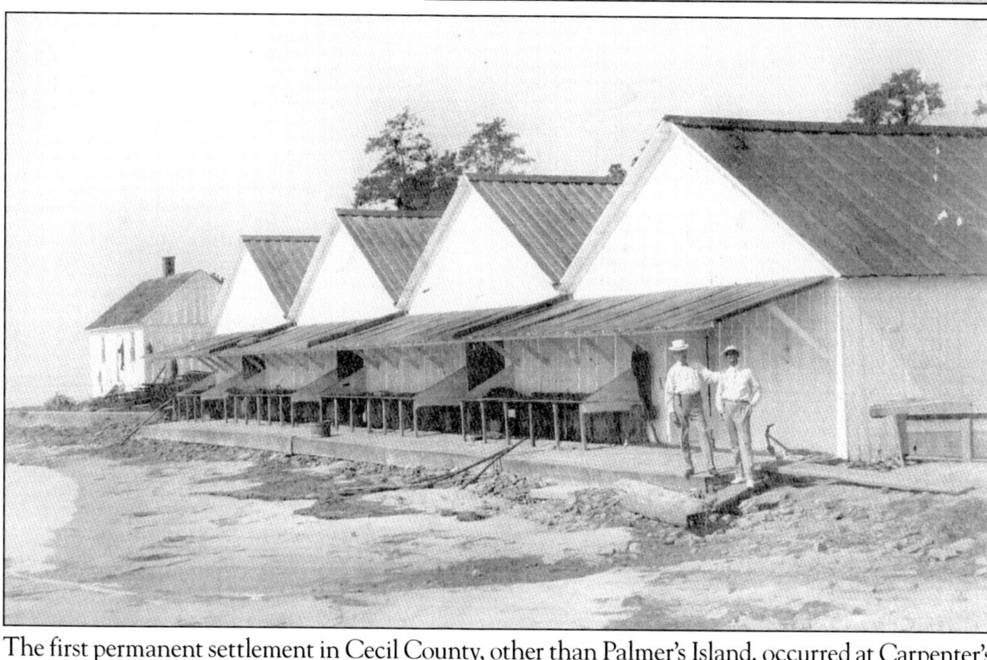

The first permanent settlement in Cecil County, other than Palmer's Island, occurred at Carpenter's Point around 1658 near the mouth of Principio Creek. The original tract of land was patented by William Carpenter, probably for the purpose of trading with Native Americans. This photograph is of the Barnes Brothers Carpenter's Point Fishery, established in the decade following the Civil War. (Courtesy of Jack Manning.)

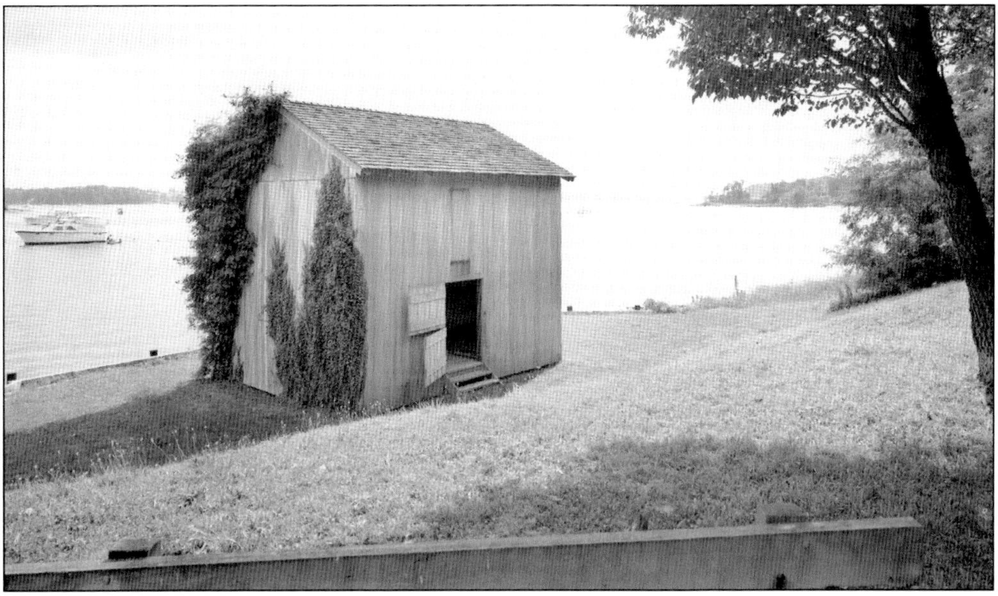

The structure of the northernmost tobacco prize house in the United States, shown in 1936, still stands at Mount Harmon Plantation on the banks of Back Creek, a tributary of the Sassafras River. Mount Harmon was a successful tobacco plantation and a local center for tobacco shipment for the Sassafras area. From 1645 to 1660, the tobacco industry boom helped the Chesapeake region grow from 100 inhabitants to about 6,000. But tobacco growth was exhausting to the soil, and as early as 1720, settlers began looking for more fertile ground farther inland. (Library of Congress.)

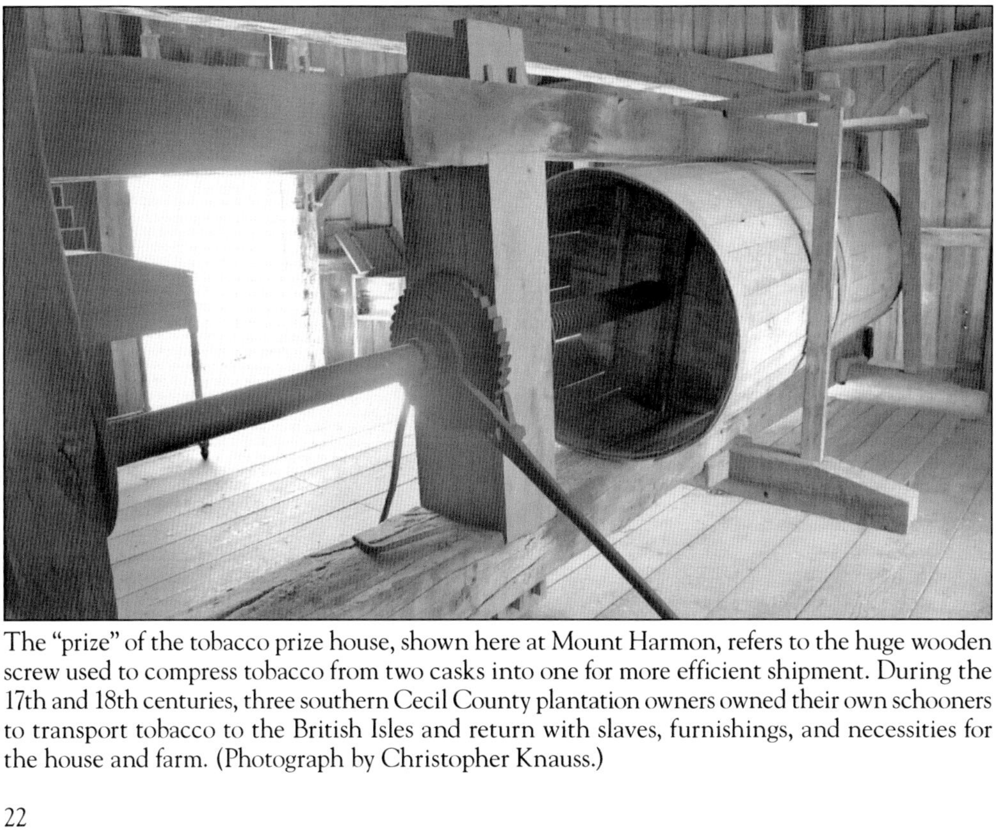

The "prize" of the tobacco prize house, shown here at Mount Harmon, refers to the huge wooden screw used to compress tobacco from two casks into one for more efficient shipment. During the 17th and 18th centuries, three southern Cecil County plantation owners owned their own schooners to transport tobacco to the British Isles and return with slaves, furnishings, and necessities for the house and farm. (Photograph by Christopher Knauss.)

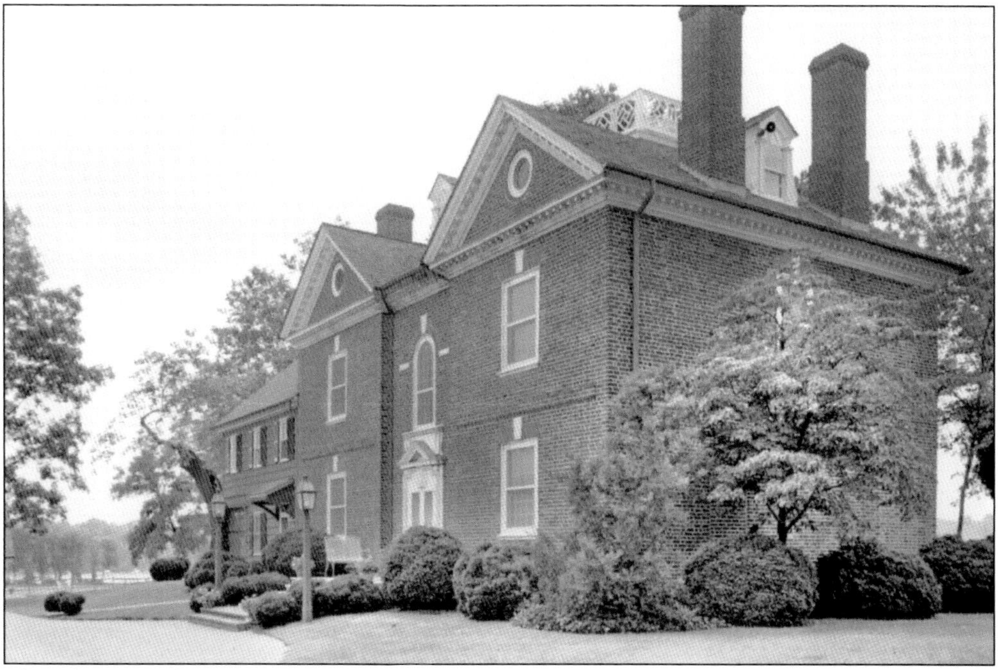

The plantation house at Mount Harmon, shown in 1936, dates to 1730 and is listed by the National Register of Historic Places. Much of the house was restored to the period of 1760–1810 by Marguerite Boden. The plantation originated as a land grant of 350 acres to Godfrey Harmon by Caecilius Calvert, the second Lord Baltimore, in 1651. The area was depicted on early maps as "World's End." (Library of Congress.)

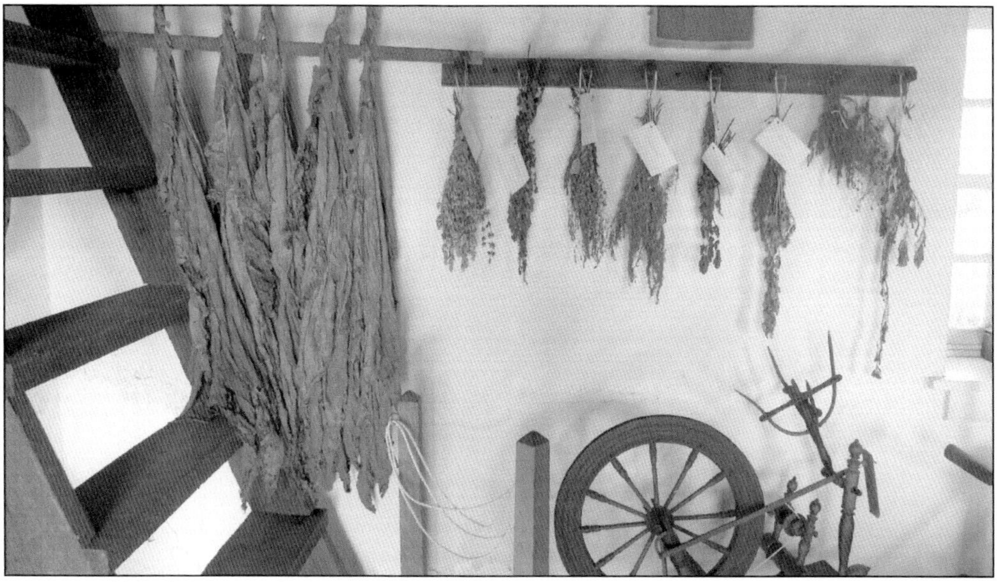

Visitors will find sheaves of tobacco, left, on display in the plantation kitchen at Mount Harmon. When gold and silver became scarce and wampum use became too complicated, early settlers relied on tobacco as currency. Concurrently, the desire for tobacco grew in England and the need for supplies grew in the colonies. The tobacco trade, by necessity, became the leading item of commerce with England. (Photograph by Christopher Knauss.)

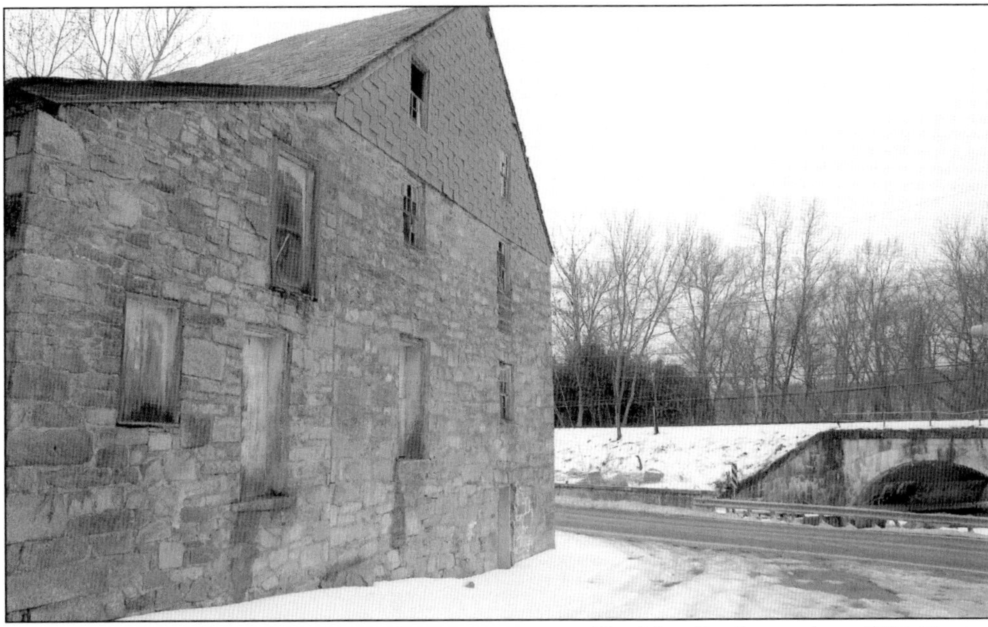

Rock Run Mill, still standing in Port Deposit, was owned by John Steel as early as 1731. During operation, the building was used for making flour, furniture, brushes, and finally sausage and scrapple. This location also served as the beginning point for the ill-fated Susquehanna Canal, the first artificial inland waterway in the United States. This canal ran from a tidewater connection near Rock Run to Love Island, just below the Mason-Dixon Line. (Photograph by Christopher Knauss.)

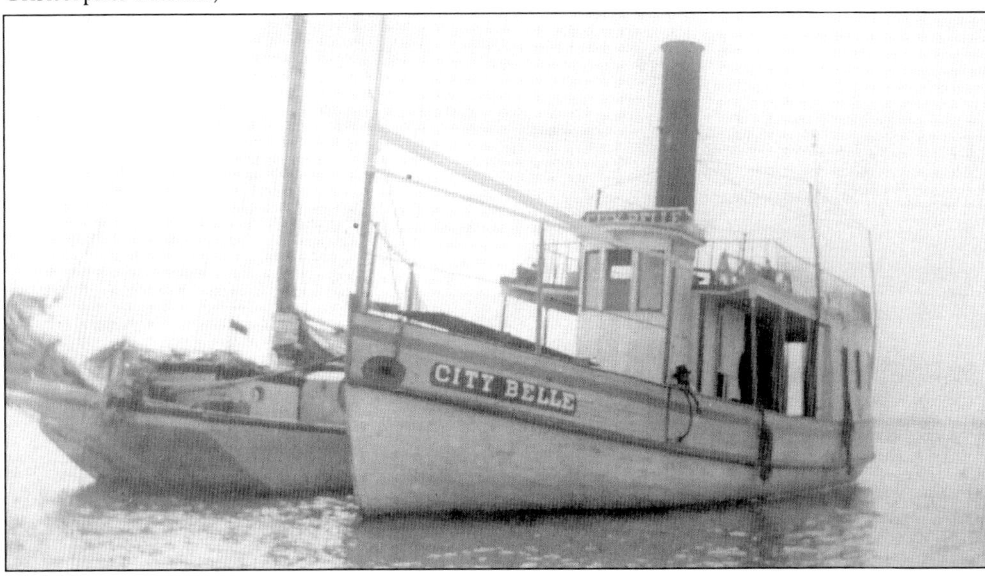

The steamboat *City Belle*, pictured *c.* 1930, carried passengers and freight across the Susquehanna between Port Deposit and Lapidum in Harford County. As early as 1727, Thomas Cresap operated a ferryboat service between Port Deposit and Lapidum, then called Bell's Ferry. Port Deposit at that time was known as Smith's Ferry, for the ferryboat and Smith's Falls, a place in the Susquehanna Capt. John Smith marked with a German cross. (Courtesy of the Port Deposit Heritage Corporation.)

Two

INDEPENDENCE AND WAR

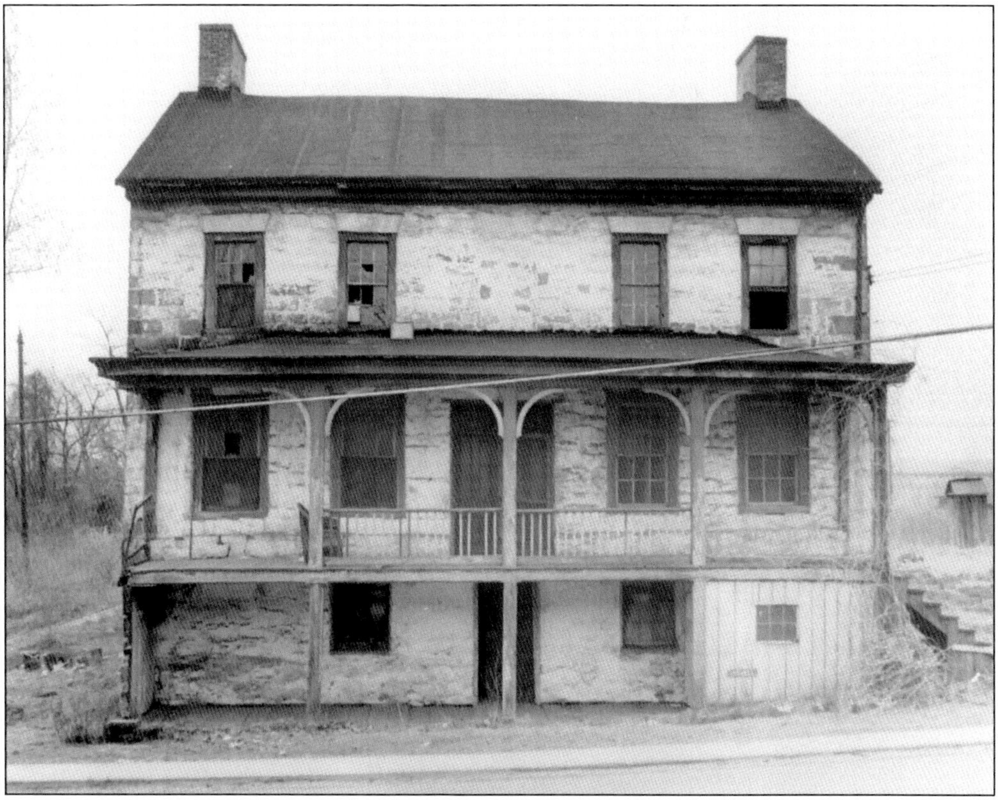

Cecil County's role in America's independence and subsequent wars loomed large. Because of the county's strategic location, it became an important place to the British navy. On a hot stormy day, August 27, 1777, some 250 ships with over 15,000 British soldiers commanded by Gen. Richard Howe landed on the shores of the Elk River. The British stayed in Cecil County for a few days, planning strategy, stocking supplies, and waiting for the storm to pass. When the British marched onward, it was to victory at Brandywine Creek and occupation of Philadelphia, America's capital at the time. Built in the early 18th century, Rodgers Tavern (shown before restoration) in Perryville was first known as the Ferry House or Stevenson's Tavern, located next to a ferry established in 1695. Here on the Post Road between Baltimore and Philadelphia, travelers crossed the Susquehanna River, lodged, and enjoyed food and drink. The tavern was a favorite stopping place for Revolutionary War figures George Washington, the Marquis de Lafayette, and the Comte de Rochambeau. (Courtesy of the Historical Society of Cecil County.)

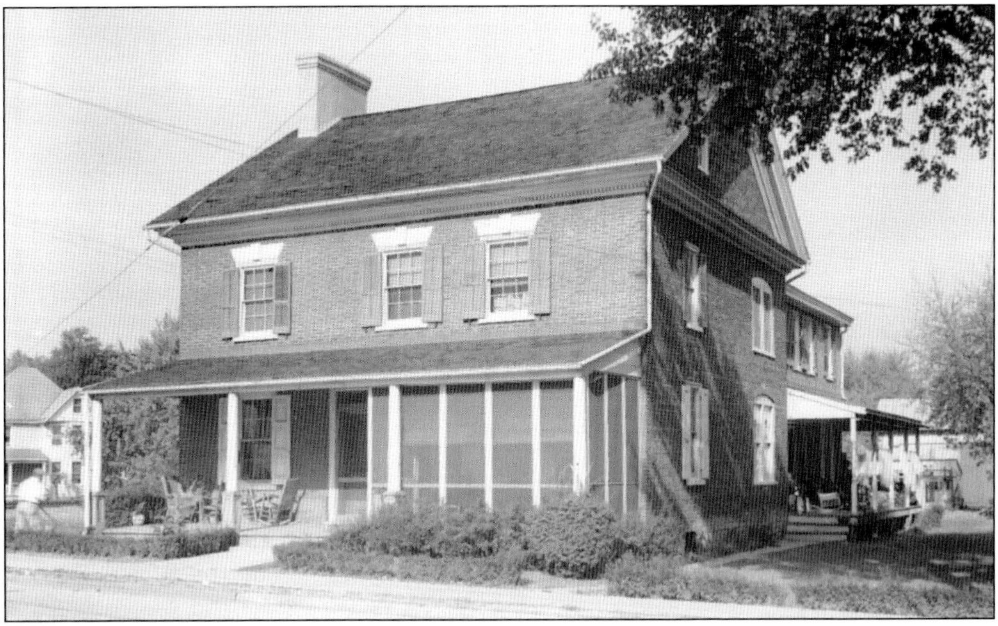

On August 25, 1777, prior to the landing of the British on the Elk River, Gen. George Washington traveled through pouring rain to reach Cecil County. He came to observe the situation, knowing the British were sailing up the Chesapeake Bay. According to local lore, Washington stayed in Elkton in this building, a hotel owned by Jacob Hollingsworth, shown in 1936. Just two days later, the British landed, and General Howe slept in the same room as Washington. (Library of Congress.)

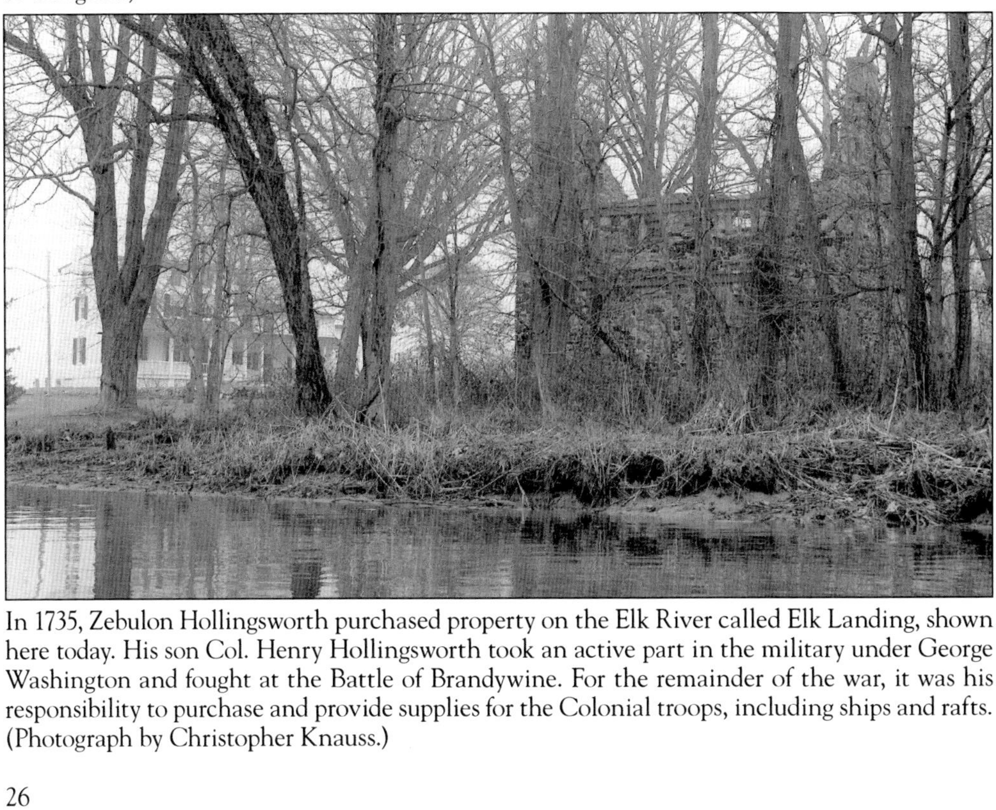

In 1735, Zebulon Hollingsworth purchased property on the Elk River called Elk Landing, shown here today. His son Col. Henry Hollingsworth took an active part in the military under George Washington and fought at the Battle of Brandywine. For the remainder of the war, it was his responsibility to purchase and provide supplies for the Colonial troops, including ships and rafts. (Photograph by Christopher Knauss.)

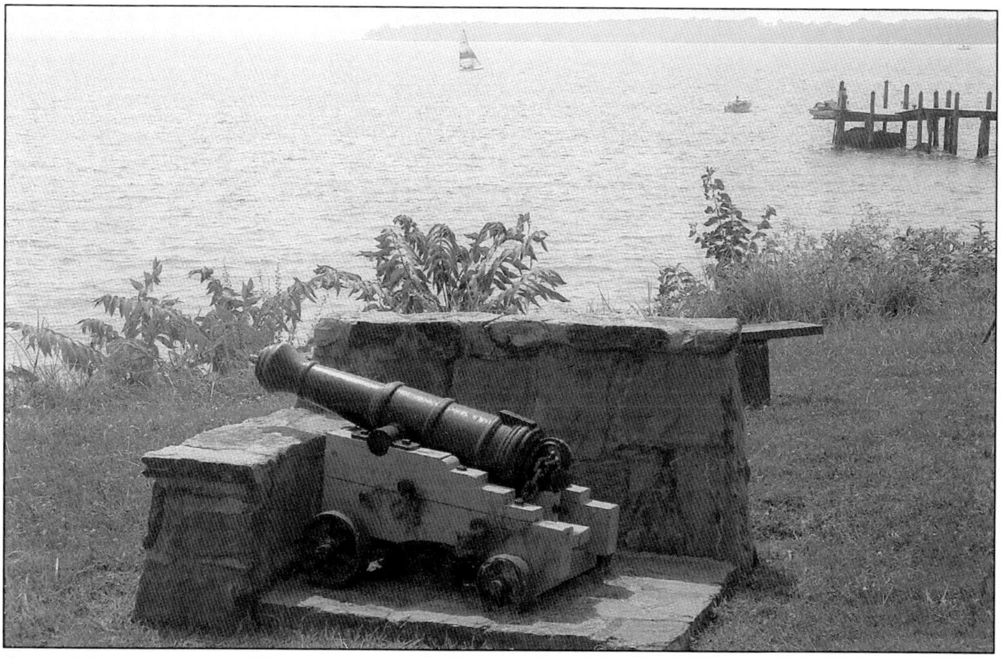

A surviving cannon is still positioned on the banks of the Northeast River in Charlestown. During the Revolutionary War, Charlestown was a major supply depot for the Continental Army. In 1778, Capt. Michael Rudulph led a squad disguised as poultry peddlers who boarded and captured a British man-of-war blockading the port of Charlestown. (Photograph by Christopher Knauss.)

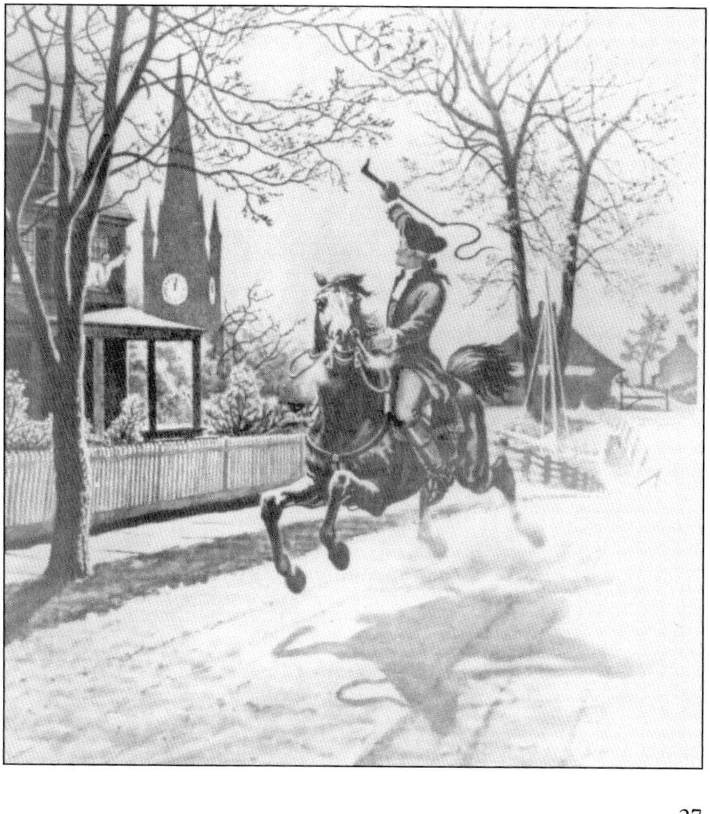

Cecil County's maritime connection with American patriot Paul Revere (depicted here) comes from John Evans, who resided on the banks of the Big Elk, where he manufactured bar iron and nails and engaged in the rolling of copper. He and Paul Revere were the only rollers of copper in the colonies at that time, and all the vessels of the American navy were coppered with material of their manufacture. (National Archives.)

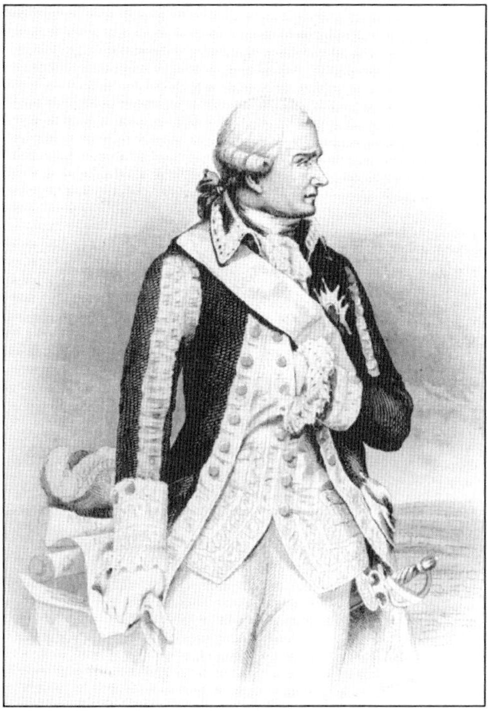

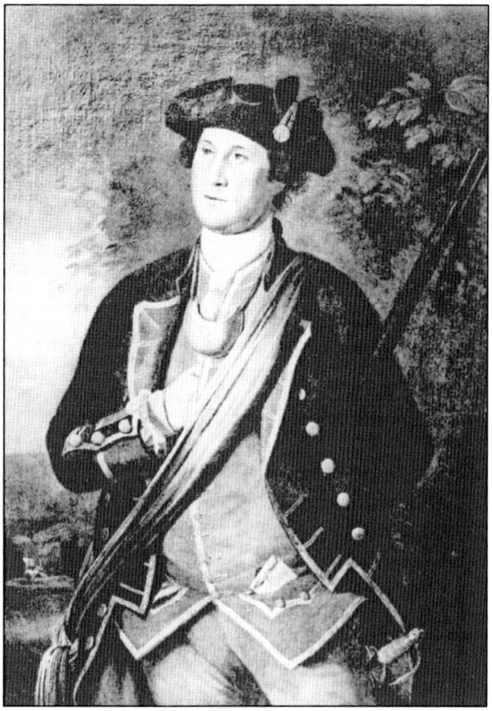

September 6–8, 1781, American Revolution allied forces camped just south of Hollingsworth Tavern in Head of Elk (Elkton). Gen. George Washington, above right, had hoped to find enough vessels there to transport French and American armies to Yorktown, but only 12 sloops, 18 schooners, and a few dozen smaller vessels awaited. Some 2,000 troops were transported by water from Plum Point to Annapolis. On September 10, some 4,000 French infantry, which had camped at Lower Ferry (Perryville), were ferried across the Susquehanna River. Meanwhile, 300 hussars and the wagon train crossed the Susquehanna at Bald Friar Ford, near the present Conowingo Dam. The troops of Comte de Rochambeau, above left, followed a similar return route northward after victory in Yorktown. Historical signage in Perryville describes the activity. (Photograph below by Christopher Knauss.)

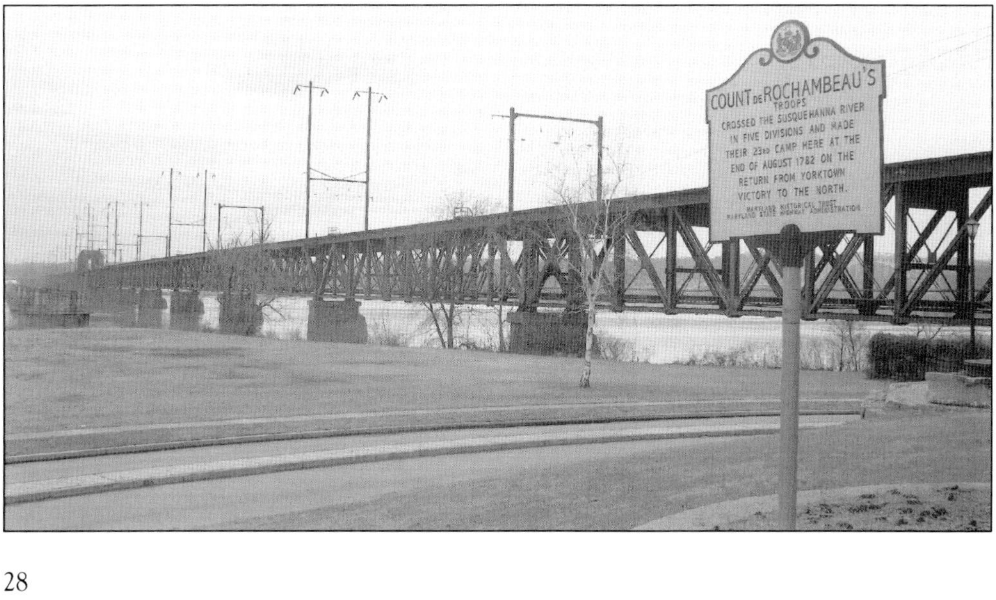

The Marquis de Lafayette was a French soldier and statesman. In 1781, Lafayette led a small American force in Virginia that evaded and then battled a larger British army under Gen. Charles Cornwallis. After the French fleet cut off Cornwallis's escape route through the entrance of the Chesapeake Bay, Lafayette cooperated with the Comte de Rochambeau and Washington in forcing Cornwallis to surrender at Yorktown.

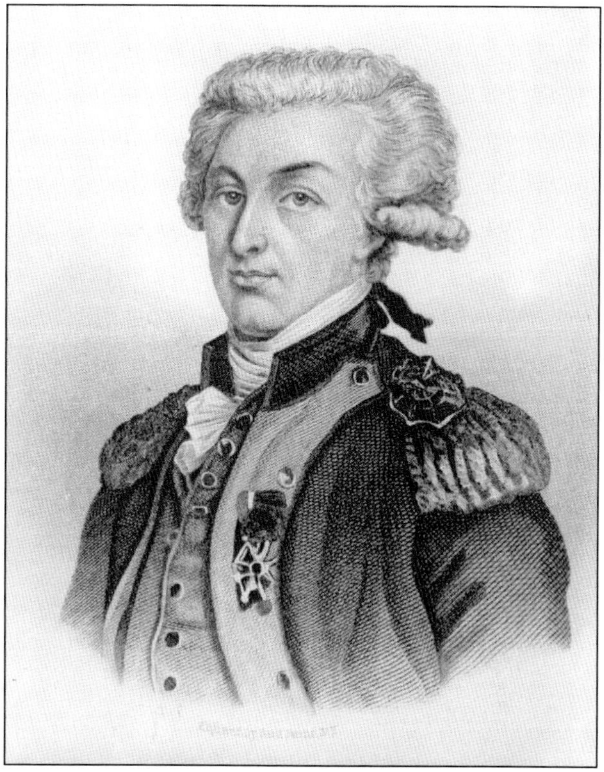

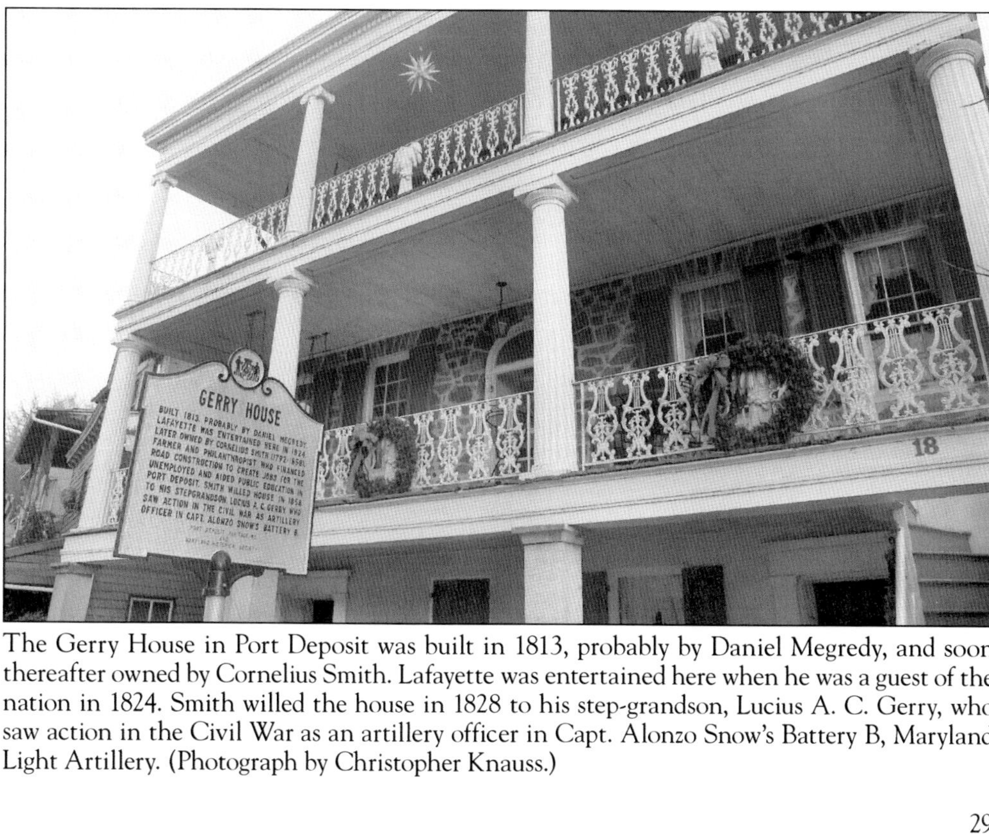

The Gerry House in Port Deposit was built in 1813, probably by Daniel Megredy, and soon thereafter owned by Cornelius Smith. Lafayette was entertained here when he was a guest of the nation in 1824. Smith willed the house in 1828 to his step-grandson, Lucius A. C. Gerry, who saw action in the Civil War as an artillery officer in Capt. Alonzo Snow's Battery B, Maryland Light Artillery. (Photograph by Christopher Knauss.)

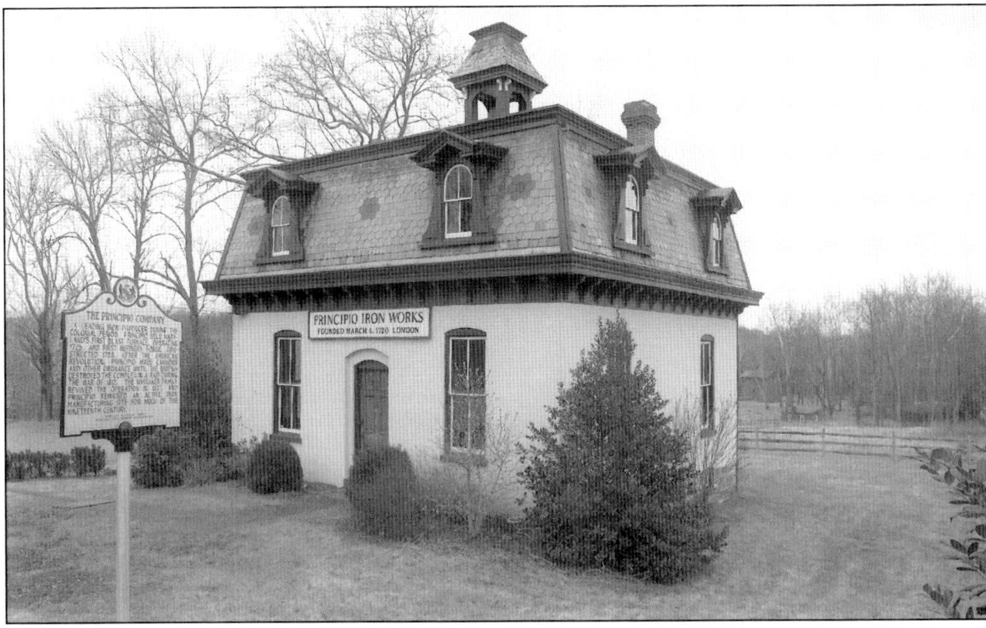

In 1720, British investors formed the Principio Company and built the Principio Furnace to provide pig iron and other cast-iron products. The company, on the banks of Principio Creek, first known as Back Creek, near Perryville, was the country's leading producer of iron during the Colonial period. The mouth of Back Creek widened into the Chesapeake Bay, providing a harbor in an era when navigable waterways provided the cheapest and easiest means of transportation. (Photograph by Christopher Knauss.)

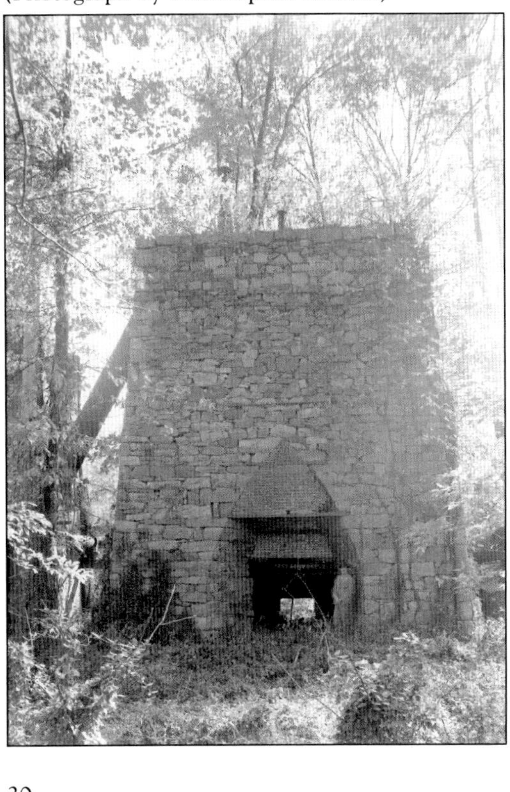

After the American Revolution, Principio made cannons and other ordnance. Government contracts included an order in 1796 to manufacture cannons for the U.S. Navy's first warships, the frigates *Constitution*, *Constellation*, and *United States*. Twenty-four nine-pound, 12 six-pound, and 40 twelve-pound cannons were ordered. The complex was destroyed by the British in the War of 1812. The Whitaker family revived the operation in the 1830s, and Principio remained an active iron manufacturing site for much of the 19th century. This photograph of the Principo Furnace was taken in 1936. (Library of Congress.)

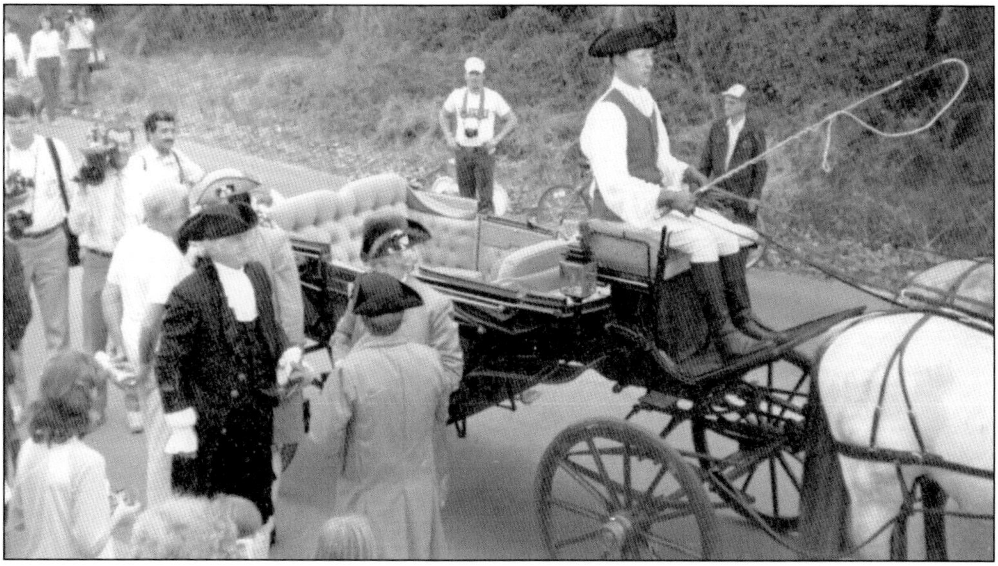

"Gen. George Washington" arrives at Rodgers Tavern in Perryville on April 18, 1989, en route to the bicentennial reenactment of his inauguration in New York. Washington set out from Mount Vernon on April 16, 1789, reaching New York City in time to be inaugurated on April 30. His journey northward was a triumphal procession as people in towns and villages turned out to greet him. Just one year after John Rodgers bought the tavern, in 1781, Washington brought officers and troops through the Lower Ferry crossing on his way to his victorious campaign against Cornwallis at Yorktown. (Courtesy of the Historical Society of Cecil County.)

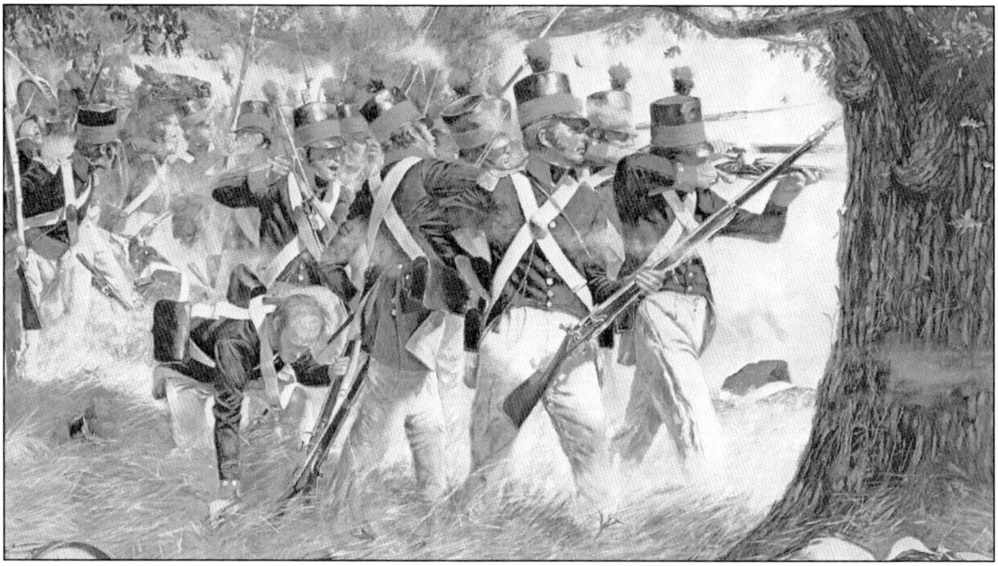

Col. John Rodgers, owner of the ferry and tavern in Perryville, was the forefather of a distinguished family of military and naval officers. In the Revolutionary War, Colonel Rodgers raised the 5th Company of the Maryland militia, which was instrumental during the early stages of the war. His son, also named John Rodgers, rose to the rank of commodore of the U.S. Navy during a career that lasted more than 40 years. His efforts in assembling 12,000 men and 100 cannons contributed to the retreat of the British at North Point in September 1814, shown here. (Courtesy of U.S. Army Center for Military History.)

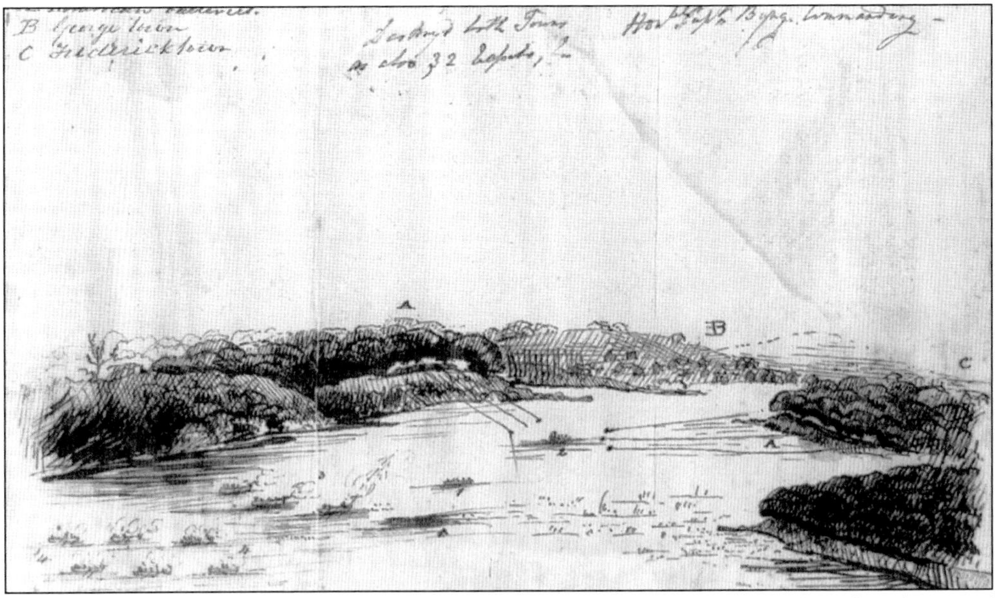

This drawing, c. 1813, depicts the attack upon Georgetown and Fredericktown by a detachment of boats from Right Hon. Sir T. B. Warrens's squadron under Rear Adm. George Cockburn in April 1813. The drawing shows the position of Cockburn's boat, as well as others, and the location of Georgetown, Fredericktown, and the American batteries on the Sassafras River during the War of 1812. (Courtesy of the Library of Congress.)

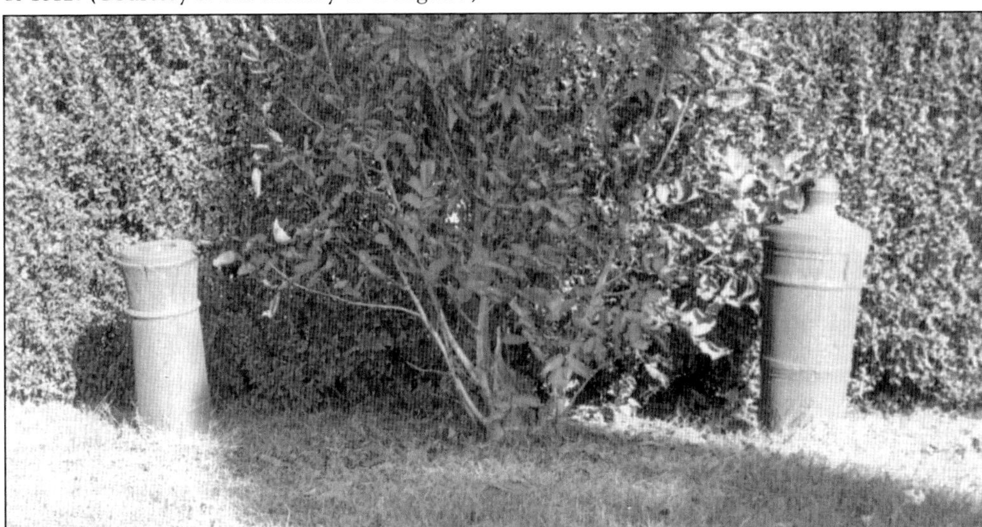

Two cannons from the six-cannon battery used in the defense of Frenchtown during Cockburn's attack on April 29, 1813, can still be seen at Brantwood Manor, a private estate built c. 1791 alongside the present-day Brantwood Golf Club. The American defense did not initially hold on the Elk River as the British landed, captured a fort, and burned Frenchtown. From there, the British tried to advance to Elkton, but they were defeated by the American defense at Fort Defiance and Fort Hollingsworth. An iron chain was placed across the river to prevent passage of larger ships. Royal marines tried rowing up the river, but American militia peppered them from the riverbanks and cannon fire forced the British to retreat. (Courtesy of the Historical Society of Cecil County.)

Commodore Jacob Jones, who married and lived near Cecilton, was born in Delaware in March 1768. Initially educated in the field of medicine, he was employed as clerk of the Delaware Supreme Court before joining the navy in 1799 as a midshipman. During the quasi-war with France, he served under Commodore John Barry in the frigate *United States* and was promoted to the rank of lieutenant in 1801. Jones was an officer of the frigate *Philadelphia* when that ship was taken by the Tripolitans in 1803. Held captive for nearly two years, he again had seagoing service after his release and, with the rank of master commandant, took command of the sloop-of-war *Wasp* in 1810. (U.S. Naval Historical Center.)

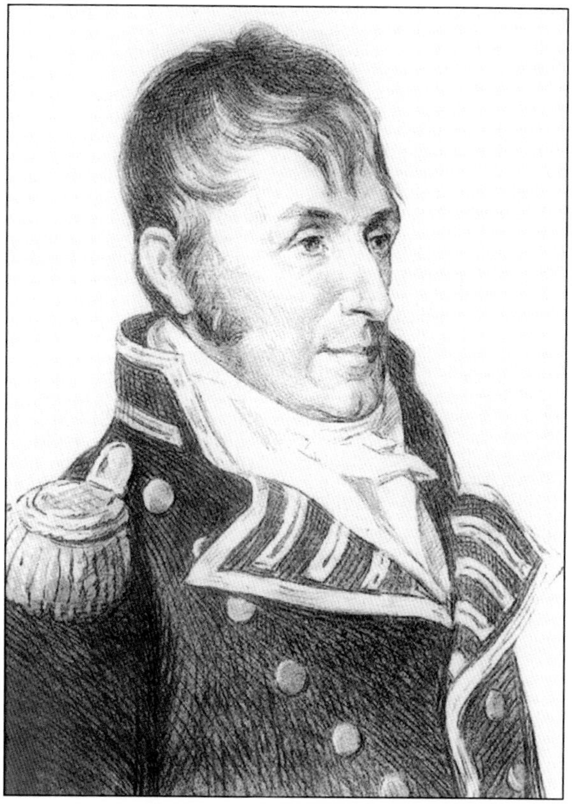

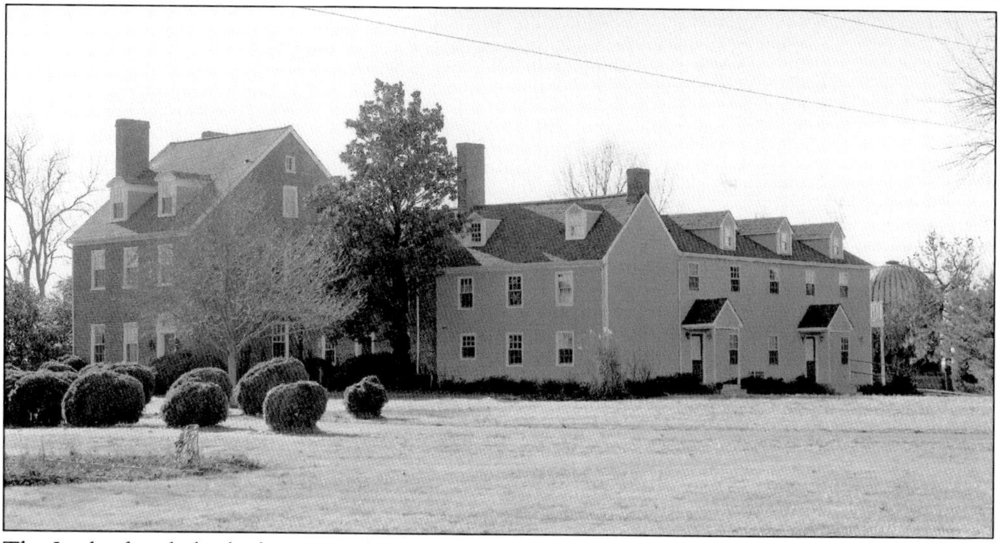

The Lusby family built the original part of the Anchorage, near Cecilton, in 1710. Ruth Lusby inherited the estate and married Commodore Jacob Jones, a hero of the War of 1812. Jones became commodore of the United States' squadrons in the Mediterranean in 1821–1823 and in the Pacific in 1826–1829. Between those tours at sea, Jones was a navy commissioner in Washington, D.C., and held important commands ashore at Baltimore and New York during the 1830s and 1840s. Most recently the Anchorage has served as a bed-and-breakfast. (Photograph by Christopher Knauss.)

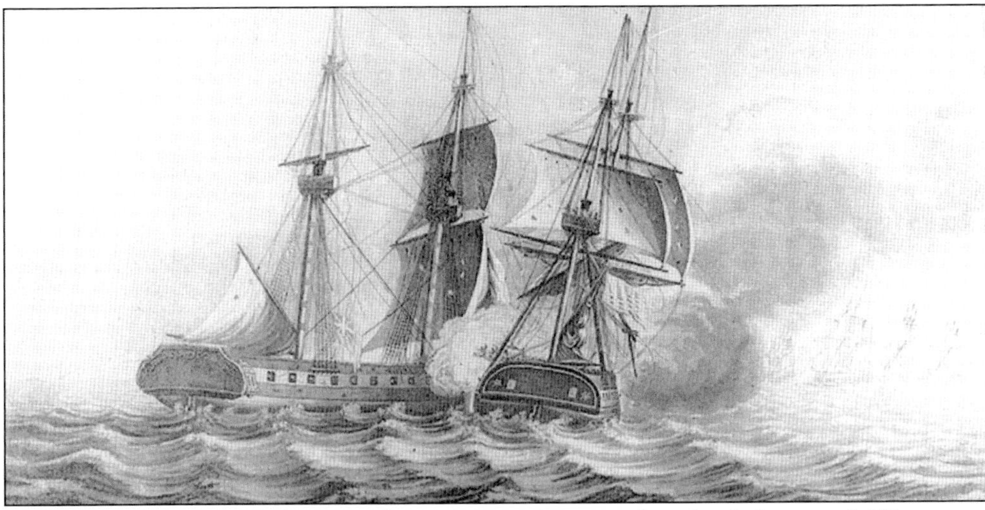

In October 1812, early in the War of 1812, Master Commandant Jacob Jones took *Wasp* on an Atlantic cruise. Despite storm damage to his ship, he attacked a British convoy on October 18 and, following an intense battle, captured the Royal Navy sloop-of-war *Frolic*. Returning to the United States, he received a gold medal from Congress, was promoted to captain, and was given command of the frigate *Macedonian*. With his ship blockaded at New York, Captain Jones was sent to the Lake Ontario theater, where he commanded the frigate *Mohawk* during the last year of the war. This rendering of the *Wasp*'s battle with the *Frolic* is described as "The Capture of H.B.M. Sloop of War Frolic, Capn. Whinyates, the U.S. Sloop of War Wasp, Capn. Jab. Jones, on the 18th of Octr. 1812." (Courtesy of the U.S. Naval Academy Museum.)

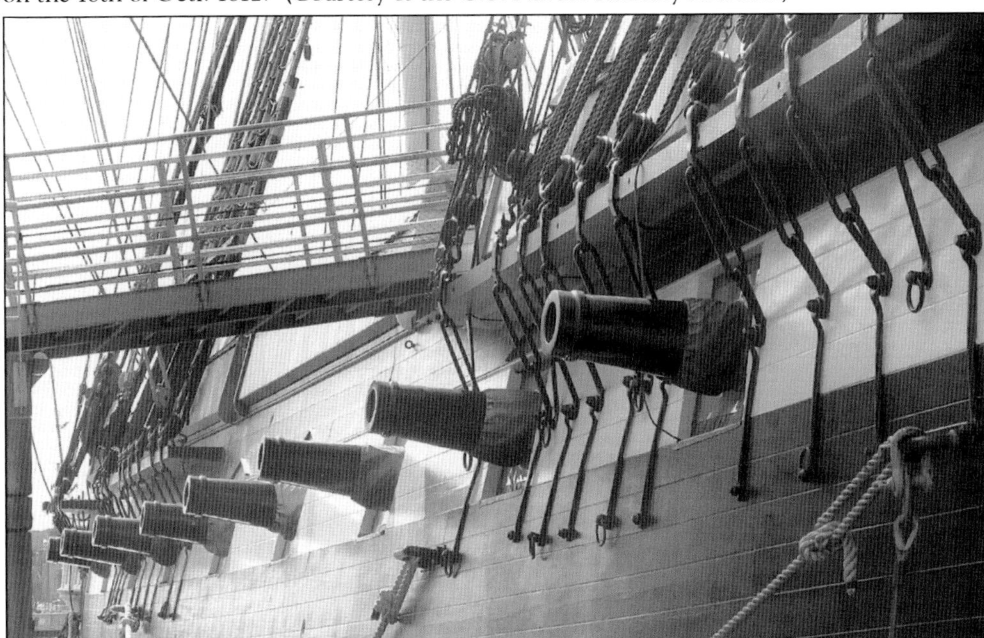

This photograph is of the Civil War–era USS *Constellation* docked at the Inner Harbor in Baltimore. The first U.S. Navy ship to bear the name *Constellation* was a frigate launched in Baltimore on September 7, 1797. John Rodgers was first lieutenant on the maiden voyage of the *Constellation*. (Photograph by Christopher Knauss.)

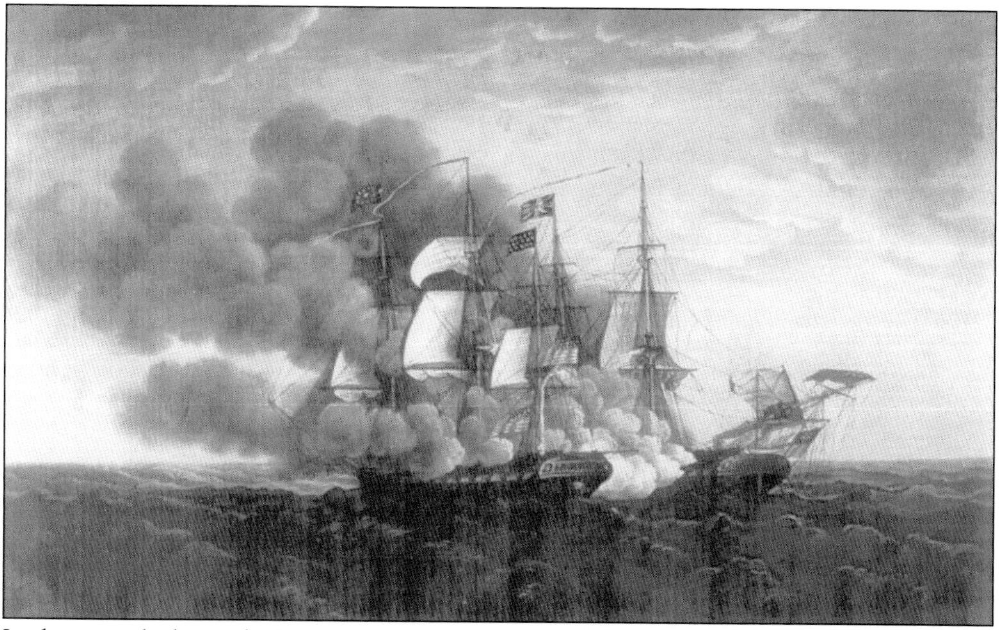

In the artwork above, the U.S. Navy frigate *Constitution* defeats the British frigate *Guerrière* in an engagement off the coast of Nova Scotia during the War of 1812. The commodore's forward cabin, portside of the *Constitution*, is shown below. Dr. Amos Evans, born on the banks of the Big Elk, served aboard the *Constitution* as surgeon, taking part in a famous chase by the British fleet June 17–19, 1812, as well as the important battle with the *Guerrière* on August 12. Of the British chase, Dr. Evans wrote in a journal: "Thus terminates a disagreeable chase of nearly three days attended by inexpressible anxiety, and alternate elevation and depression of spirits, as the winds were propitious or otherwise." For his service in the war, Dr. Evans was presented with two silver medals, given by vote of Congress. (Courtesy of the Library of Congress.)

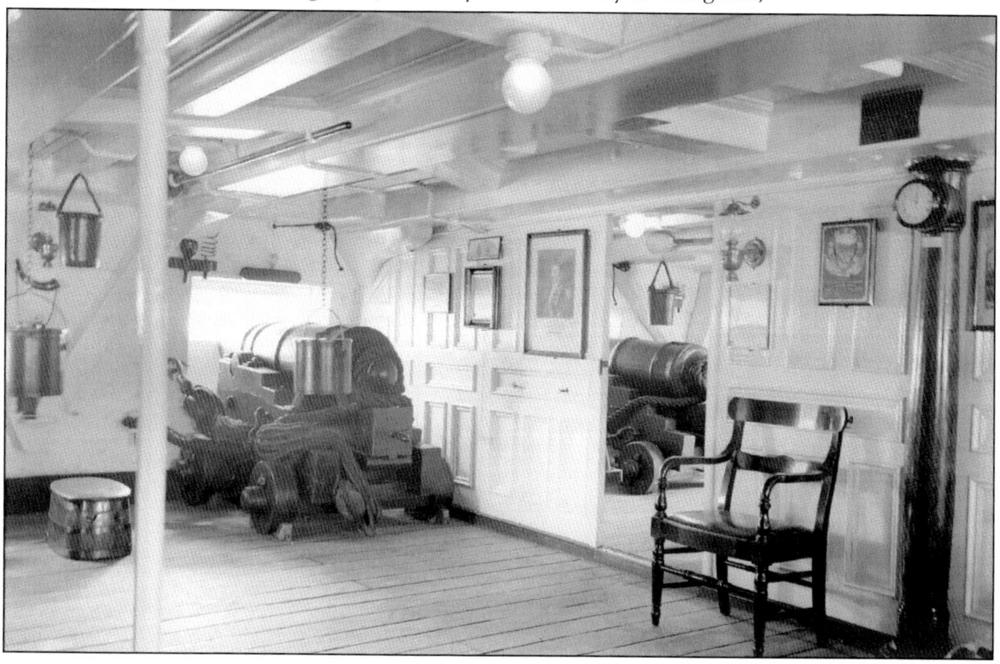

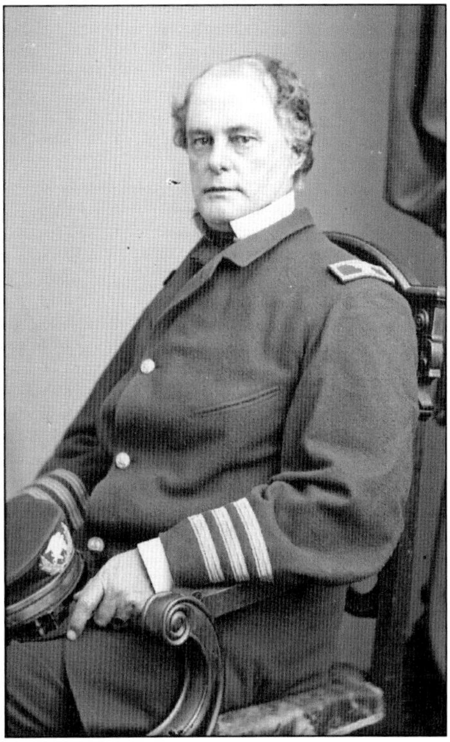

Rear Adm. John Augustus Rodgers, son of Commodore John Rodgers and grandson of Col. John Rodgers, entered the navy as a midshipman in 1828. Service in the Mediterranean onboard *Constellation* and *Concord* opened his long career of distinguished service. In the mid-1850s, he succeeded Commander Cadwalades Ringgold in command of the North Pacific Exploring and Surveying Expedition. In the early months of the Civil War, Rodgers organized the Mississippi Flotilla and supervised construction of the first ironclad gunboats on the western rivers. He took command of the ironclad *Galena* in April 1862 and operated with distinction in the James River. (Courtesy of the Library of Congress.)

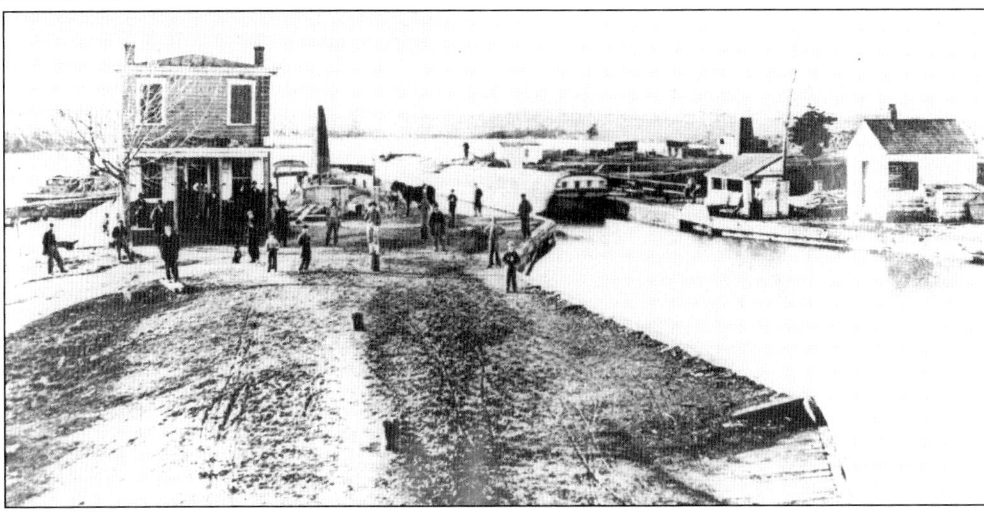

On April 17, 1861, Virginia seceded from the Union, and Washington, D.C., was undefended by troops or fortifications. Federal troops were blocked in Baltimore en route to Washington. Bridges between Baltimore and the Susquehanna River had been destroyed by Confederate troops. By April 20, the government commandeered all the propeller steamers in Philadelphia capable of negotiating the locks of the Chesapeake and Delaware Canal. The "troop ships" sailed down the Delaware through the canal and arrived at Perryville. The troops then moved by rail to Baltimore, then by steamer to Annapolis, and again by rail to Washington, D.C. The canal provided a vital link of men and supplies for Union forces, which continued throughout the war. The canal also aided in military transportation in World Wars I and II. (Courtesy of the U.S. Army Corps of Engineers.)

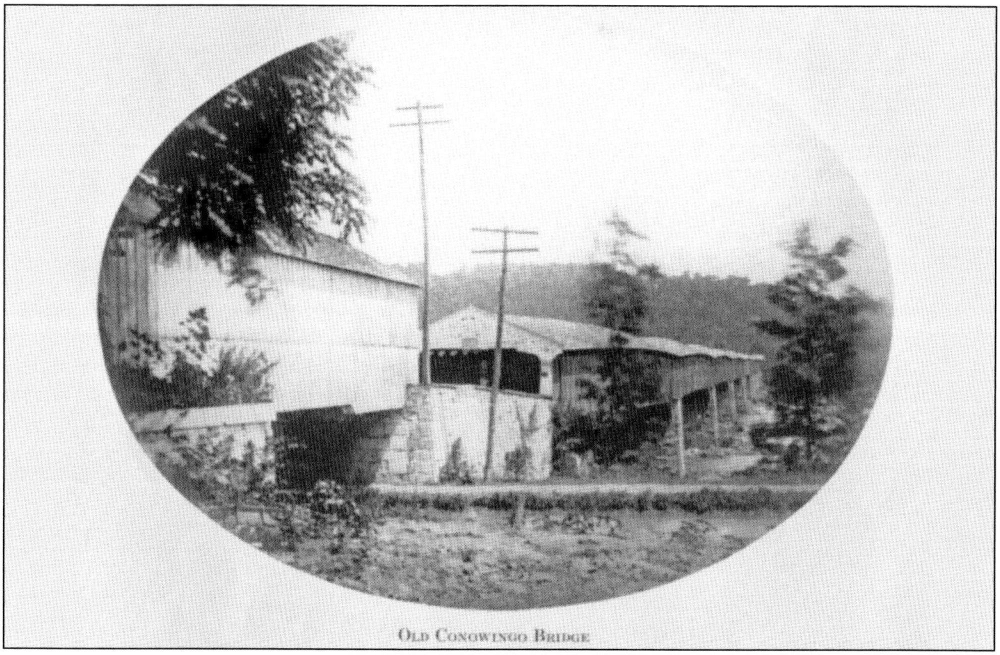

This covered bridge was constructed over the Susquehanna River near Conowingo in 1859. The covered bridge replaced the original bridge built in 1820 and destroyed by a flood in 1846. During the Civil War, Federal troops were stationed at the bridge for three years to prevent Southern sympathizers from crossing into Northern territories. The covered bridge was destroyed by fire in 1907, and an iron bridge was built. The iron bridge was dynamited in 1928 to make room for the Conowingo Dam. (Courtesy of the Historical Society of Cecil County.)

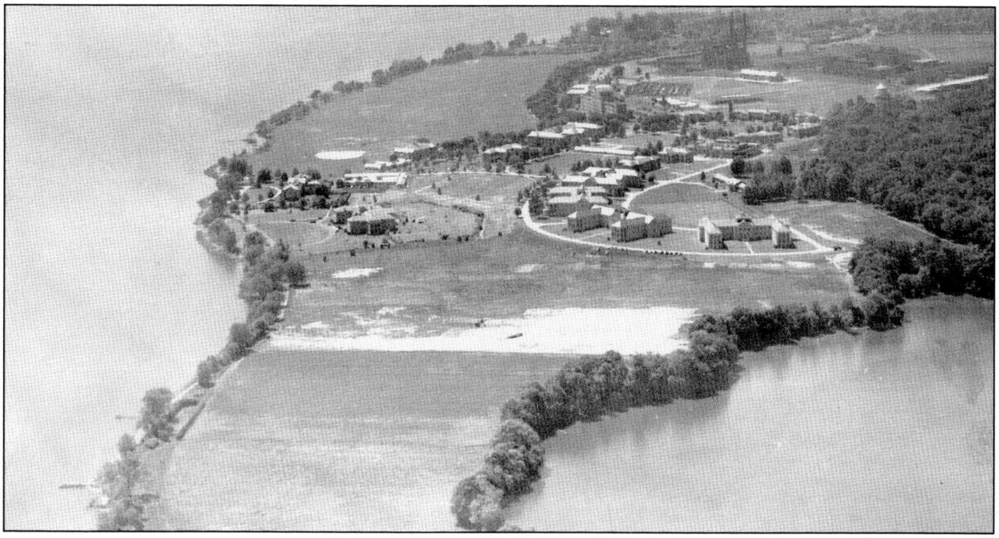

During the Civil War, the Union army operated the ferry across the Susquehanna River at Perryville. By the winter of 1861, there were 1,600 troops on Perry Point protecting the ferry and railroad. In 1918, the federal government officially purchased Perry Point and leased it to Atlas Powder Company to make ammonium nitrate. The peninsula now is home to the Perry Point Veterans Affairs Medical Center and the Perryville Community Park. (Courtesy of the Historical Society of Cecil County.)

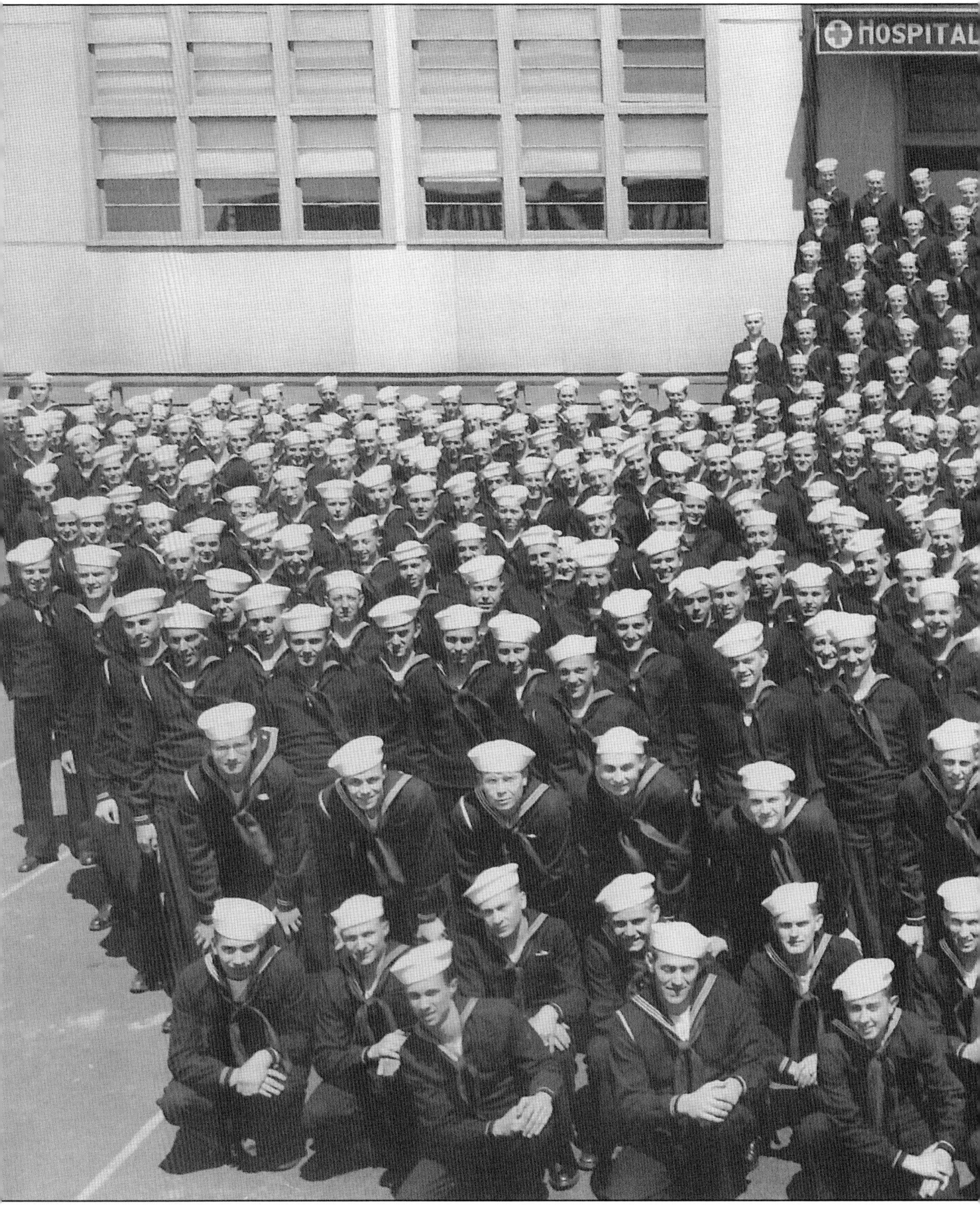

In early 1942, President Roosevelt approved the purchase of the Tome School for Boys and adjacent land in Port Deposit for a naval training center. The base was named Bainbridge in memory of Commodore William Bainbridge, commander of the frigate *Constitution* and founder of the first naval training school. Bainbridge became the navy's principal training center on the East Coast. By the end of World War II, more than half a million sailors had passed through the

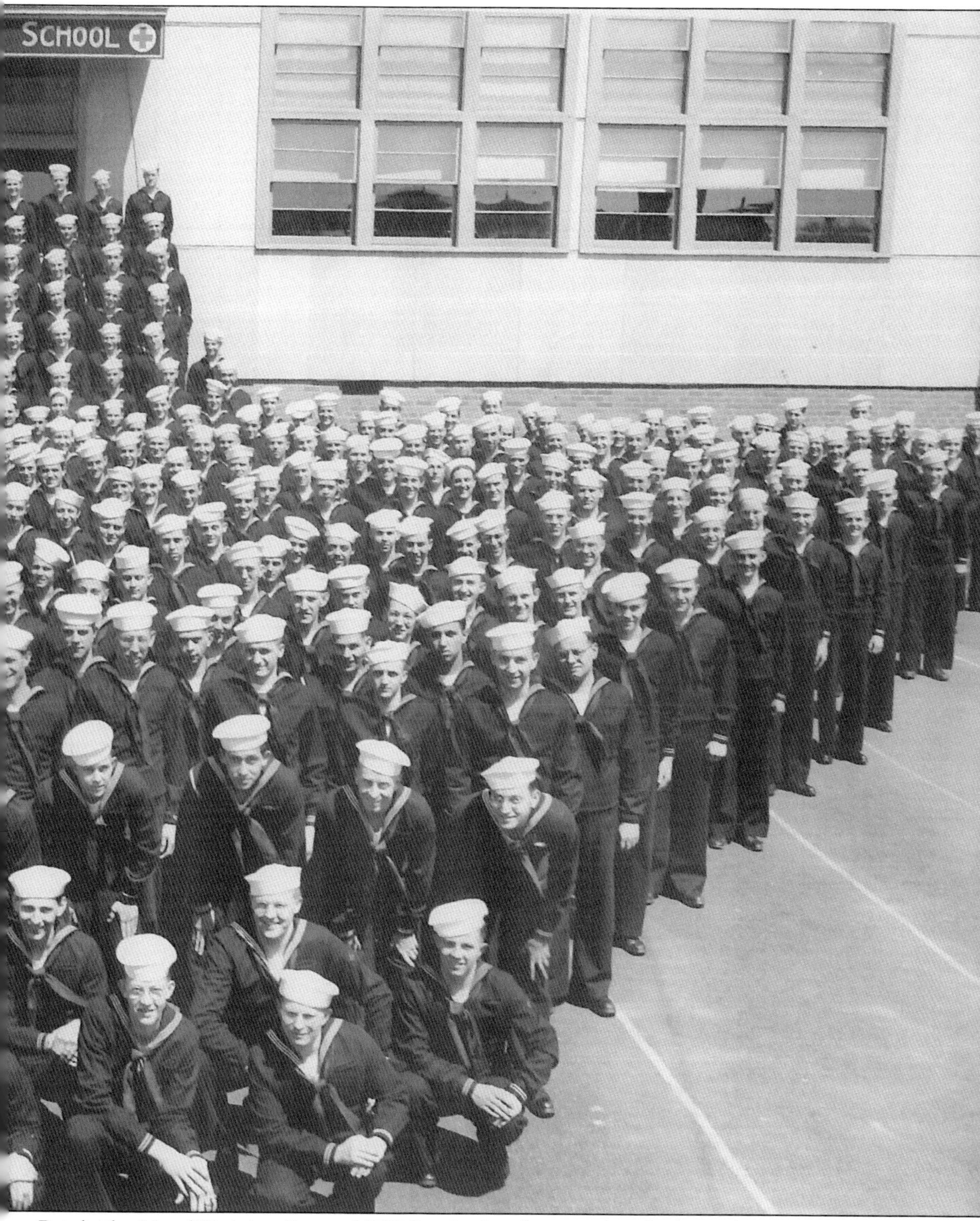

Bainbridge Naval Training Center. NTC Bainbridge also served as the home for several service schools providing technical training for recruits and fleet sailors. Radiomen, hospital corpsmen, dental technicians, electricians, storekeepers, and yeomen were among those taught at Bainbridge. (Courtesy of the Historical Society of Cecil County.)

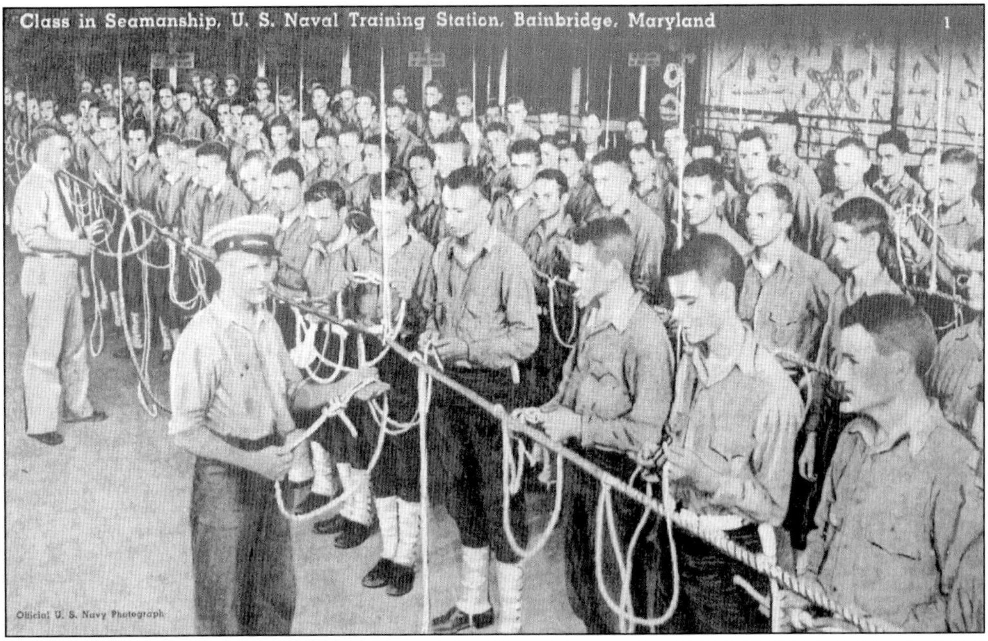

Between construction ground breaking on May 19 and August 14, 1942, NTC Bainbridge had 506 buildings constructed. The Recruit Training Command, Bainbridge's largest subordinate activity, consisted of four large camps each named after naval heroes: Rodgers, Perry, James, and Barney. Each camp was an entity in itself with its own drill hall, swimming pool, mess hall, drill field, classrooms, barracks, and recreational facilities and with the capacity to berth, mess, and train a regiment for 5,000 sailors. (Courtesy of the Port Deposit Heritage Corporation.)

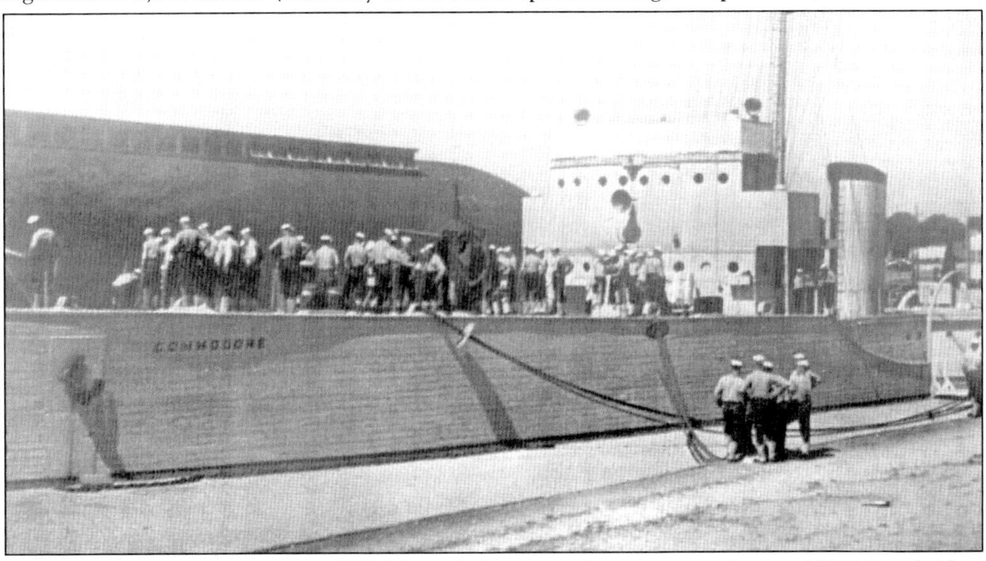

The *Commodore*, also known as USS *Never Sail*, was used as a training boat at NTC Bainbridge. Bainbridge ceased operations after World War II in 1947 but reopened in 1950–1951 as a WAVES (Women Activated for Voluntary Emergency Service) training center and a Naval Academy prep school in response to the Korean War. During the Korean War, Bainbridge reached its peak population of 55,000 people. The facility closed all operations in 1976. (Courtesy of the Port Deposit Heritage Corporation.)

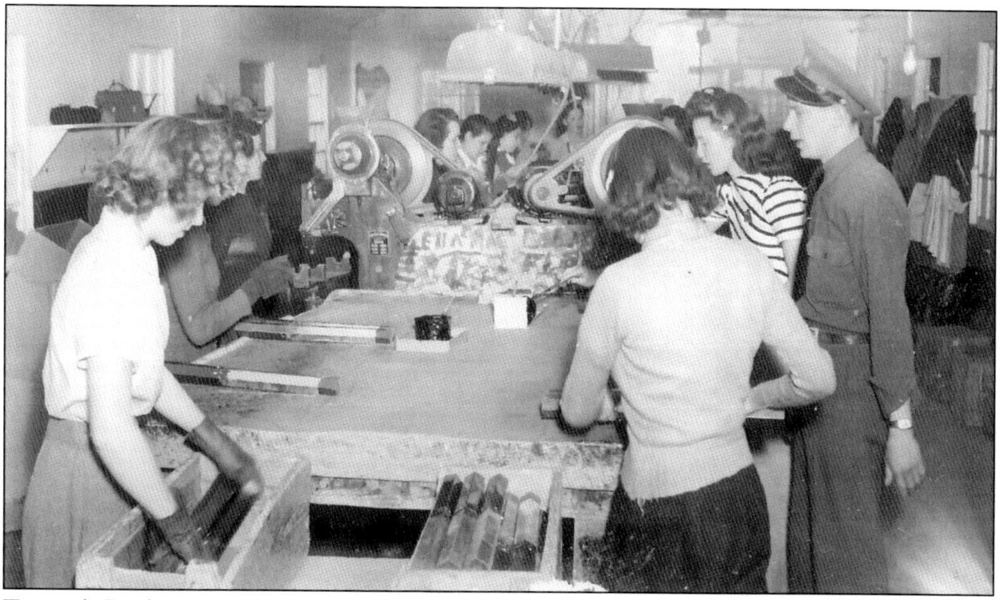

Triumph Explosives Industries, here *c.* 1942, was a 1,200-acre, World War II–era munitions manufacturer just east of Little Elk Creek near Elkton. Wartime products included shell loading, tetranitrate, lead oxide, pentolite, grenades, primers and detonators, explosives, fuses, bombs, grenades, and pyrotechnics. U.S. Navy staffers at the site included Navy Inspector of Ordnance, Navy Cost Inspector, and Officer in Charge of Construction of Civil Works. An accident at Triumph Industries in the midst of heavy war production in May 1943 killed 15 and injured 100. (Courtesy of the Historical Society of Cecil County.)

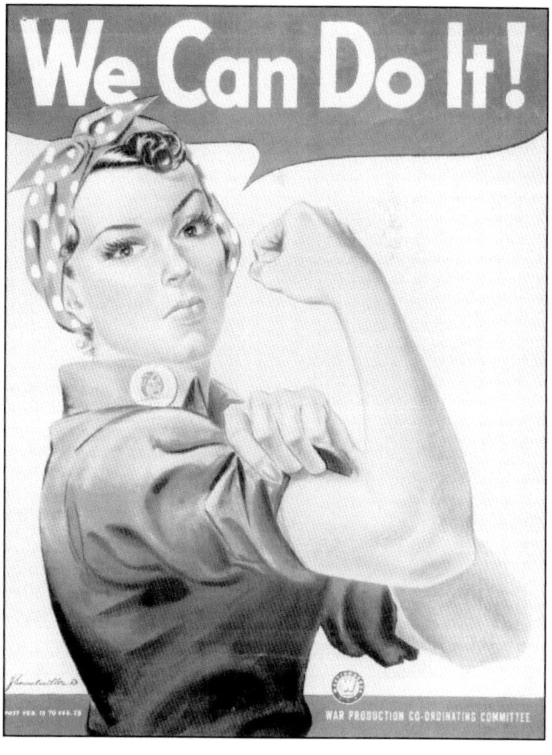

The outcome of World War II may have been different if more than 18 million women hadn't worked in home-front defense industries to free men for overseas battlefields and to keep the nation running. Women in Cecil County and across America gave up their jobs to work in the defense industry, performing jobs previously reserved for men. Other women who previously hadn't been in the workforce added jobs in the defense industry to their traditional responsibilities of cooking, cleaning, and taking care of children. The "Rosie the Riveter" poster was the most famous image of working women during World War II. "Rosie" represented women who were working as welders, machinists, mechanics, pipe fitters, electricians, and boilermakers. (Courtesy of the Library of Congress.)

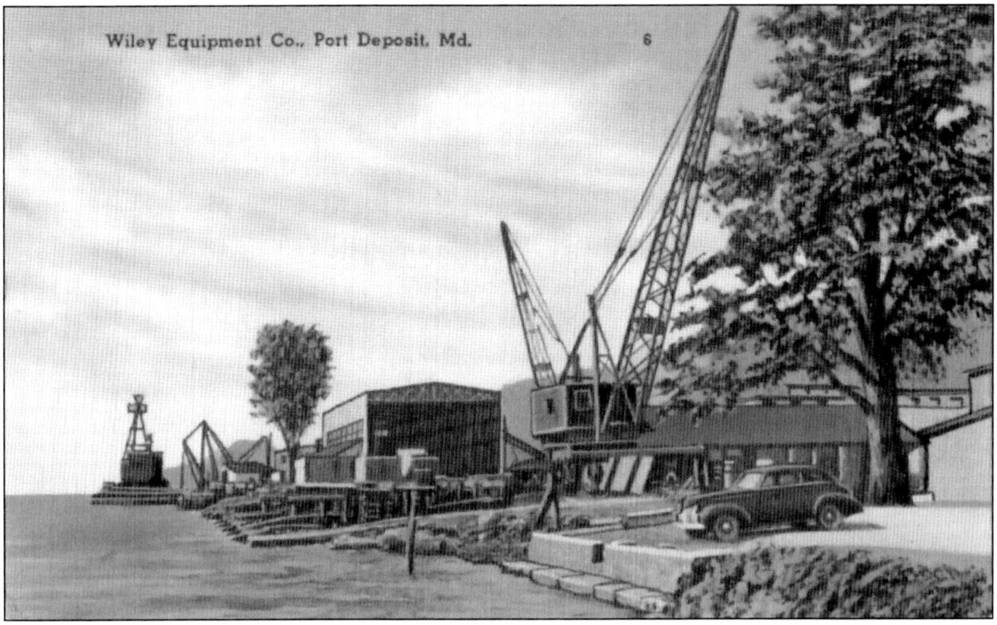

Records indicate that in August 1941 the federal government had over $1 billion worth of contracts with Maryland companies for war production. One of the companies was Port Deposit's Wiley Manufacturing, which occupied much of the waterfront of the town. Wiley Manufacturing constructed heavy-duty cranes, hoisting engines, steel barges, derrick boats, and motor vessels and had sales of $10 million at its peak during World War II. (Courtesy of Jack Manning.)

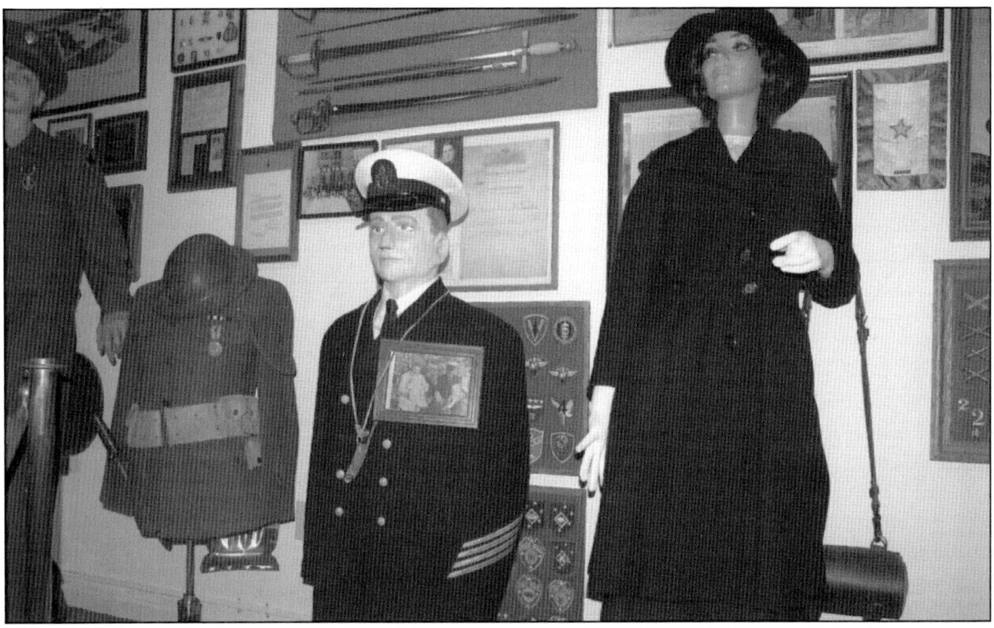

The uniform of Chief Boatswain's Mate Charles Bernard Storke, of Elkton, is part of the display at the Sheriff John F. DeWitt Military Museum at the Historical Society of Cecil County in Elkton. Storke served in World Wars I and II. The museum is dedicated to Cecil County veterans of all wars with military memorabilia dating back to before the Civil War. (Photograph by Christopher Knauss.)

Three

FLOATING COMMERCE

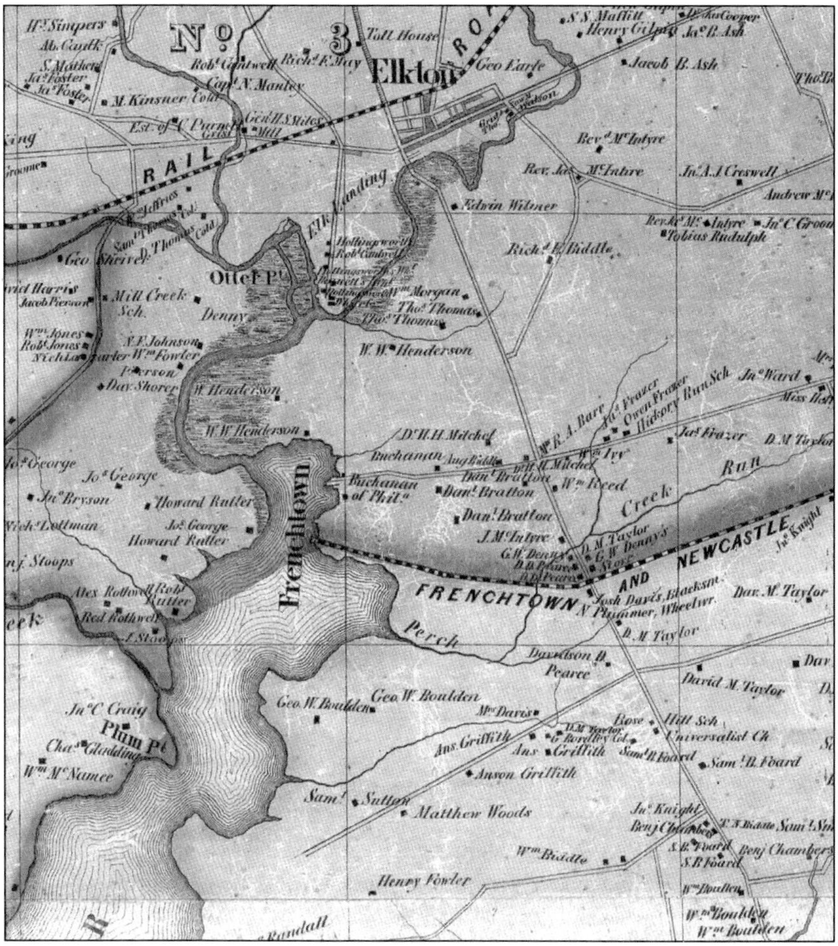

During the period of settlement and the Revolutionary War, Cecil County developed into a farming community at the head of the bay. The main exports were animal skins, tobacco, and other agricultural products, usually shipped from the town ports that developed at strategic locations. Farming was so important to the economy that squirrels and crows became a destructive problem, and legislators put a bounty on their heads. As money was scarce, citizens were allowed to pay their taxes with squirrels and crows. In 1806–1807, William McDonald and Andrew Henderson established the first line of packets between Baltimore and Philadelphia. It consisted of four sloops that ran to Frenchtown on the Elk River. From there, freight was carried by wagons to New Castle and then to Philadelphia by water. In June 1813, less than two months after the British had burned Frenchtown, the first steamboat on the water of the bay or its tributaries, the *Chesapeake*, traveled from Baltimore to Frenchtown loaded with passengers and freight. (From Martenet's 1858 map of Cecil County; courtesy of the Library of Congress.)

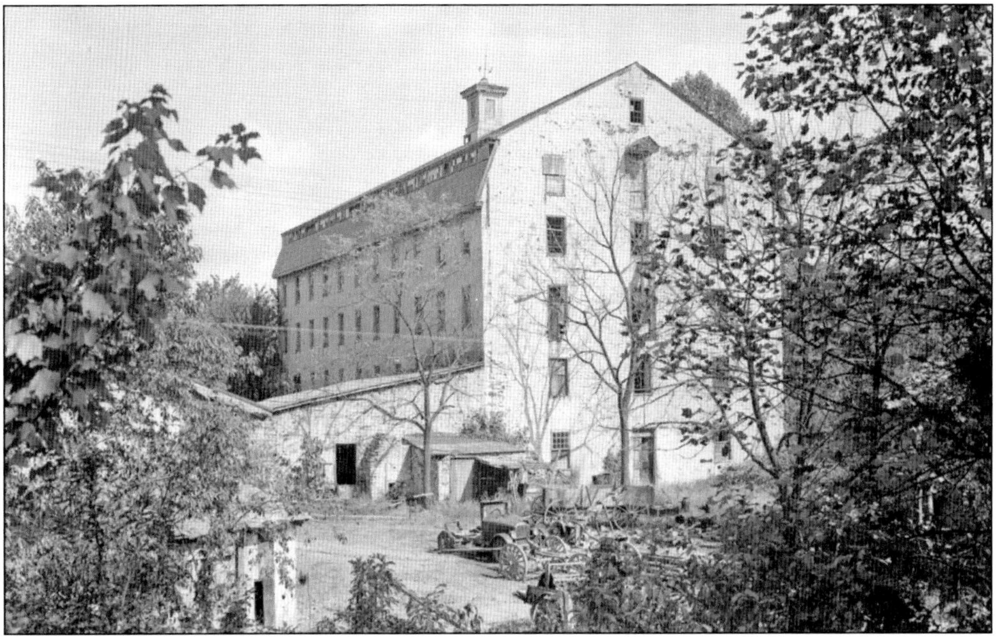

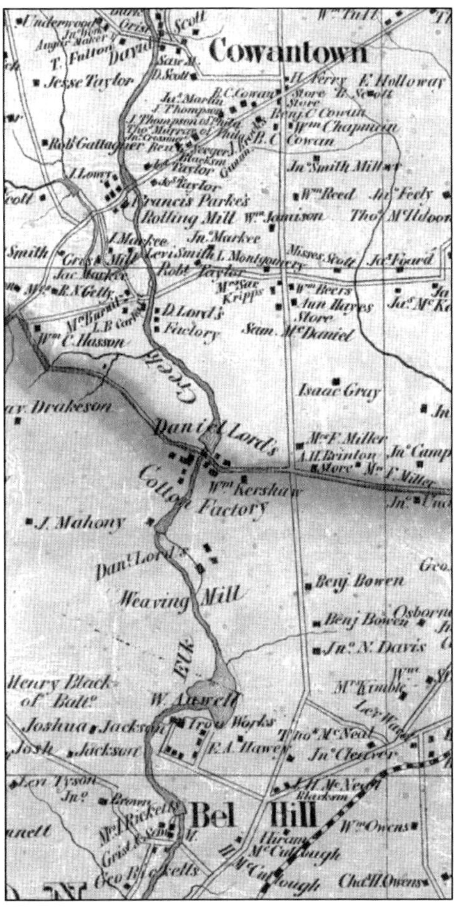

The 1936 photograph above is of the main mill at Elk Mills, a cotton factory on the Big Elk Creek owned by Daniel Lord. The village that evolved around Lord's Factory became known as Elk Mills. As early as 1807, there were 53 grist and merchant mills in Cecil County. Elkton was one of the largest wheat markets in the country with 250,000 bushels sold in a year. Water from the streams created the power to run the mills. (Above, courtesy of the Library of Congress; at left, from Martenet's 1858 map of Cecil County, courtesy of the Library of Congress.)

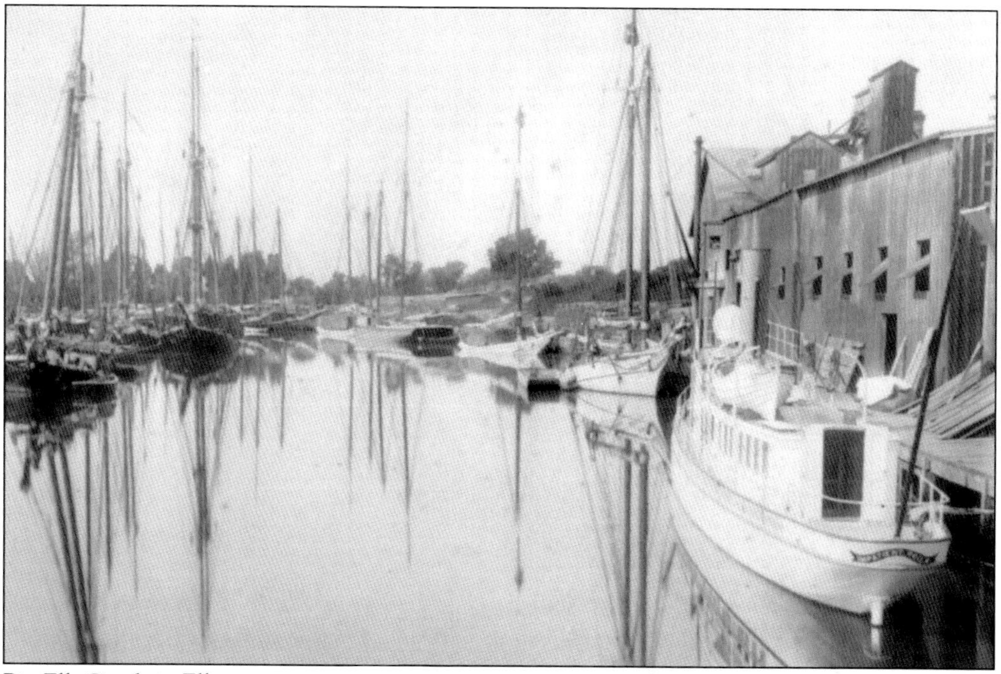

Big Elk Creek in Elkton was once an important waterway. Early pioneers who reached the head of navigable waters settled in Elkton. The town thrived because of the waterway and industry located along the creek. Scott Fertilizer Plant (above) and Radnor Pulp and Paper (below) tenanted the creek bank at the southwest corner of Bridge and Main Streets. Sailing craft, steamers, tugs, and barges carried goods to and from the wharfs. In the first 10 months of 1888, the Pulp Mill reported that 132 vessels had discharged goods at its wharves. In 1905, some 29,000 tons of freight valued at $327,000 were transported on the waterway. (Courtesy of the Historical Society of Cecil County.)

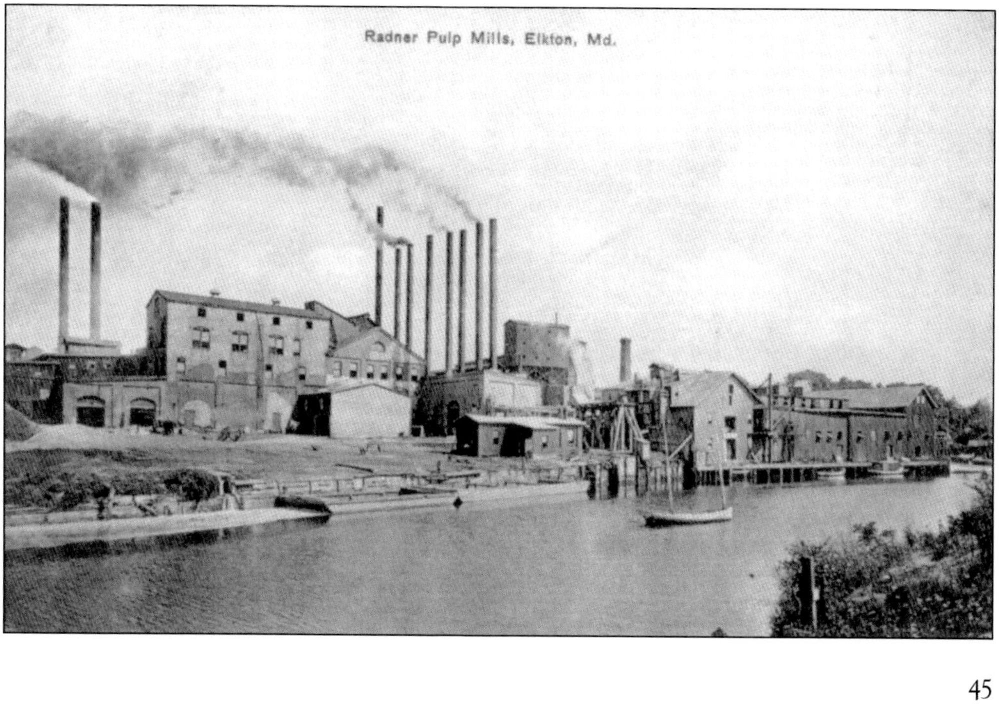

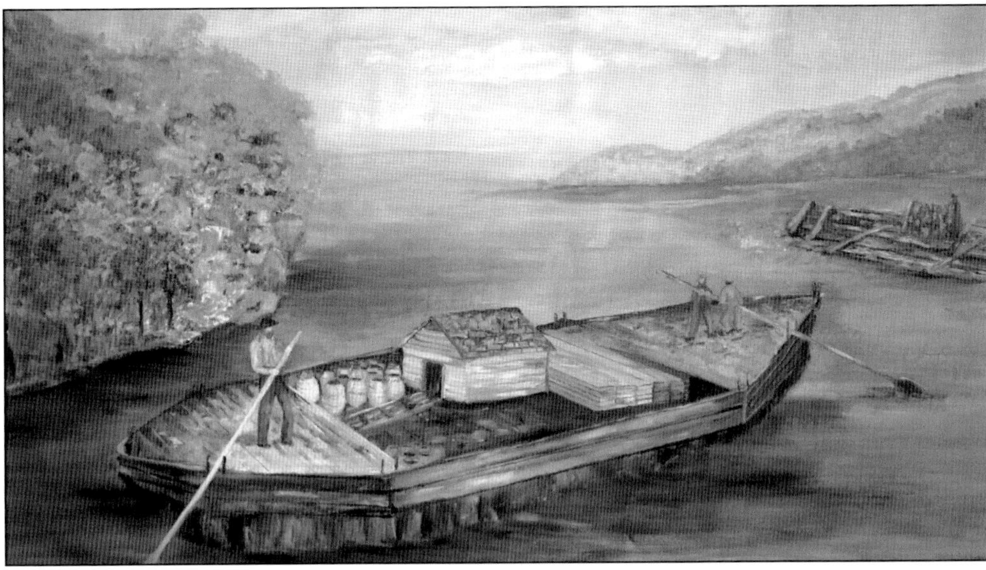

The first ark that floated down the Susquehanna River was built by a German miller named Richard Breider in 1796. It was loaded with flour to be taken to Baltimore. Arks were crudely constructed with heavy timbers and planks and were so huge and hard to maneuver that most were at the mercy of the current. Typical sizes ran from 75 to 100 feet long, 15 to 20 feet wide, and 3 to 5 feet deep. These vessels could not go upstream, so upon reaching their destination, they were broken up and sold for lumber, often made into housing and furniture. (Painting by Grace C. Humphries, 1974.)

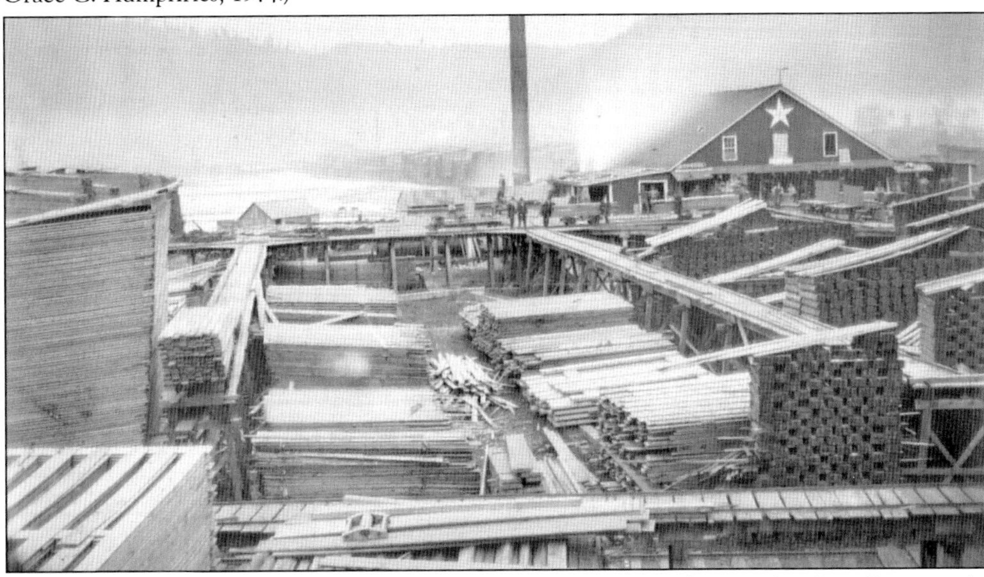

Much of the lumber floating down the Susquehanna River was deposited at Port Deposit, the impetus of the town's name. Since it was located at the farthest point downstream on the Susquehanna and the farthest navigable point upstream for ships from the Chesapeake Bay, Port Deposit was a junction point for products such as lumber, grain, coal, whiskey, and tobacco. In 1821, a total of 525 arks and 925 rafts reached Port Deposit carrying goods totaling $1,121,000. Eventually railroads and the Conowingo Dam brought about the end of this industry. (Courtesy of the Historical Society of Cecil County.)

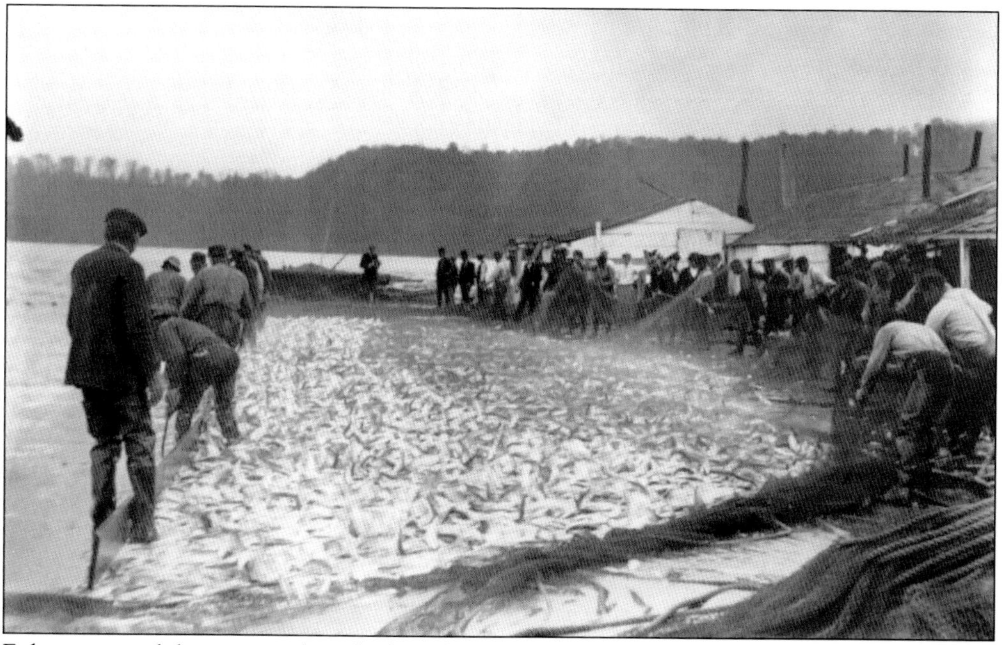

Fishermen tend their nets and catch along the Susquehanna River in Port Deposit prior to sorting and cleaning, *c.* 1908. Abundant catches of herring and shad during their spawning runs were daily occurrences. Capt. John Smith wrote of the fishery in his diary: "Abundance of fish lying so thicke with their heads above the water, as for want of nets, our barge running against them, we attempted to catch them in frying pans; but found we had a bad instrument to catch fish with." (Above, courtesy of the Port Deposit Heritage Corporation; below, courtesy of the Historical Society of Cecil County.)

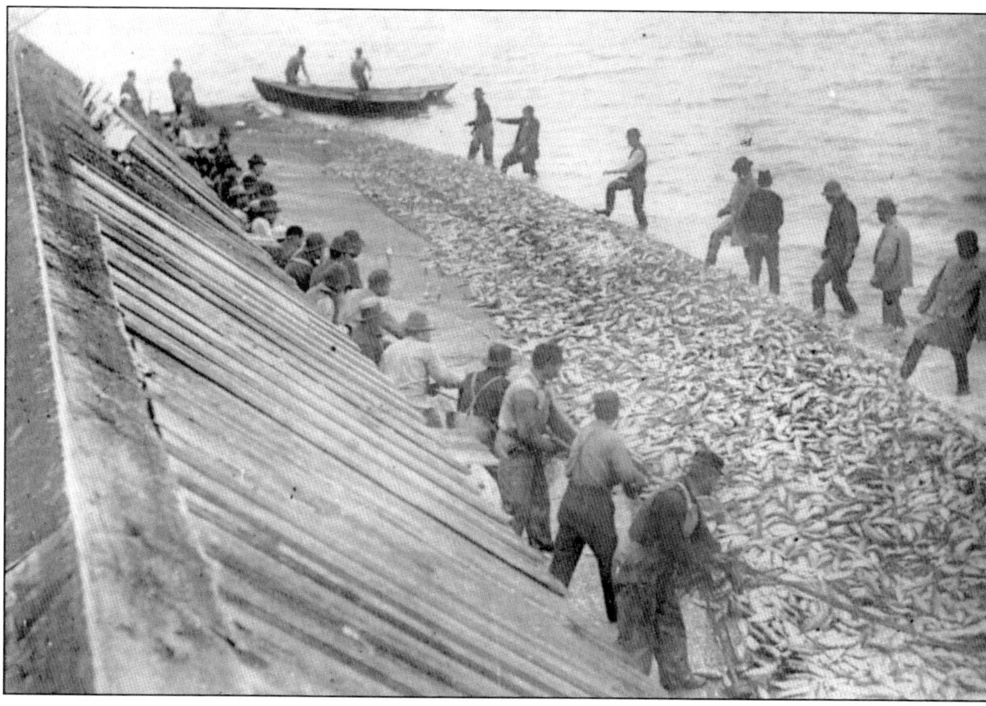

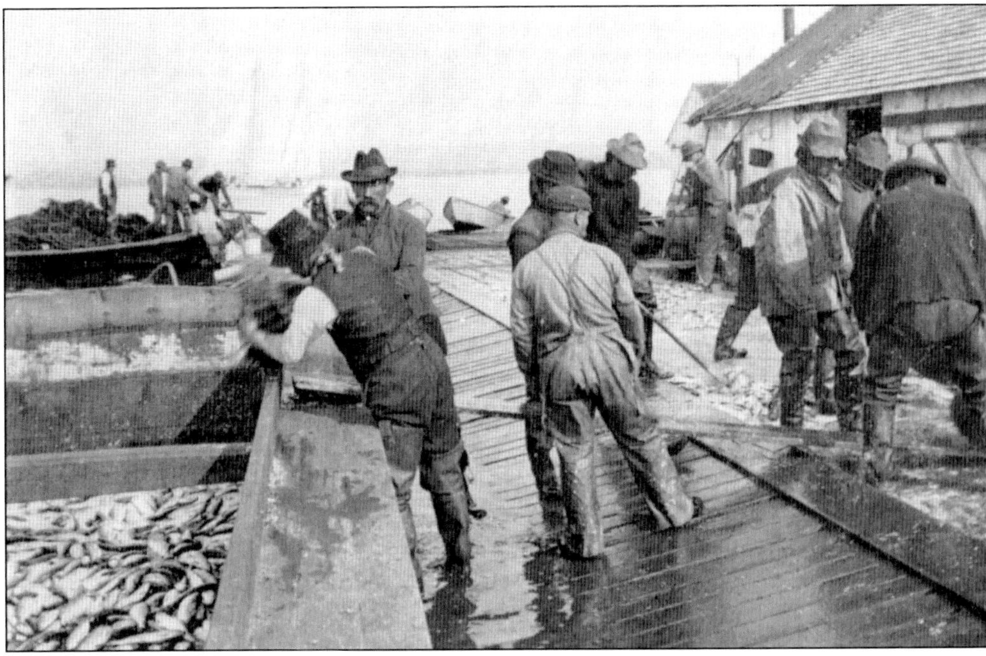

Between 1820 and 1830, the fishing industry in Port Deposit peaked with the invention of floats. Fish floats were large wooden platforms, usually about 75 feet long, that floated on the Susquehanna River and served as small towns for fishermen during the six-week fishing season. Living quarters consisted of small shacks. Each float had a large kitchen and storage bins for fish and food. A steam engine provided power to haul the nets. (Courtesy of the Historical Society of Cecil County.)

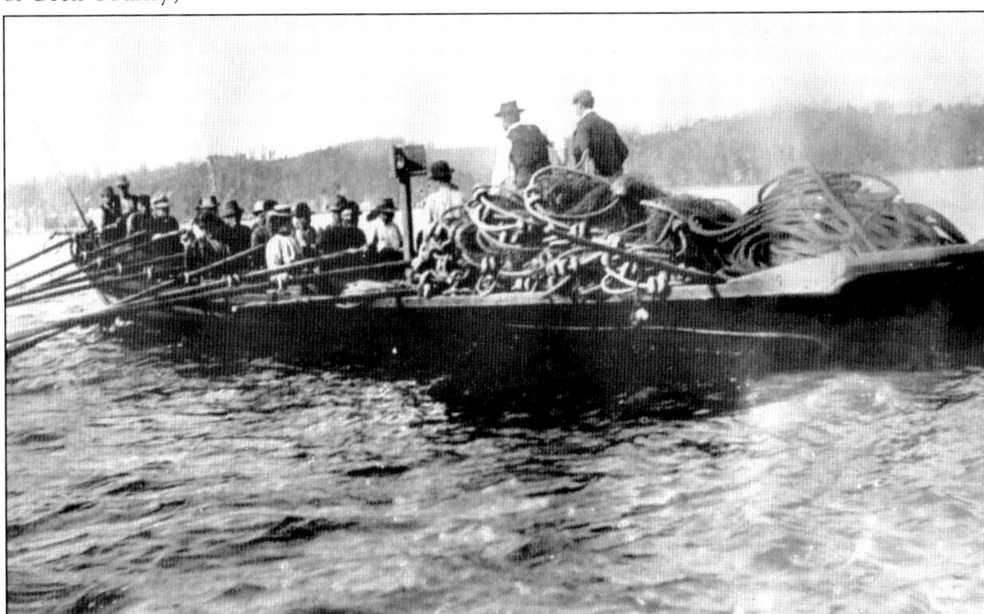

Family and friends sometimes visited the fishermen on the fishing floats for social outings. As late as 1902, a trip to the floats anchored midstream in the Susquehanna River for commercial fishing was a favorite spring excursion. (Courtesy of the Historical Society of Cecil County.)

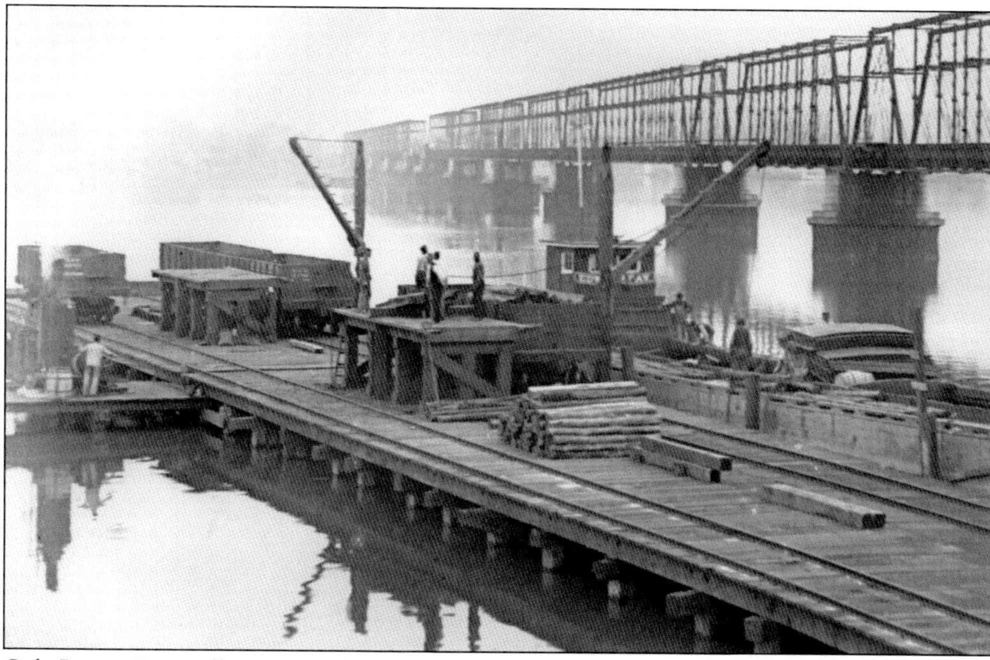

Cole Pier in Perryville was a working construction wharf in the early 20th century. In the 19th century, it was the site of the railroad wharf for the steam ferry *Maryland* connecting Perryville with Havre de Grace. The *Maryland*'s two tracks could hold 14 freight cars. The bridge in the background was the first railroad bridge across the Susquehanna, which was originally built of wood in 1867 and converted to metal in 1880. (Courtesy of the Historical Society of Cecil County.)

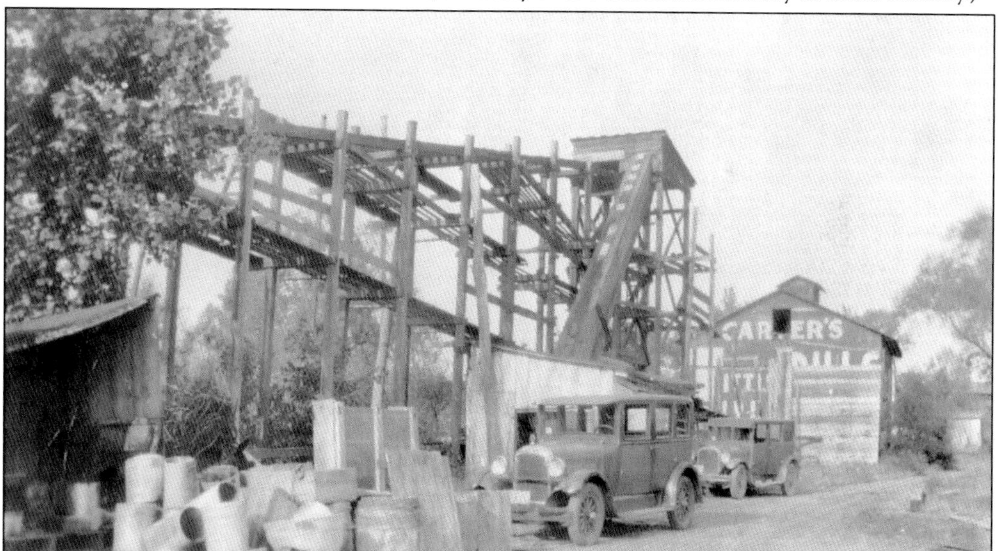

Ice harvesting began in Perryville about 1875 and become a mainstay of the town's economy, with at least 100,000 tons of ice harvested each winter. Ice was collected, stored, and transported, often by schooner, to cities along the Eastern Seaboard. Icehouses were filled in the winter with ice cut from surrounding ponds and waterways. The ground under the houses was dug out 10 to 12 feet and covered with straw. The insulation helped the ice remain frozen for months. (Courtesy of the Historical Society of Cecil County.)

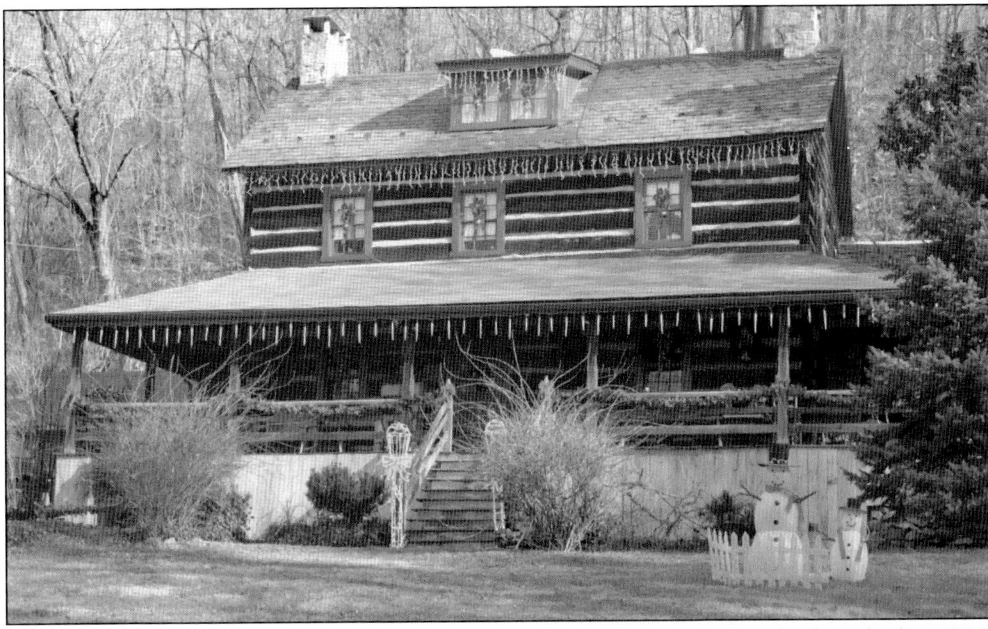

The Union House Restaurant in Port Deposit, which is still operating, dates back to the late 1700s when it was owned by James Gillespie and his wife, Martha, and was known as Gillespie's Log House. During the early 1800s, one of Gillespie's descendants operated it as a tavern and hotel, serving the many merchants and seamen who traveled down the Susquehanna on river arks, as well as travelers crossing the river on bridges and ferries. (Photograph by Christopher Knauss.)

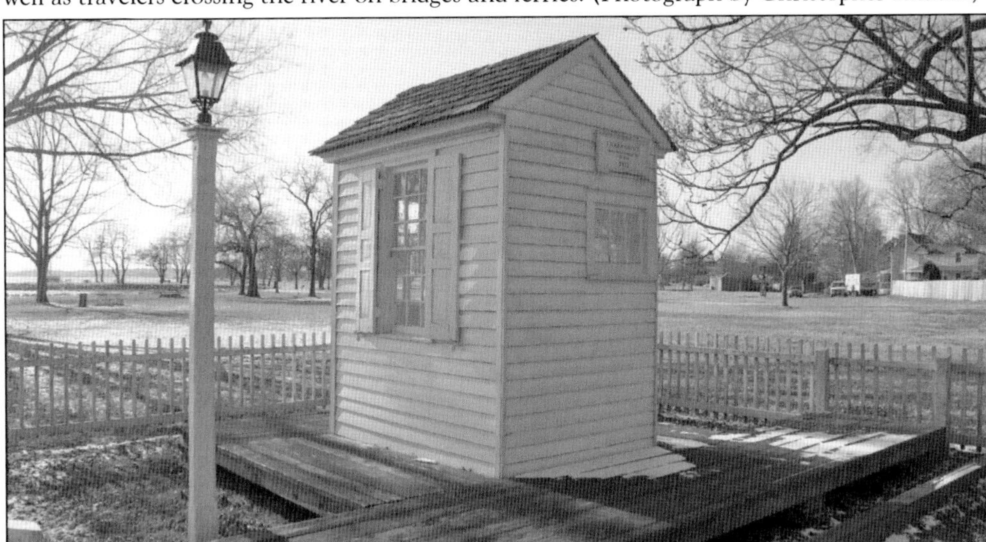

One of the first railroads in the country extended from New Castle, Delaware, to Frenchtown on the Elk River. It provided an important commercial link between the North and South. On March 31, 1830, the New Castle and Frenchtown Turnpike and Rail Road Company was formed, and the new railroad opened in 1831, using horses for about a year before switching to steam locomotives. The Chesapeake and Delaware Canal, which opened in 1829, became a major competitor to the railroad. This photograph is of the New Castle–Frenchtown Railroad Ticket House located at Battery Park in New Castle. (Photograph by Christopher Knauss.)

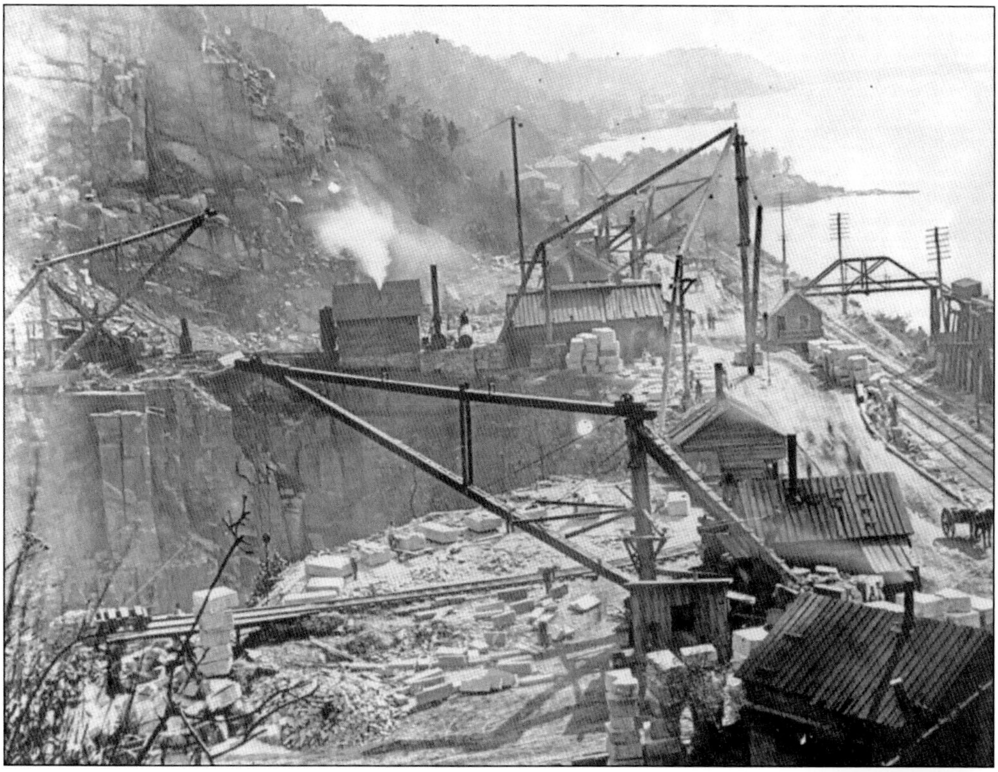

Construction of a bridge between Port Deposit and Lapidum in Harford County began in 1818 near the present-day Veterans of Foreign Wars. The bridge construction called for solid foundations, which led to the first Port Deposit granite quarry. In 1829, the Maryland Canal Company ran a quarry at the north end of Port Deposit, the beginning of the town's lucrative trade in granite, which was shipped down the Susquehanna. Granite deposits of the town were used in the construction of churches, schools, homes, and other buildings. The Concord Point Lighthouse in nearby Havre de Grace was constructed from Port Deposit granite. (Above, courtesy of the Historical Society of Cecil County; at right, photograph by Christopher Knauss.)

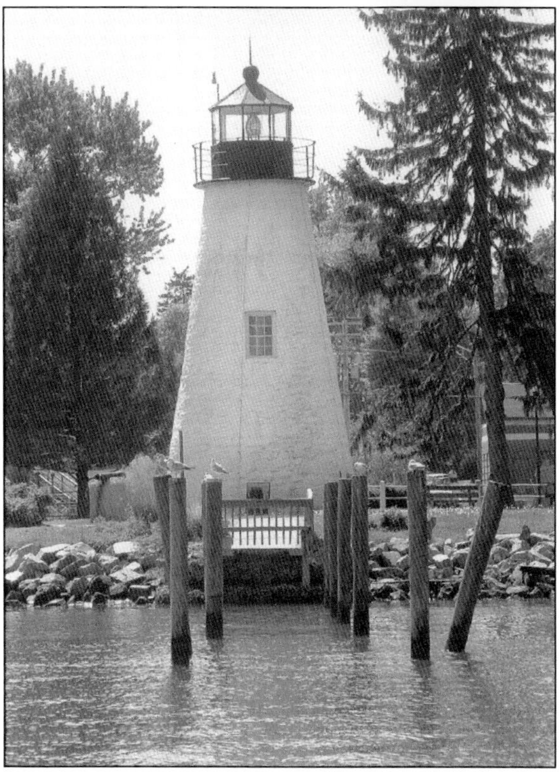

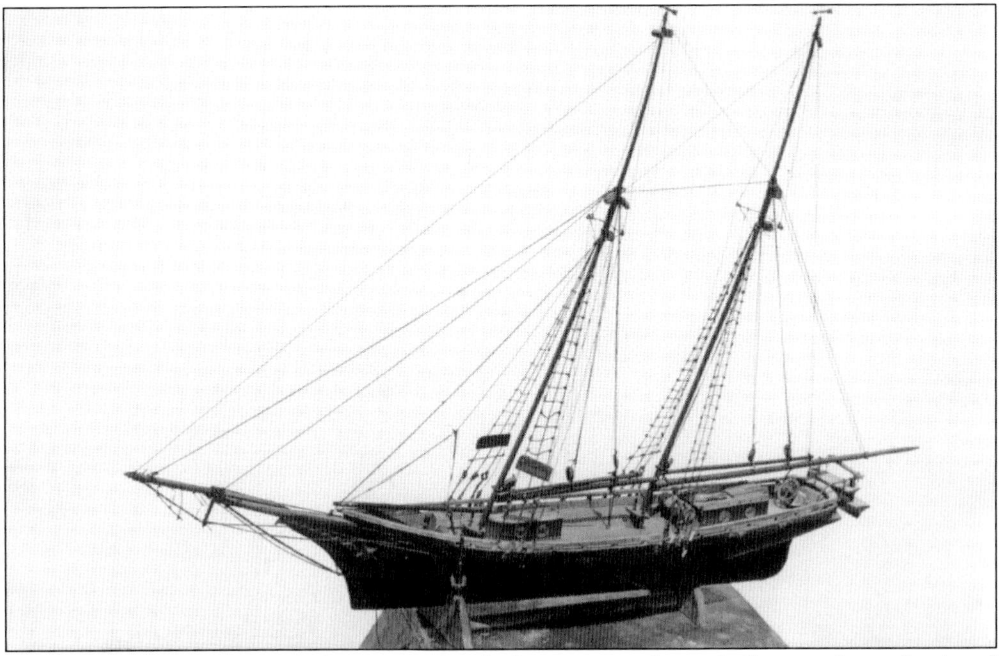

The pungy is a smaller form of schooner used to dredge oysters and carry bulk cargo. It was developed in the 1840s and 1850s in the Accomac region of Virginia's Eastern Shore. The pungy was a common site in Baltimore's harbor during World War I and up until the 1930s. Its use eventually gave way to boats like the bugeye and the skipjack. The pungy *Mystic* was owned and operated by George Wingate of North East until 1904. This model of the *Mystic*, c. 1975, was made by one of the crew for Wingate. (Courtesy of the Historical Society of Cecil County.)

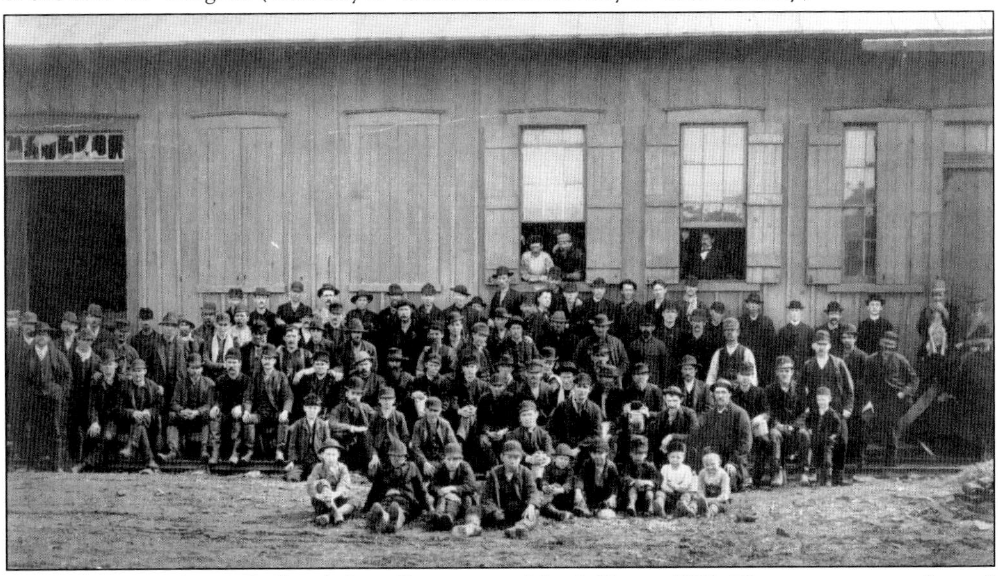

Workers pose at the McCullough Iron Company in North East c. 1880. The company was formed in 1861 and continued until 1898 as a successful business, shipping products from their location along the Northeast River. Through its various mills, the company eventually controlled the bulk of the United States trade in the manufacture of galvanized and sheet iron. (Courtesy of the Historical Society of Cecil County.)

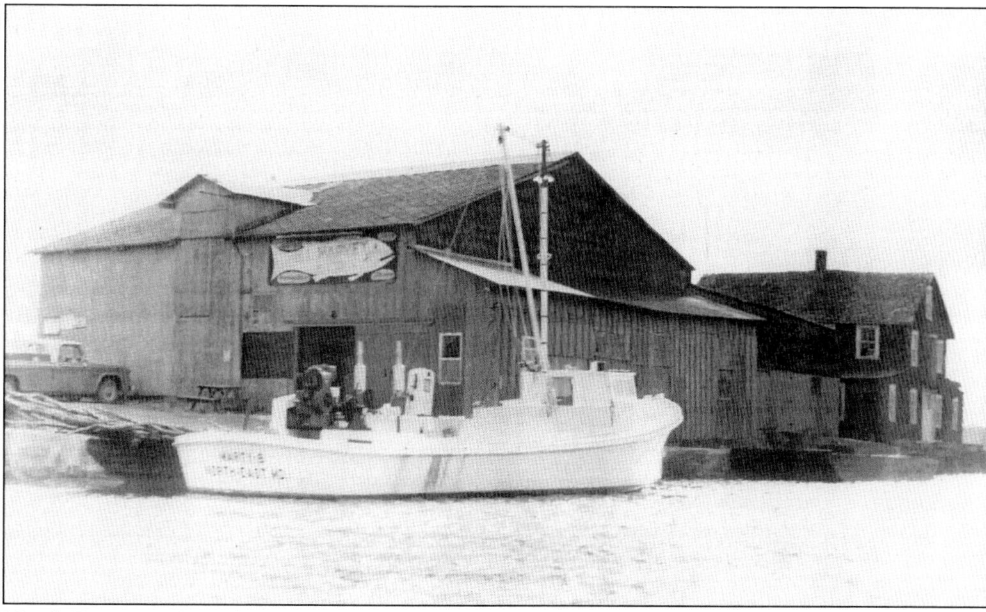

North East served as a bedroom community for nearby munitions and engineering plant workers, but the driving force behind the town's economy was fishing. The annual haul of herring and shad by the fleet of boats owned by H. L. Harvey's seafood company was enormous. Thousands of tons of fish and their eggs were pulled from nearby waters. (Courtesy of Jack Manning.)

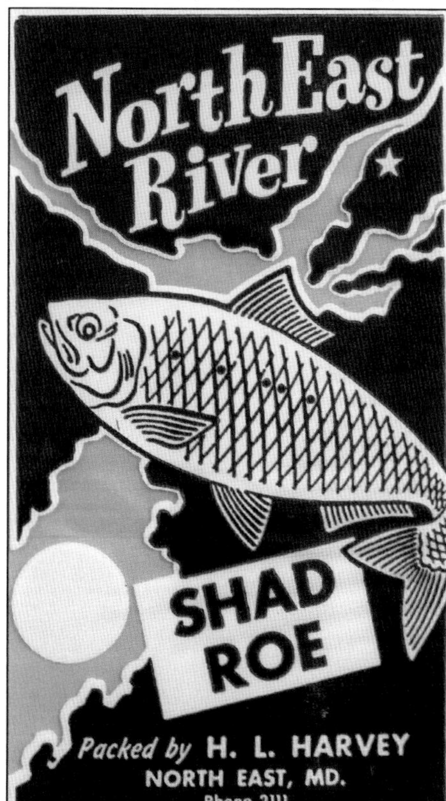

The upper Chesapeake Bay waters around Cecil County were a vital fishing area in the early 1900s. Employees of the H. L. Harvey Company processing plant in North East packed this shad roe bag. The Harvey business opened in 1880. The town purchased the property in 1977 for the North East Community Park. The plant site now is the home of the Upper Bay Museum, which houses an extensive collection of hunting, boating, and fishing artifacts native to the region. (Photograph by Christopher Knauss.)

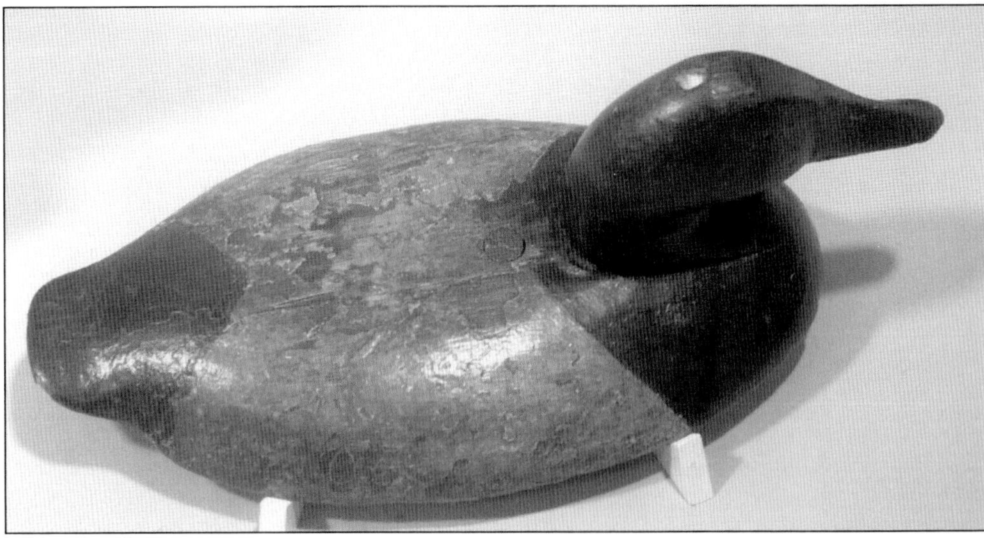

Acting as a funnel for the Atlantic flyway, the upper Chesapeake Bay saw millions of birds pass through during the famed market hunting period of the late 19th and early 20th century. Susquehanna Flats decoy carvers like Capt. Ben Dye, of Perryville, preferred soft Pennsylvania white pine, which was floated down the river as large, log rafts fastened with dowels. Dye used the end of a raft log to carve this decoy, which is the reason for the unusual dowel. (Courtesy of the Chesapeake Bay Maritime Museum.)

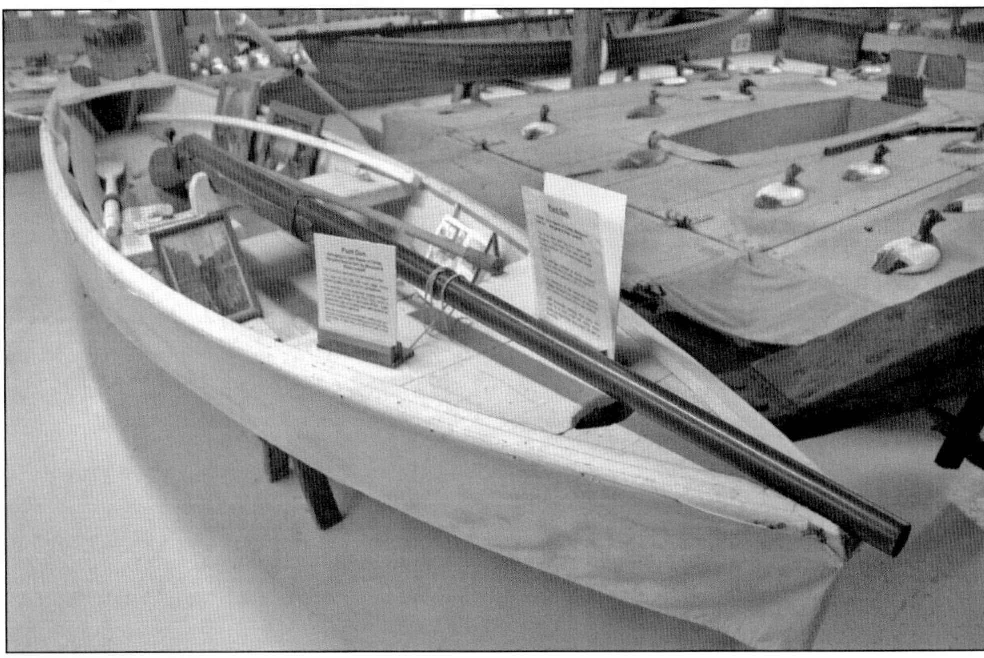

Punt guns, like this one on display at the Upper Bay Museum in North East, were used by market duck hunters. One shot could kill over 50 canvasbacks. A hunter aimed the punt gun mounted in the boat by shifting his weight and maneuvering the boat up to the flock. This type of activity was usually done illegally at night as it was the only time the tactic was successful. The invention of the automatic loading shotgun and federal laws in the early 1900s brought the end of the punt gun. (Photograph by Christopher Knauss.)

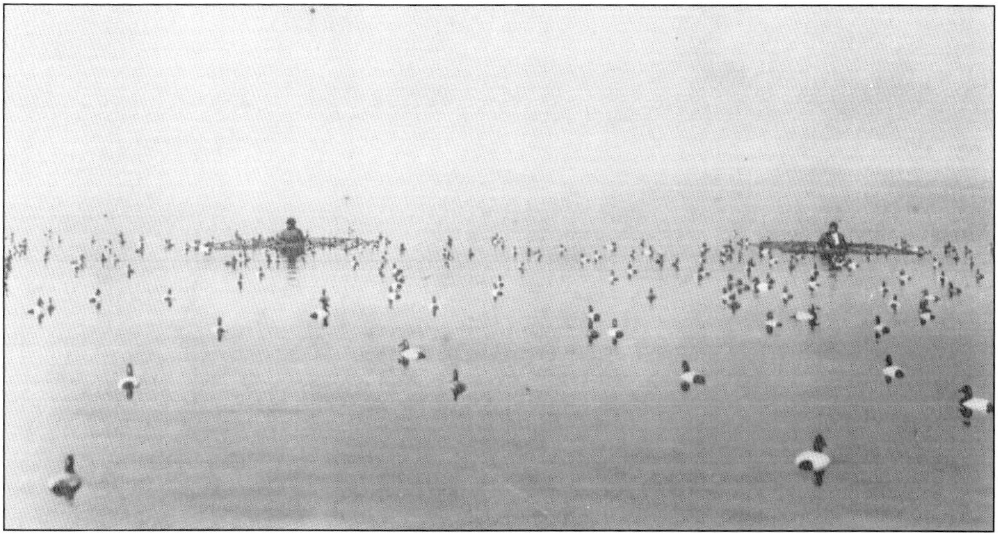

Elite hotels and men's clubs along the Eastern Seaboard served waterfowl in the 19th and early 20th centuries. Market gunners from rural areas supplied many of the ducks. For years, market hunting provided valuable income to Cecil County families. The sinkbox—a floating blind that hid part of the hunter beneath the water surface—was popular during the market gunning days. This sinkbox double-rig, *c.* 1900, was employed near Carpenter's Point. (Courtesy of Jack Manning.)

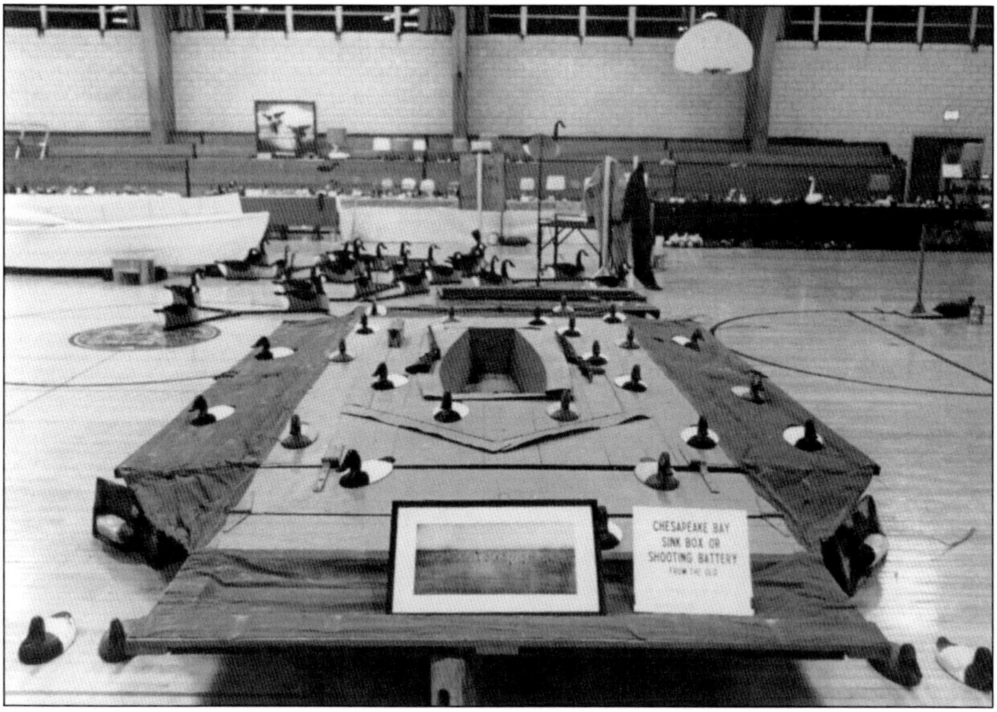

This sinkbox was displayed at one of the first Upper Bay Decoy Shows in North East. The annual show began in 1968 and continues today. Many Upper Bay decoys wore brands that identified ownership. The brands were marks of decoy makers, market hunters, gunning clubs, and gunning scows. Some of these brands are very rare, and an otherwise ordinary decoy wearing one of these brands can today be a valuable artifact. (Courtesy of Jack Manning.)

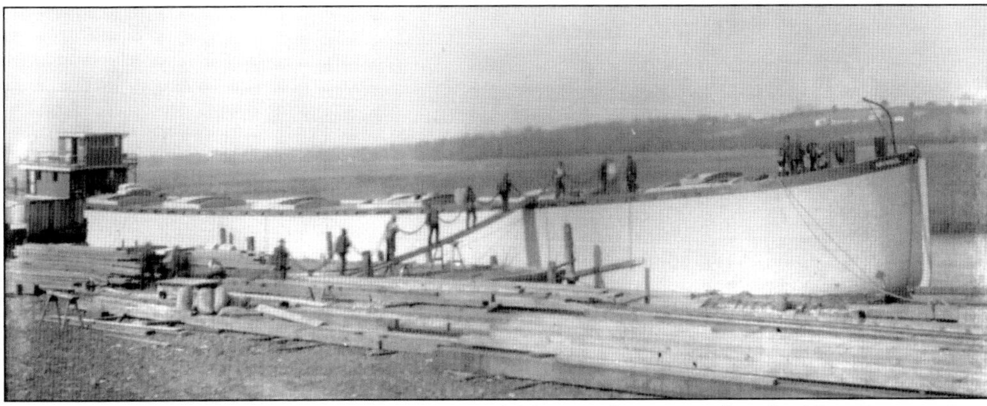

With timber, iron, and plenty of waterways available, Cecil County's boatbuilding history dates back to Colonial days. As early as 1744, the state assembly supplemented the incorporation of Charlestown to use Seneca Point for a shipyard. In 1877, Henry Deibert brought his family and seven workmen to Elk Landing to build canal boats. By 1902, the Deiberts had built as many as 70 barges, ranging from 100 to 200 feet in length. They were built of oak and yellow pine. Other boatbuilders at Elk Landing included Rudolph and Bennett and Patridge and Hollingsworth. After the government stopped dredging the Elk River, large shipbuilding ended at Elk Landing. The Deiberts moved their operation to Long Creek in Chesapeake City. (Courtesy of the Historical Society of Cecil County.)

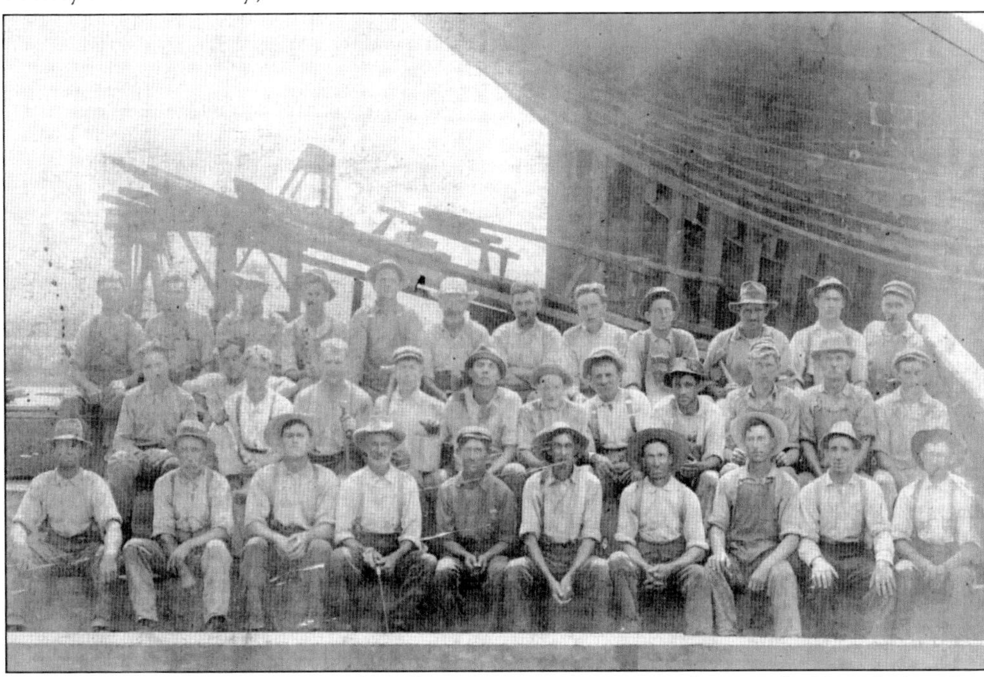

Employees of the Deibert Boat Yard in Elkton pose in this vintage photograph. Identified workers include Joe Simmons, Hilard Jamison, Hooper Heath, Billy Clayton, Clarence Leveredge, John Jamison, George Bedwell, Stewart Bedwell, Elwood Davis, Dolph Moore, Isaac Simmons, Sam Clements, Alexander Bedwell, Bart Ward, Havery Rothwell, Oscar Fowler, Earl Draper, George Deibert, Howard Clark, Charles Crawford, Calvin Ward, William Deibert, John Shafier, Alfred Simmons, John Ward, John Simmons, and Edward Plummer. (Courtesy of the Historical Society of Cecil County.)

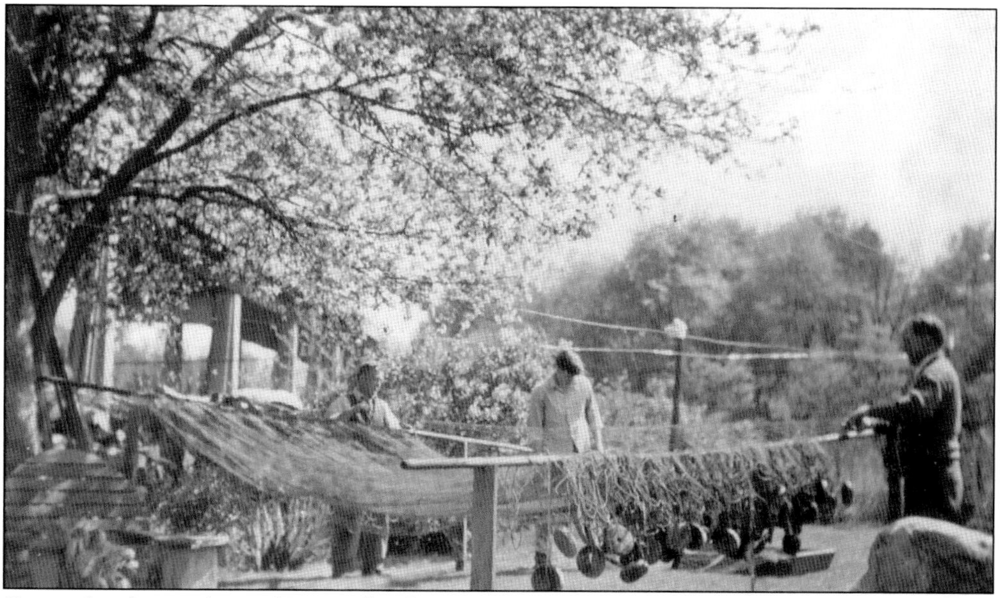

Owens family members of Perryville clean, dry, and repair a fishing net used commercially to harvest perch, shad, and striped bass in the upper bay tributaries. Early fishing seines were short and made of hemp or flax twine, which was spun on the spinning wheels in use at the time. Longer seines became commercially viable when increases in coastal city populations and better transportation created a greater demand for the area's fish. (Courtesy of Barbara Brown.)

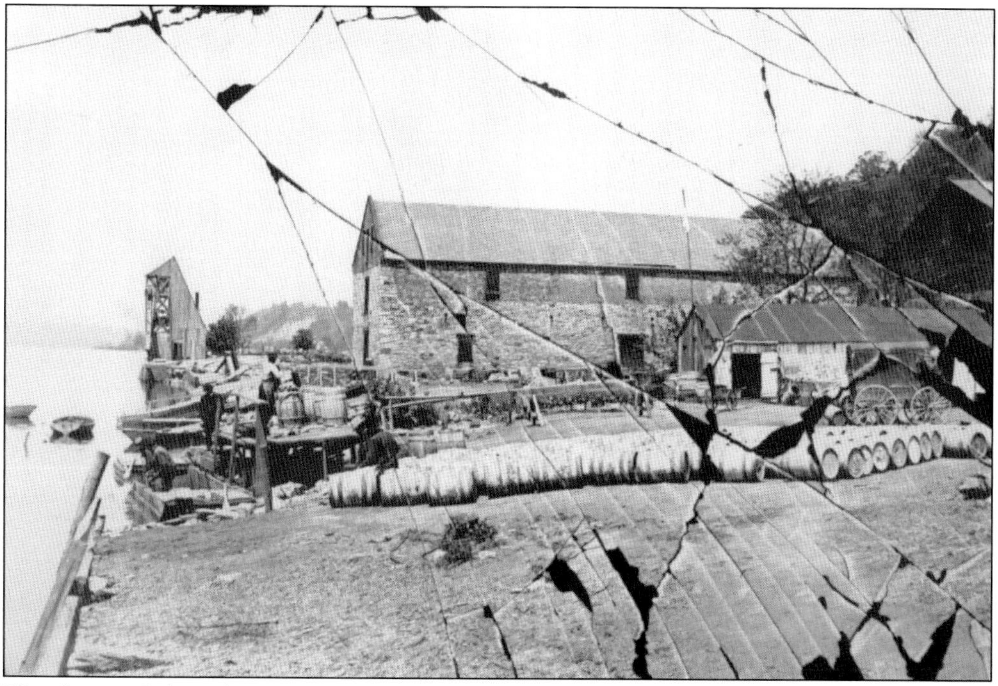

This shattered glass-plate negative image reveals extensive barrels of herring and shad roe waiting for delivery at the north end of Port Deposit. The roe was shipped to Baltimore, Philadelphia, and New York, usually on any boat the processors could put their hands on, such as a scow, a bugeye, a schooner, or, later, steam vessels. (Courtesy of the Port Deposit Heritage Corporation.)

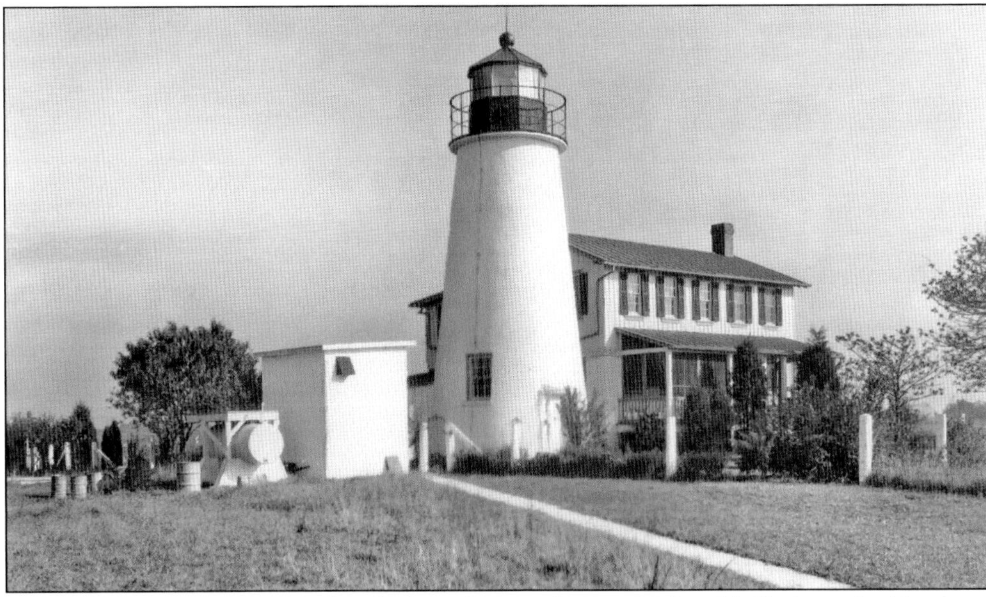

Turkey Point Lighthouse is 35 feet high and situated on a 100-foot bluff where the Northeast and Elk Rivers converge. Originally the tower had a panel of red glass to warn ships they were approaching the shallows. The beacon was visible for 13 miles and was the highest of 74 lighthouses on the bay. It was authorized by Congress in 1831 and built in 1833 with a tower and keeper's quarters by John Donohoo. Today only the lighthouse and the oil house remain. (Courtesy of the Historical Society of Cecil County.)

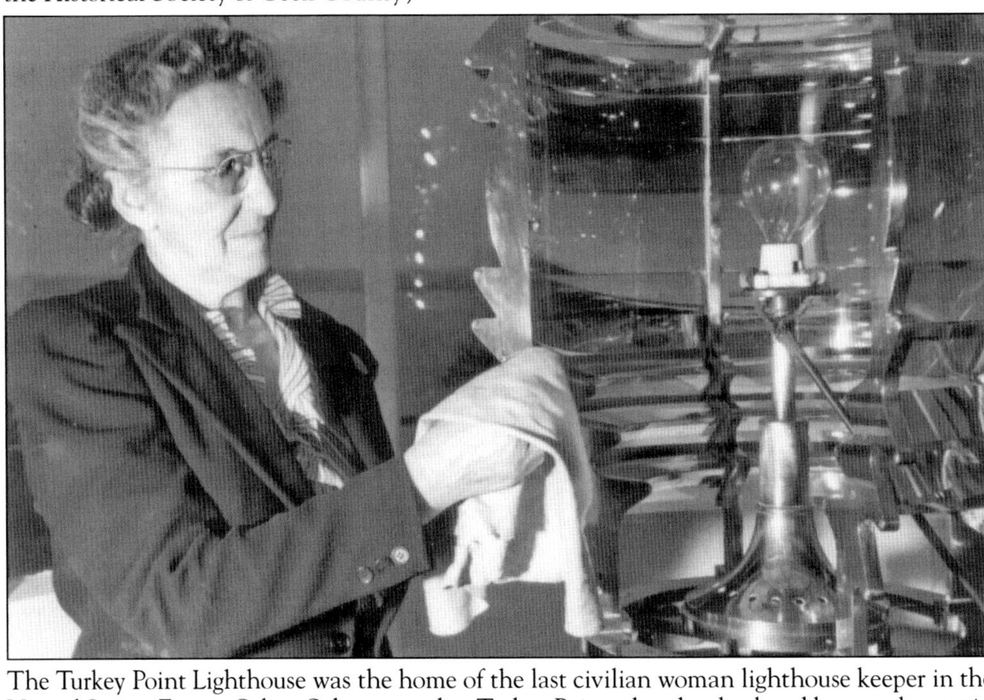

The Turkey Point Lighthouse was the home of the last civilian woman lighthouse keeper in the United States, Fannie Salter. Salter moved to Turkey Point when her husband became keeper in 1919. When he died in 1925, she successfully appealed to her senator and received the appointment. Salter served from 1925 until she retired in 1947. (Courtesy of the U.S. Coast Guard.)

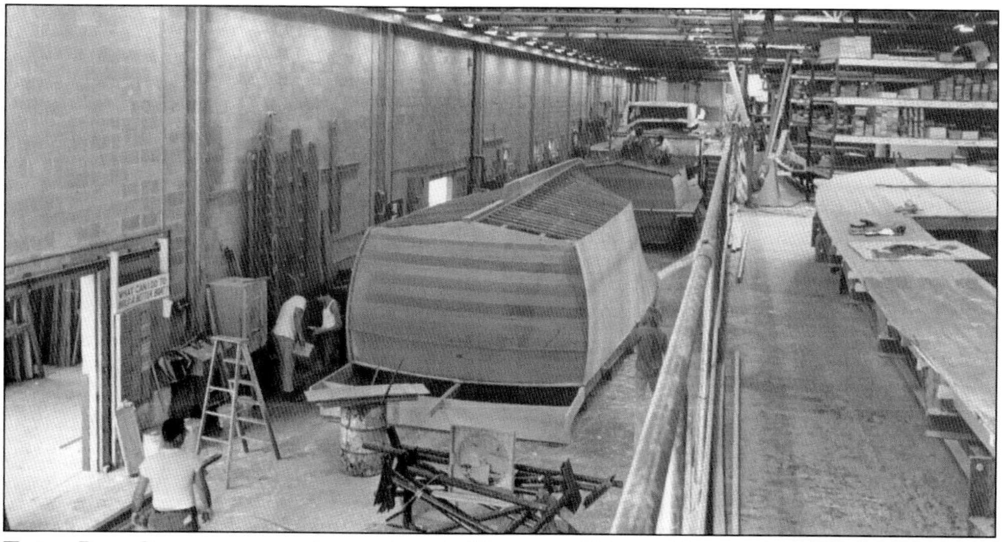

Trojan Boat Company opened operations in Elkton in 1964 on 26 acres on Oldfield Point Road on Big Elk Creek. The facility consisted of one main plant building, a guard shed, and a solvent waste storage area. Between 60 and 80 employees produced inboard pleasure boats. The company crafted wooden boats up until 1972, when it switched to fiberglass, merging with Whittaker Corporation for capital financing. The company survived the change and began making well-built fiberglass boats, the most successful in sizes from 28 to 36 feet. From about 1972 to 1992, Whittaker plants produced about 2,200 twin-inboard 32-foot sedans. (Courtesy of the Historical Society of Cecil County.)

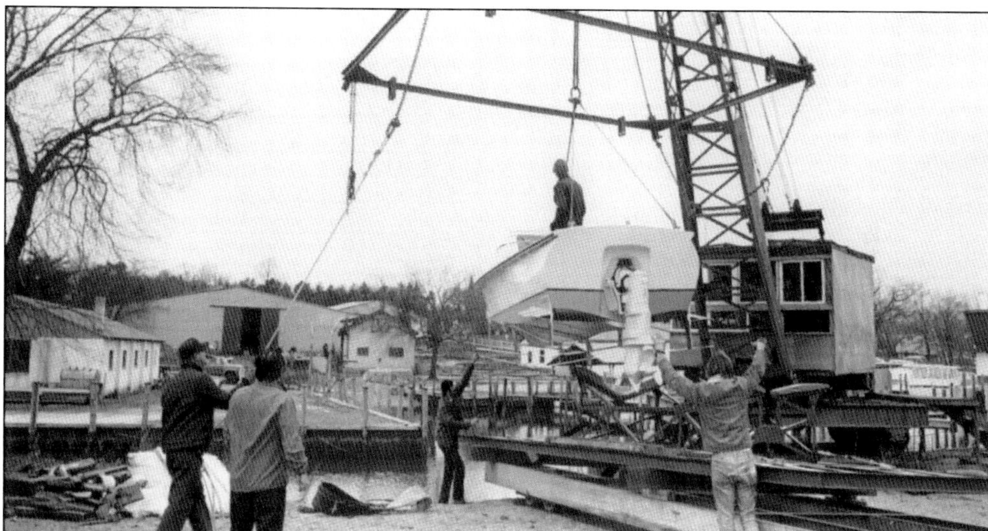

Trojans Boats originally began in 1949 when two men Jim McQueen and Harper Hull, bought the Cottrell-Spoore Boatworks in Troy, New York. In 1954, the company introduced the famous Trojan Sea Breeze, which generated 800 orders. In the 1960s, the 31-foot Sea Voyager came out, and 10,000 of these wooden cruisers were produced over the next decade. By 1968, Trojan facilities in Lancaster, Pennsylvania; Elkton, Maryland; and Niagara-on-the-Lake, Ontario, Canada, made Trojan the second largest producer of inboard boats in the world. (Courtesy of the Historical Society of Cecil County.)

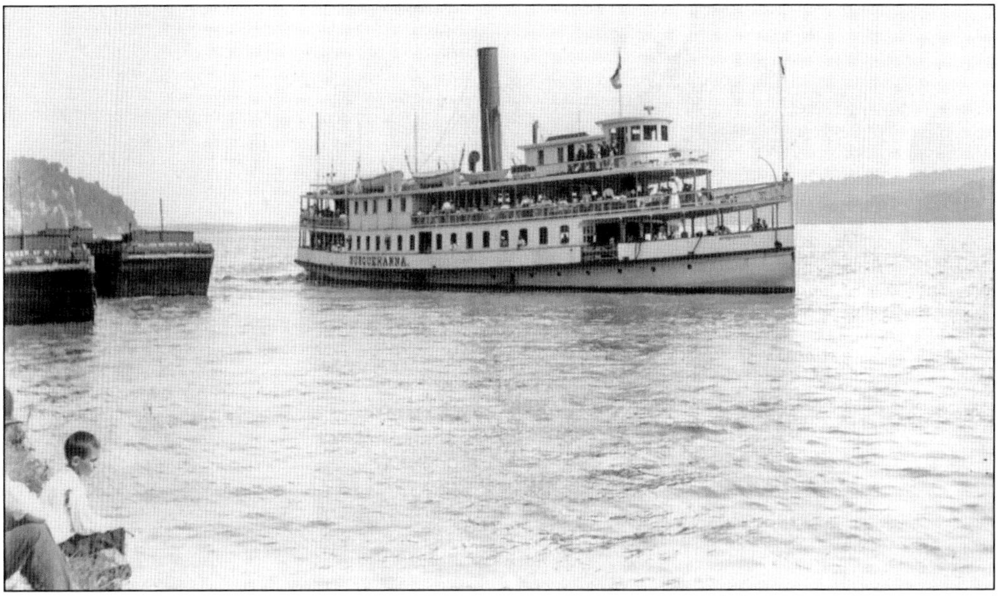

The steamer *Susquehanna* floats near Port Deposit, *c.* 1905. One of the original inventors of the steamboat was a native of southern Cecil County. Born in 1743, James Rumsey became a mechanical engineer and inventor. In 1786, Rumsey built a pump-driven boat and successfully steamed upstream on the Potomac River. The following year, he received a patent on his steamboat invention, which was described as a way to propel a boat by a stream of water, forced by steam through a cylinder parallel to the keel. He received an exclusive right to use his invention for 10 years. (Courtesy of the Historical Society of Cecil County.)

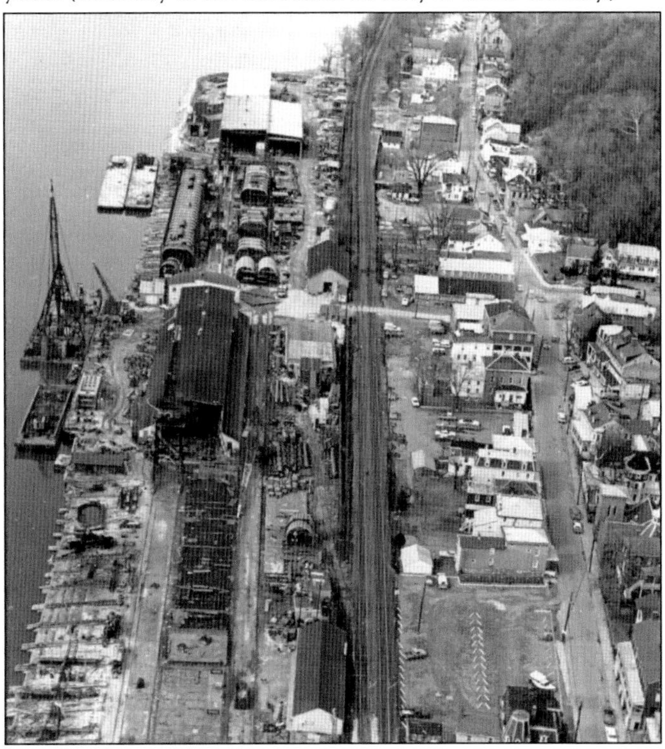

This February 1977 aerial photograph by George Hipkins depicts the expansive Wiley Equipment Company in Port Deposit. The dark, thin structure at the top left is a tunnel being built for the Washington, D.C., subway system. Glen M. Wiley of Lancaster, Pennsylvania, founded Wiley Manufacturing Company in Port Deposit in 1939. One of the largest ships built at Wiley Manufacturing in Port Deposit was MN *Miss Circle Line*, built for Circle Line–State of Liberty, Inc., of New York. This 152-foot ferry could carry 1,037 passengers and took over eight months to build in 1964. (Courtesy of the Historical Society of Cecil County.)

Four

THE CANAL

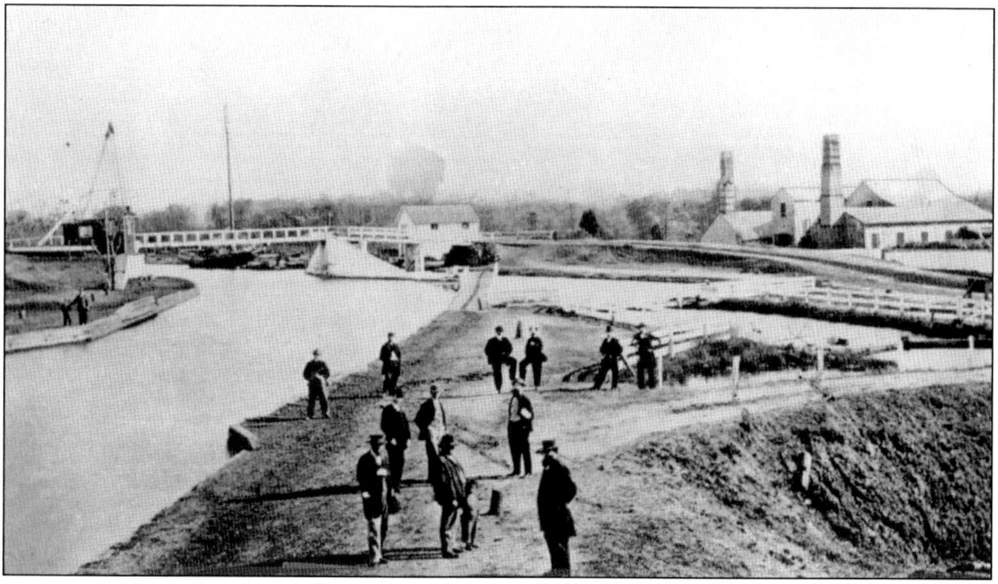

In the mid-1600s, Augustine Herrman, a Dutch envoy and mapmaker, observed that two great bodies of water, the Delaware River and Chesapeake Bay, were separated only by a narrow strip of land. Herrman proposed that a waterway be constructed to connect them. The canal would reduce, by nearly 300 miles, the water routes between Philadelphia and Baltimore. More than a century later, the project began. The 14-mile-long, 10-foot-deep, and 66-foot-wide canal opened for business in 1829. Toll-takers charged ships for the opportunity to use the canal. Today the Chesapeake and Delaware Canal is 35 feet deep and 450 feet wide and owned by the federal government. It's the busiest canal in the nation with the passage of 15,000 vessels per year from ports around the globe. A group of men congregate on the causeway in this scene at the Chesapeake and Delaware Canal in Chesapeake City, c. 1865. In the background are the High Bridge and canal steam pump. As early as the 17th century, settlers to the New World understood progress through industry and commerce would depend upon practical transportation of goods across both land and water. (Courtesy of the U.S. Army Corps of Engineers.)

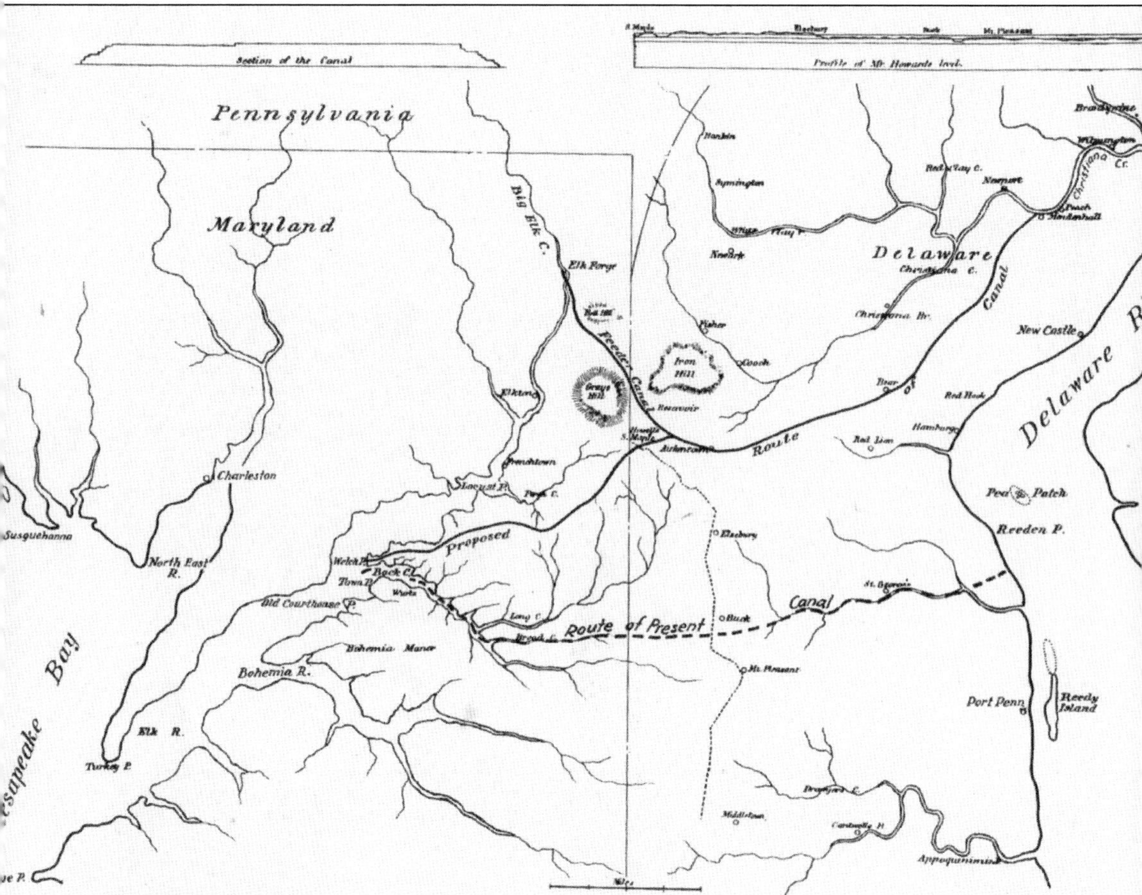

Reproduced from map published in "A Memoir on the Chesapeake and Delaware Canal" by Joshua Gilpin, dated 1821.

ROUTE PROPOSED IN 1804 TO CONNECT ELK RIVER WITH "CHRISTIANA CREEK"

In the mid-1760s, surveys of possible water routes across the Delaware/Maryland Peninsula were made, but no other work was completed. The issue of constructing the canal was raised again in 1788 by regional business leaders, including noted Philadelphians Benjamin Franklin and Benjamin Rush. In 1802, following actions by the legislatures of Maryland, Delaware, and Pennsylvania, the Chesapeake and Delaware (C&D) Canal Company was incorporated. More surveys followed, and in 1804, construction of the canal began, including 14 locks to connect the Christina River in Delaware with the Elk River at Welch Point in Maryland. Work was suspended in 1806 and later abandoned for a new location connecting Broad Creek with St. George's Creek, substantially the route of the present canal. Canal construction began in earnest in April 1824, and in several years, some 2,600 men were digging and hauling dirt from the ditch. Laborers toiled with pick and shovel working for an average daily wage of 75¢. In 1829, the C&D Canal Company opened the waterway for business. (Courtesy of the U.S. Army Corps of Engineers.)

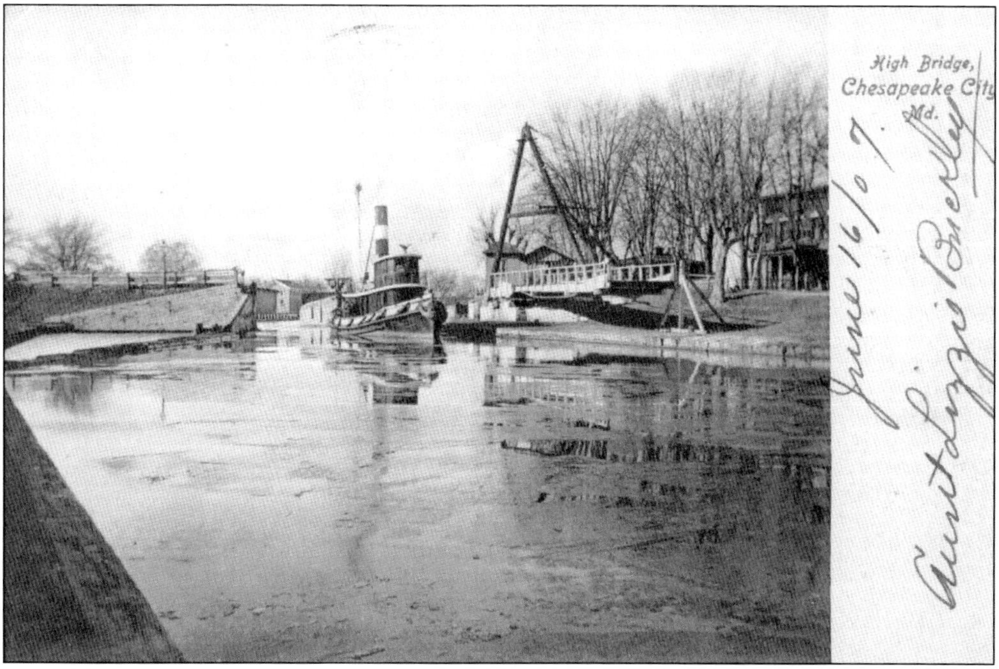

The tugboat *Startle* heads east through High Bridge in Chesapeake City in this *c.* 1905 postcard. High Bridge crossed the canal between the canal lock and the raceway of the waterwheel built in 1852. (Courtesy of Jack Manning.)

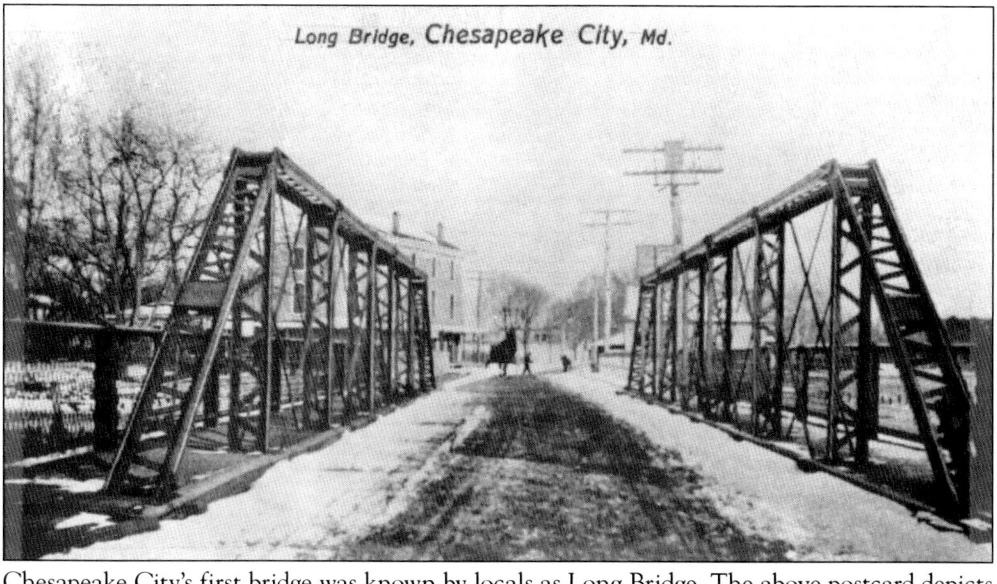

Chesapeake City's first bridge was known by locals as Long Bridge. The above postcard depicts the view across Long Bridge over Back Creek in South Chesapeake City from what is now Pell Gardens. To the left is the Masonic Hall built in 1870. The hall was near the east end of Long Bridge, which ran across the mouth of the basin from the dock area (Pell Gardens) to the Corps of Engineers property today. (Courtesy of the U.S. Army Corps of Engineers.)

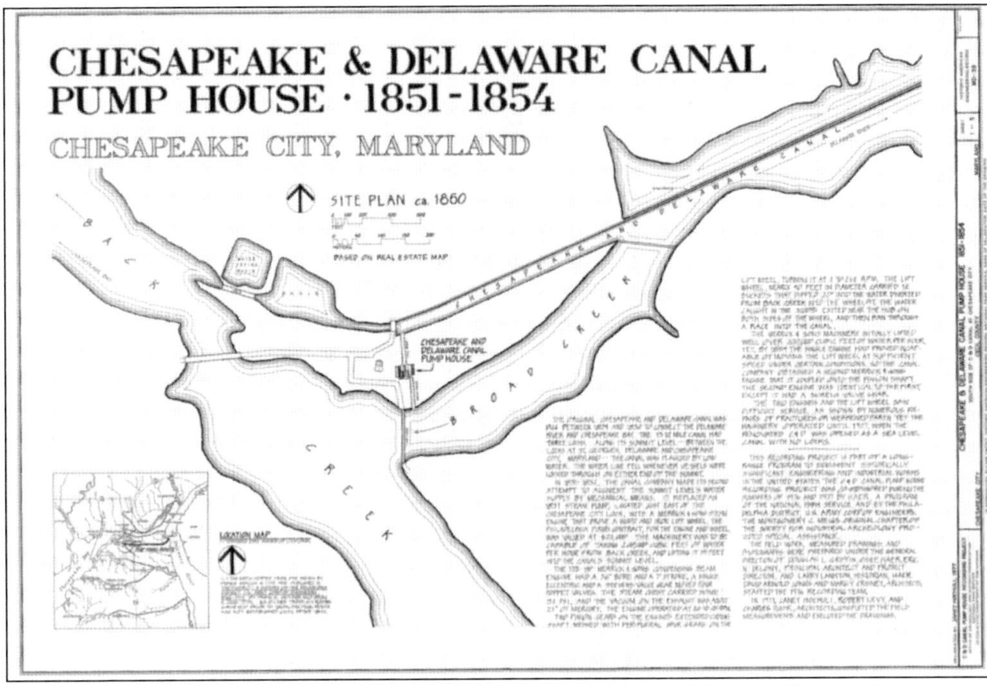

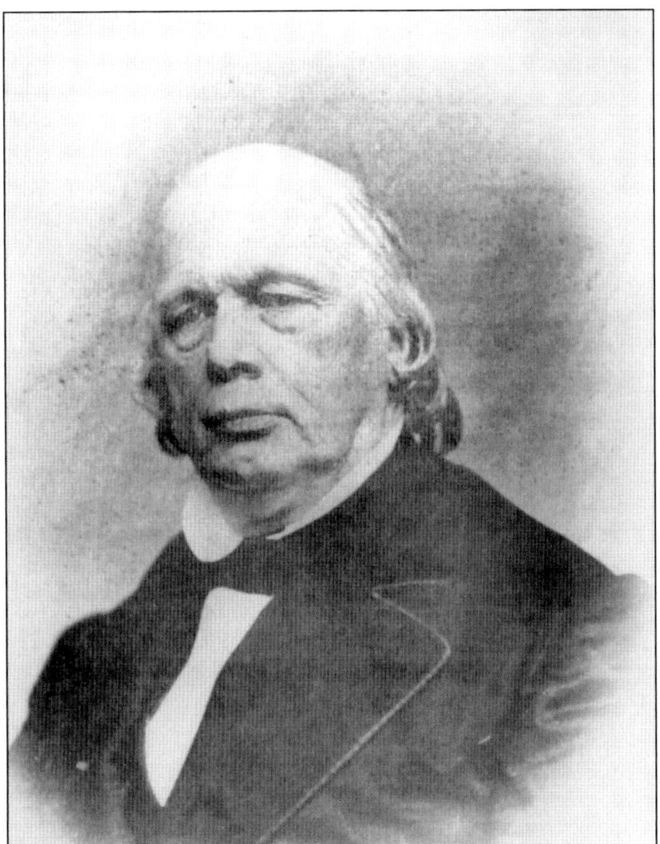

The canal's water levels were a continual problem, and a means to lift water from Back Creek into the canal was necessary. A steam-operated pump was purchased in 1837, and in 1852, a steam engine and large waterwheel were installed at the pump house in Chesapeake City. Measuring 39 feet in diameter and 10 feet wide, the iron-and-wood waterwheel had 12 troughs that filled with water as it turned; the water then spilled over the hub into the raceway and into the uppermost canal level. By 1854, a second steam engine was in use. The waterwheel and steam engines remained in continuous use through the mid-1920s. Samuel Merrick (left) and Sons, of Philadelphia, constructed the pumping machinery. (Courtesy of the U.S. Army Corps of Engineers.)

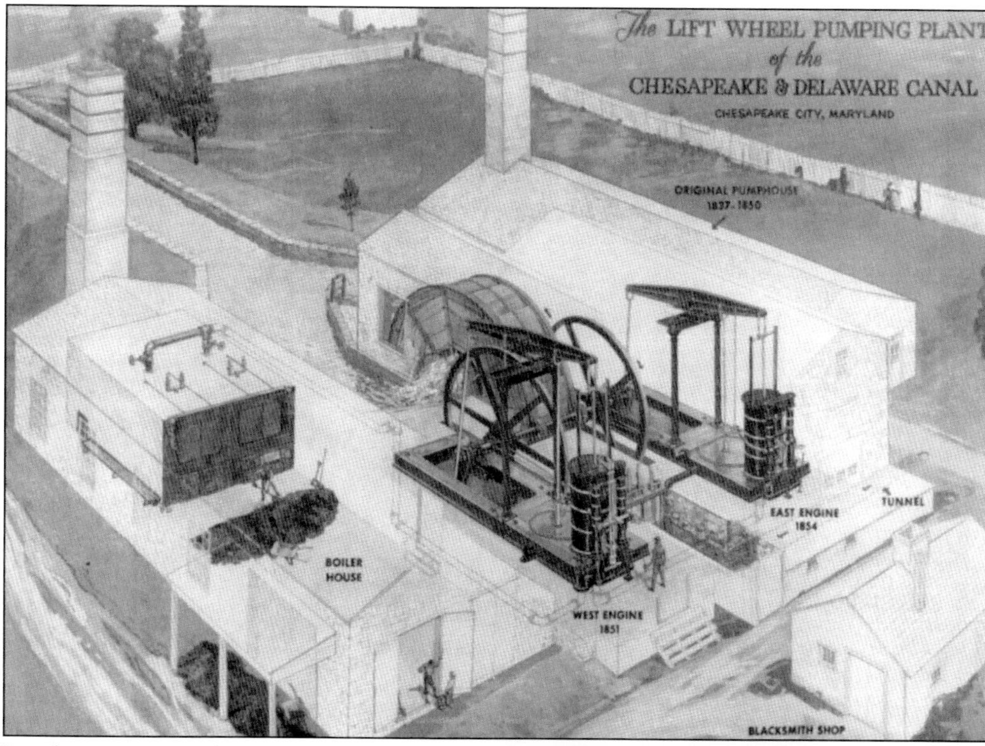

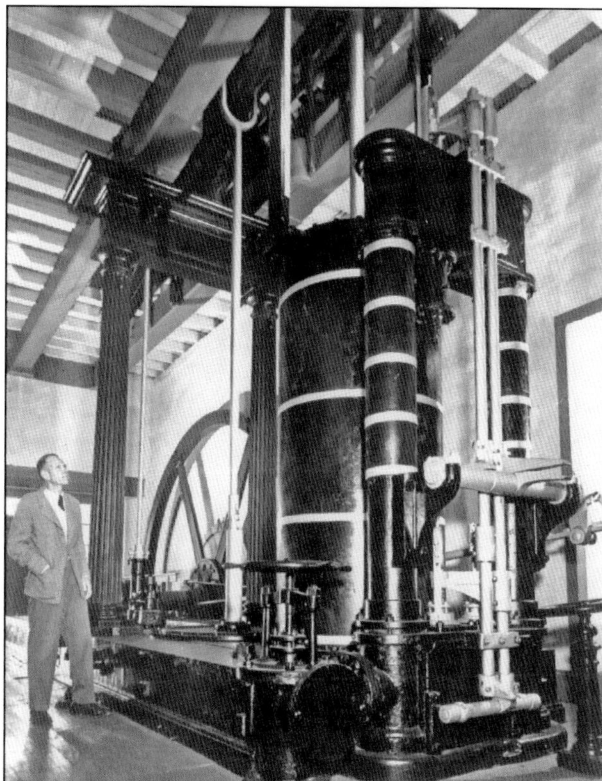

Resident engineer Clarence Brown appears alongside the west steam engine used to power the waterwheel, *c.* 1965. With the addition of the second engine in 1855, the speed of both engines was timed at 18 revolutions per minute, the scoop wheel at two revolutions, and the wheel's dip was increased to 28 inches. The wheel could lift 170 tons of water per minute, running 18 to 24 hours per day. (Courtesy of the U.S. Army Corps of Engineers.)

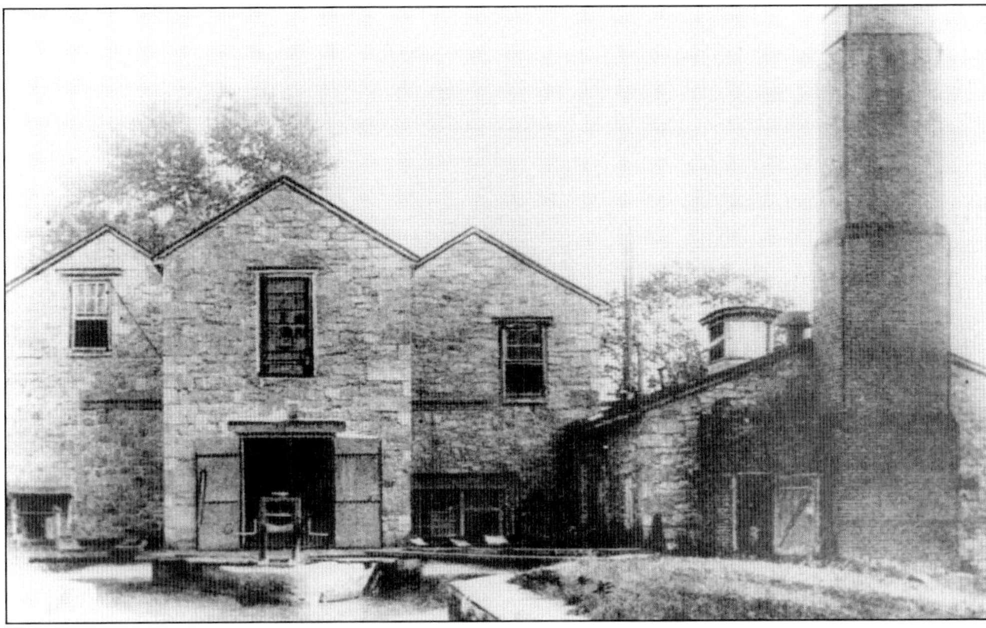

This photograph, c. 1890, is a view of the building housing the waterwheel pump. The tall stack extending out of the picture to the right was used to improve the draft of the boiler. The original boilers were a type used by Oliver Evans in high-pressure steam engines designed in 1814. The two 150-horsepower engines consumed 8 tons of coal daily. The original boilers were replaced in 1865 by two locomotive boilers that operated until 1895. In 1895, Pusey and Jones of Wilmington, Delaware, installed a pair of large round boiler tubes that had a combined capacity of 500 horsepower. They were in use until 1927, when the pumping plant shut down. (Above, courtesy of the U.S. Army Corps of Engineers; below, photograph by Christopher Knauss.)

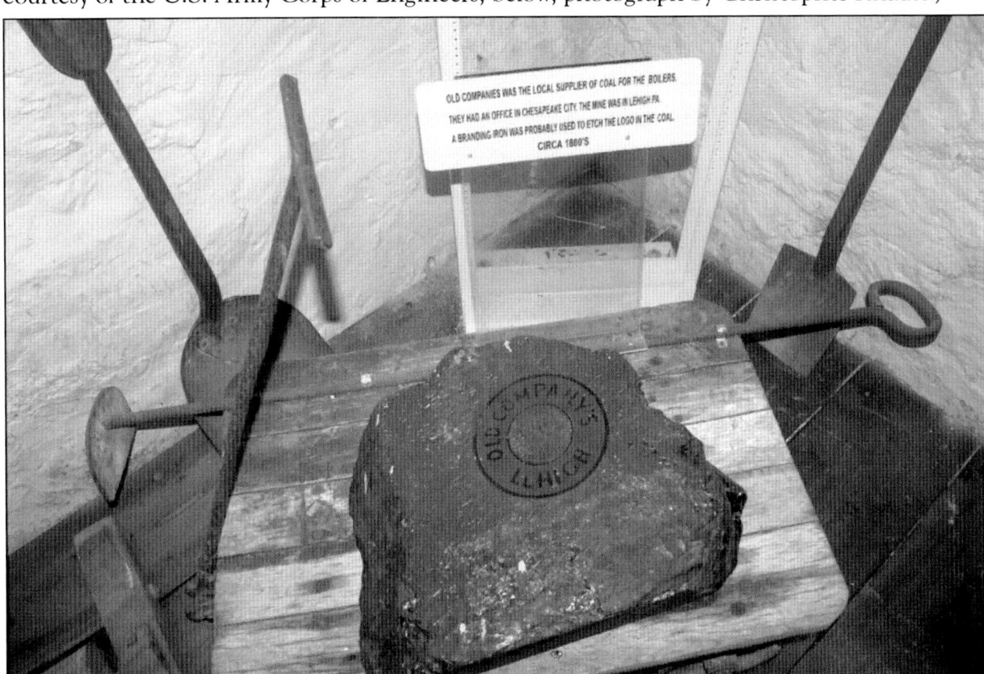

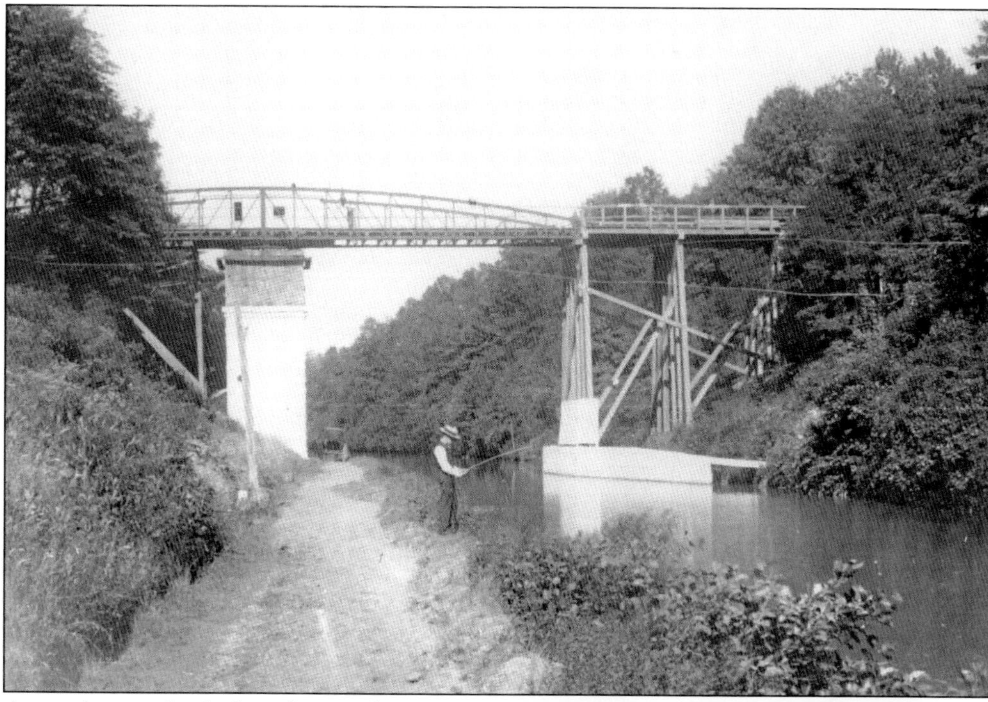

An angler tries his luck in the canal, c. 1915, with a view of Buck Bridge at Summit, which also shows the mule towpath. Before steam power, teams of mules and horses towed freight and passenger barges, schooners, and sloops through the canal. Cargo included practically every useful item of daily life: lumber, grain, farm products, fish, cotton, coal, iron, and whiskey. Packet lines were eventually established to move freight through the waterway. The base of Buck Bridge was the original location of the stone memorial plaque, right, before it was moved to its present location at the lock pump house in Chesapeake City. (Above, courtesy of the U.S. Army Corps of Engineers; at right, photograph by Christopher Knauss.)

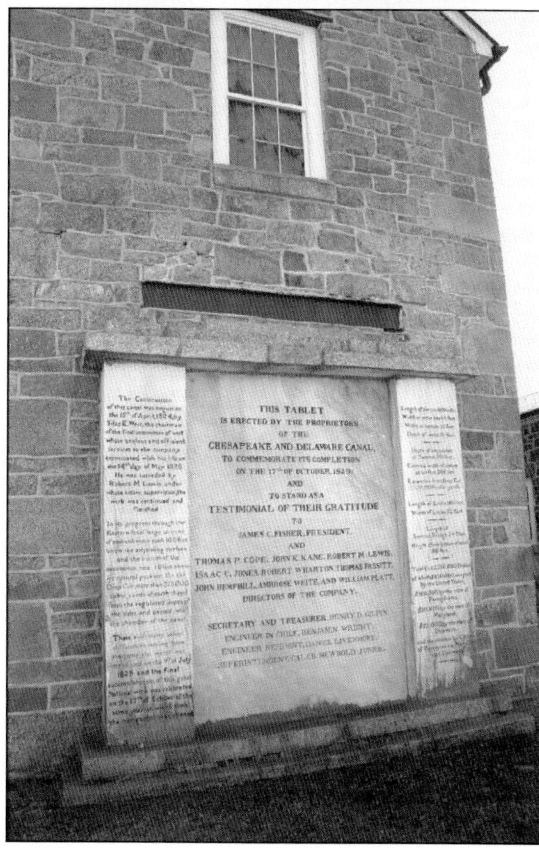

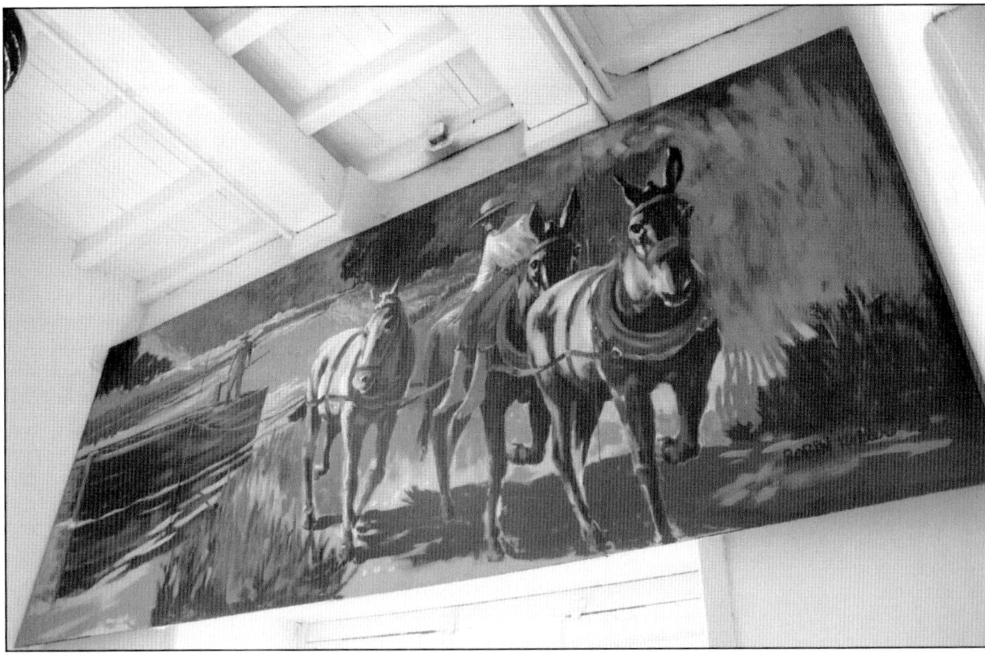

Robin Heller's painting of a mule team pulling a barge in the early years of the Chesapeake and Delaware Canal, prior to the use of steam tugboats, is displayed at the C&D Canal Museum in South Chesapeake City. A towpath ran along the north side of the canal. (Photograph by Christopher Knauss.)

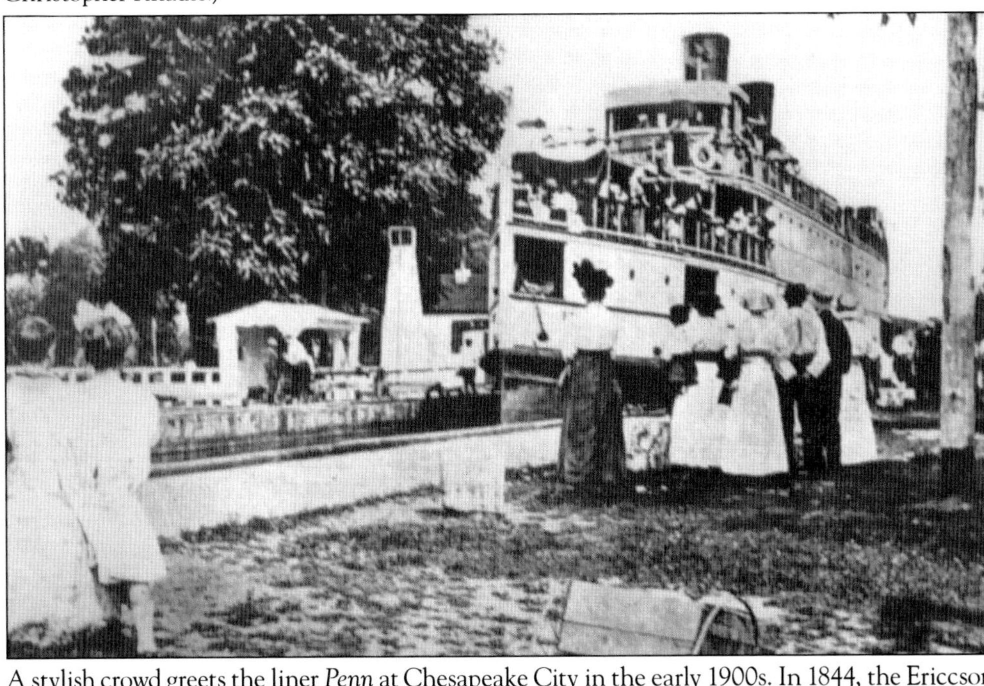

A stylish crowd greets the liner *Penn* at Chesapeake City in the early 1900s. In 1844, the Ericcson Line of the Baltimore and Philadelphia Steamship Company began offering service through the canal with a fleet of narrow, shallow-draft vessels designed to fit the canal locks. (Courtesy of the U.S. Army Corps of Engineers.)

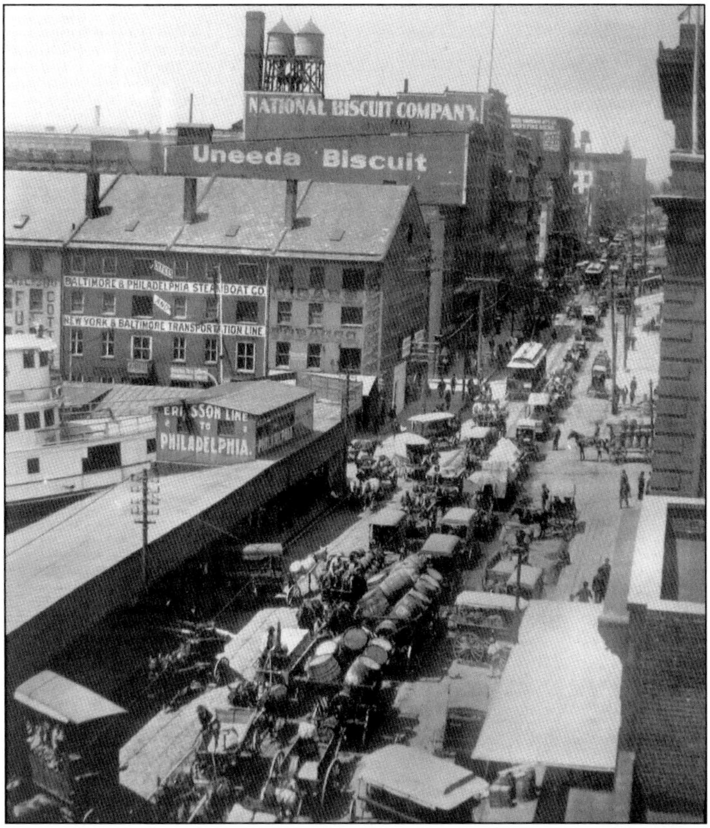

The steamship line was named after John Ericcson, the Swedish inventor who designed the propellers for the ships. Ericcson went on to more enduring fame as designer of the Civil War ironclad the *Monitor*. Below, the North's *Monitor* battles the South's *Merrimac* in the first fight between ironclad ships of war, in Hampton Roads, March 9, 1862. The right photograph is of the Ericcson steamboat terminal at Pratt and Light Streets in Baltimore. (At right, courtesy of Tolchester Beach Revisited Museum; below, courtesy of the Library of Congress.)

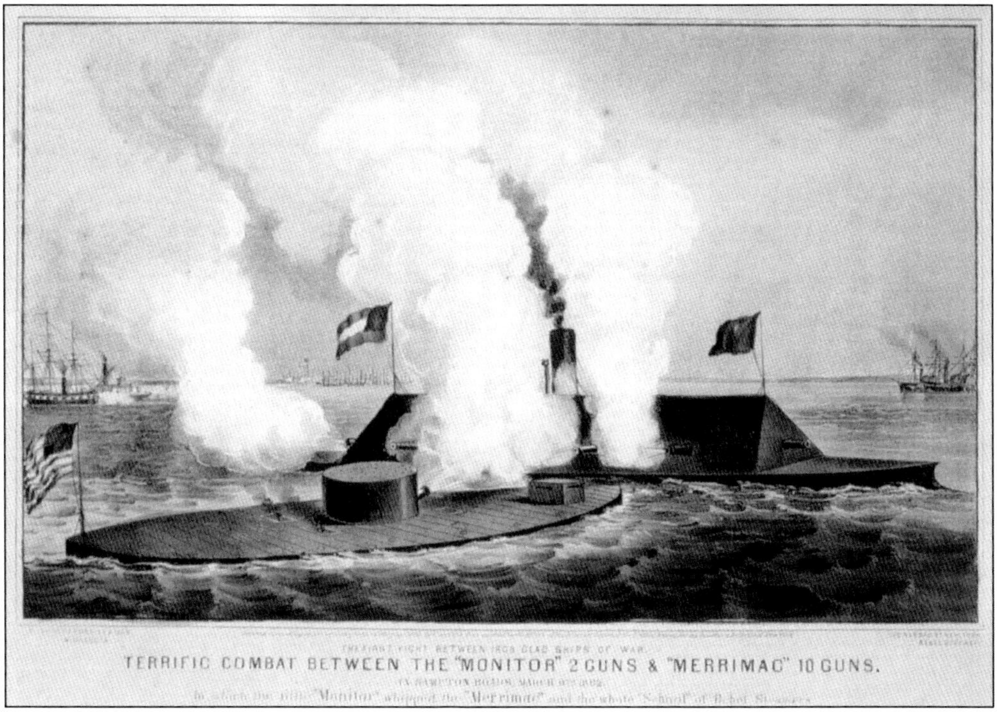

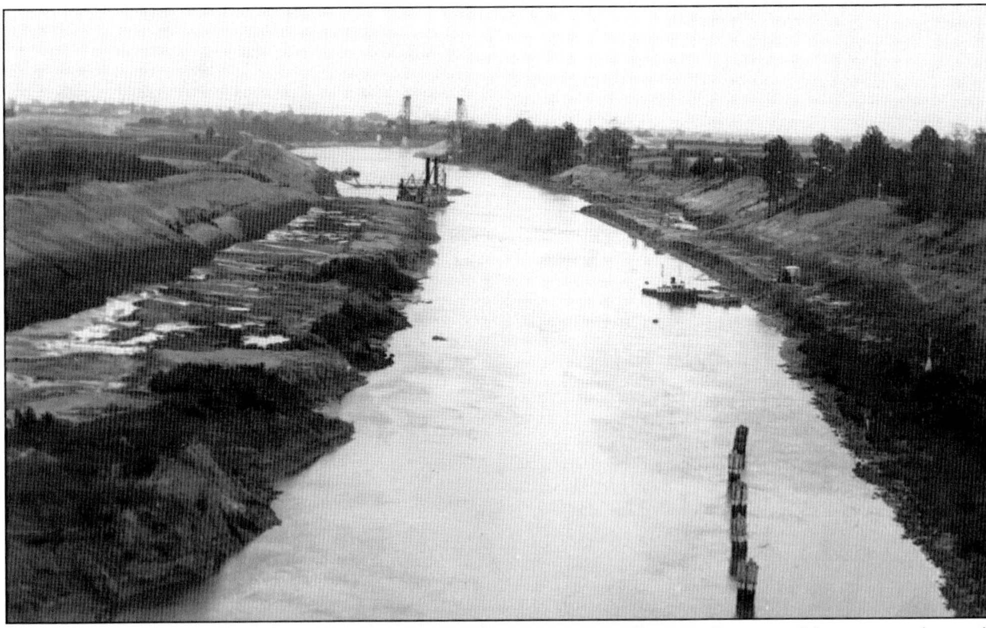

The advent of steam power brought about the development of larger ships unable to pass through the suddenly restricting locks of the canal. The federal government purchased the canal in 1919 for $2,514,000. In 1921, the Army Corps of Engineers began work on a $10,710,000 project to widen the canal to 90 feet, deepen it to 12 feet, provide a new and straighter eastern entrance at Reedy Point, Delaware, remove the locks, and construct one railroad and four highway lift bridges. (Courtesy of the U.S. Army Corps of Engineers.)

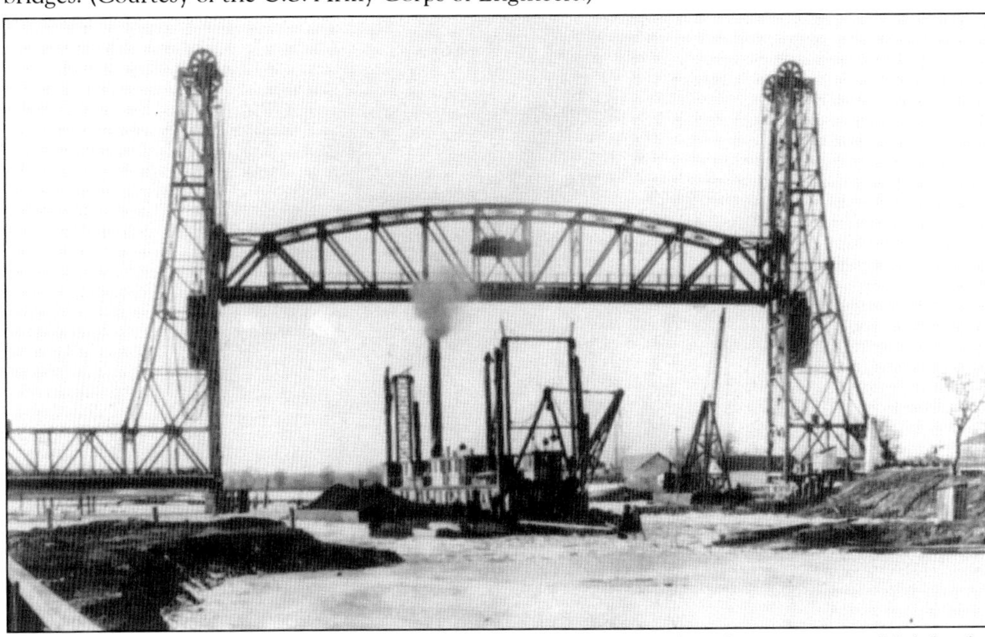

In 1927, the Chesapeake and Delaware Canal was made sea level and a new vertical lift bridge spanned the canal linking the end of George Street to the north side of Chesapeake City. Old buildings, streets, and many homes were sacrificed to the widening of the canal. (Courtesy of the U.S. Army Corps of Engineers.)

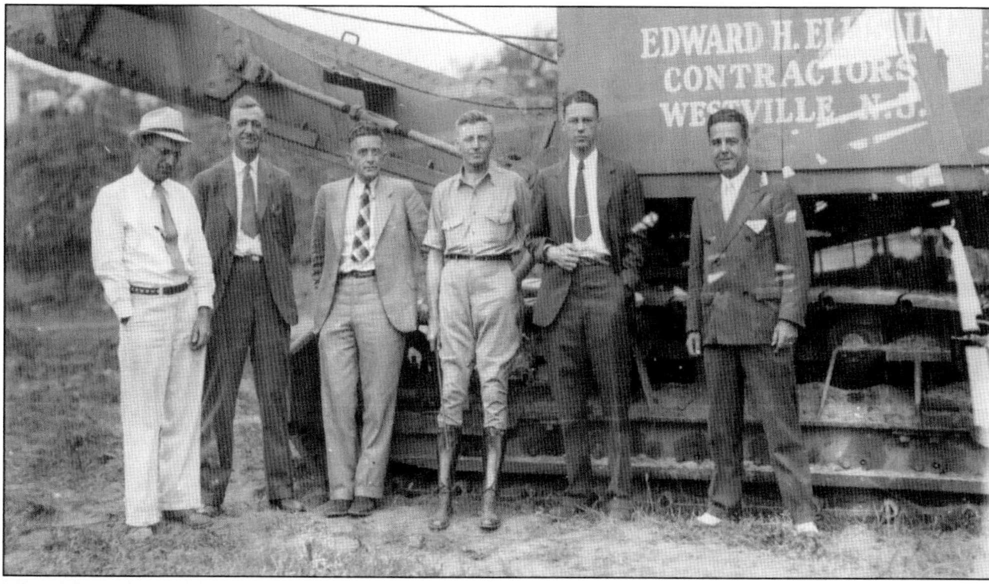

The Edward H. Ellis Company of Westville, New Jersey, was involved in the improvements to the canal that started in 1936 and were completed in 1938. Congress authorized the project to make the canal 27 feet deep and 90 feet wide from the Delaware River to the Elk River and 400 feet wide to deepwater in the vicinity of Pooles Island in the Chesapeake Bay. The project also called for an extension of the entrance jetties at Reedy Point, for alterations of the bridges over the canal, and for enlargement of the anchorage at Chesapeake City. (Courtesy of the U.S. Army Corps of Engineers.)

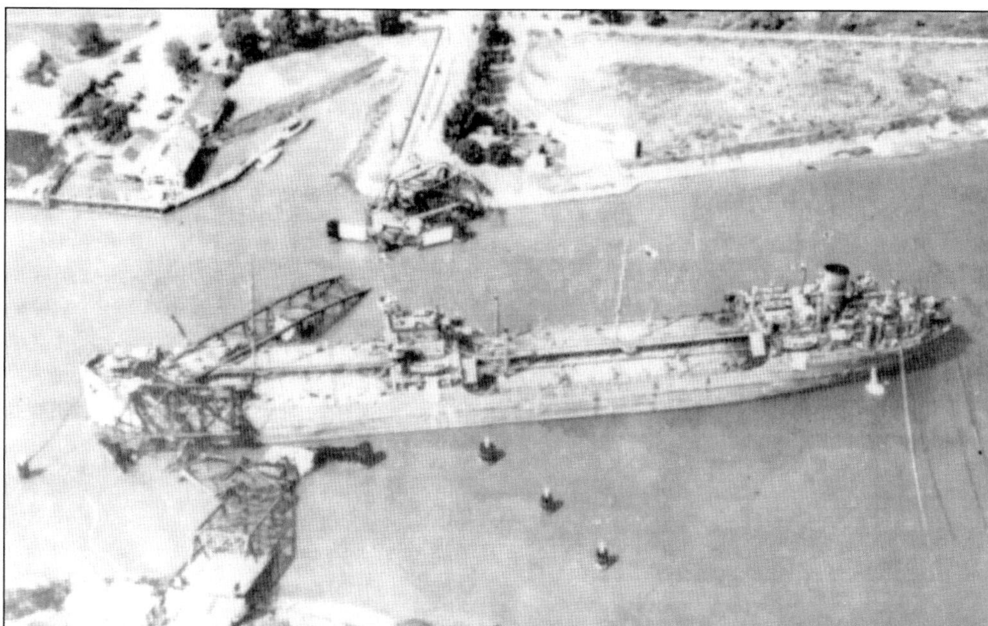

The mechanical lift bridge on the canal at Chesapeake City was toppled by a ship collision on July 28, 1942. A tanker, the *Franz Klasen*, struck the bridge, completely destroying it. It was replaced by the current suspension arch bridge, which was completed in 1949. (Courtesy of the Historical Society of Cecil County.)

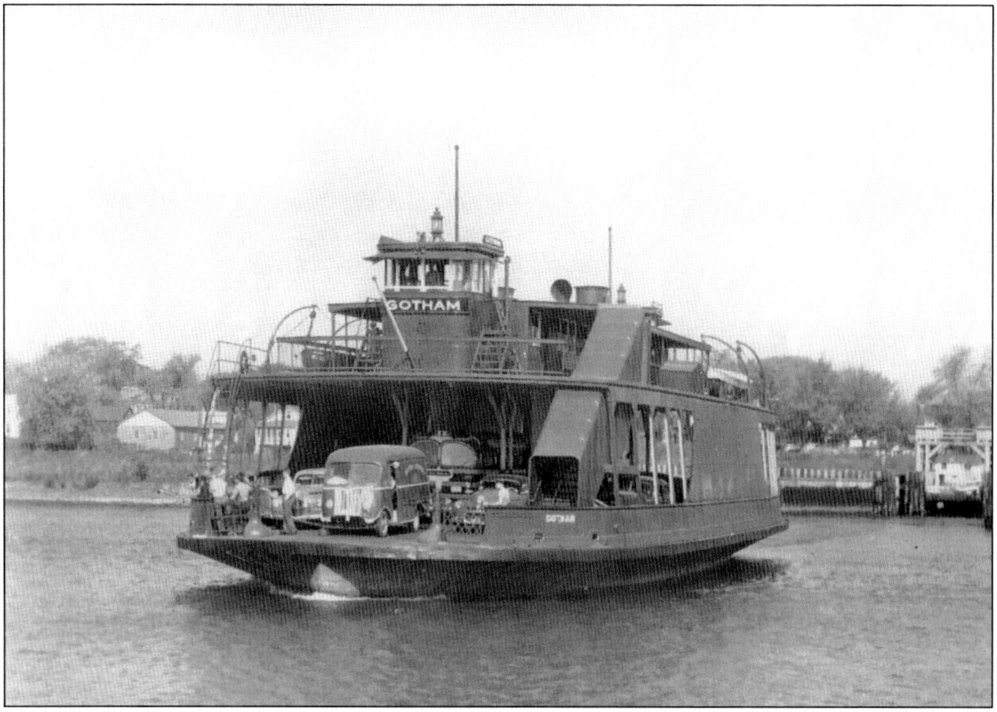

The *Gotham* ferryboat, seen *c.* 1944, carried cars and passengers across the canal between north and south Chesapeake City when the current bridge over the canal was being constructed. (Courtesy of Robert Hazel.)

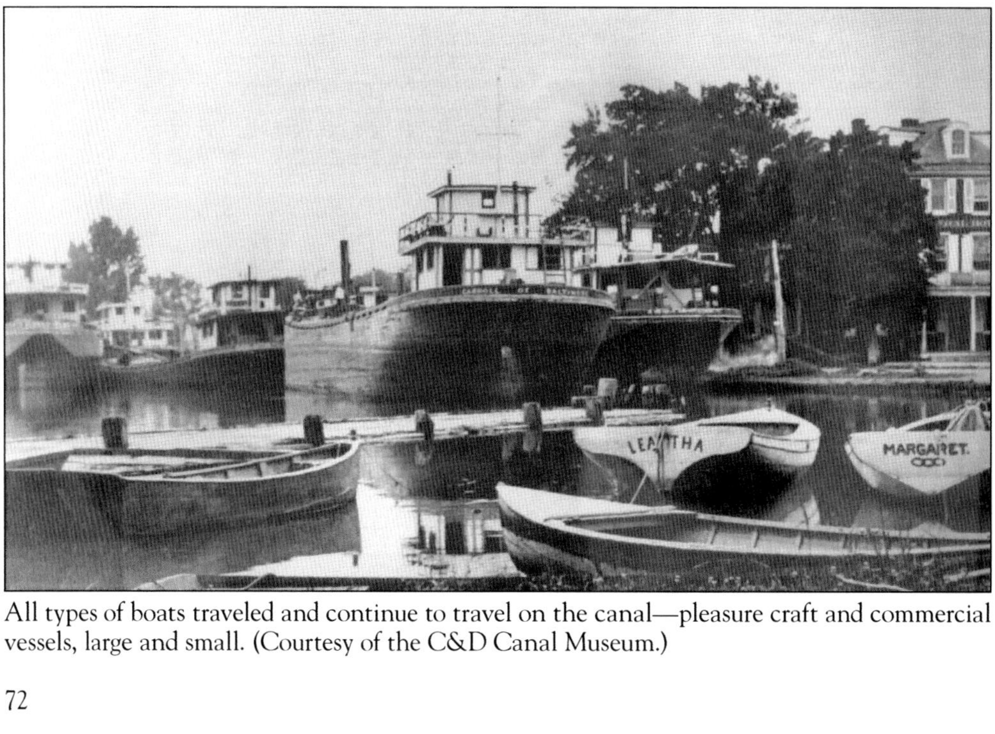

All types of boats traveled and continue to travel on the canal—pleasure craft and commercial vessels, large and small. (Courtesy of the C&D Canal Museum.)

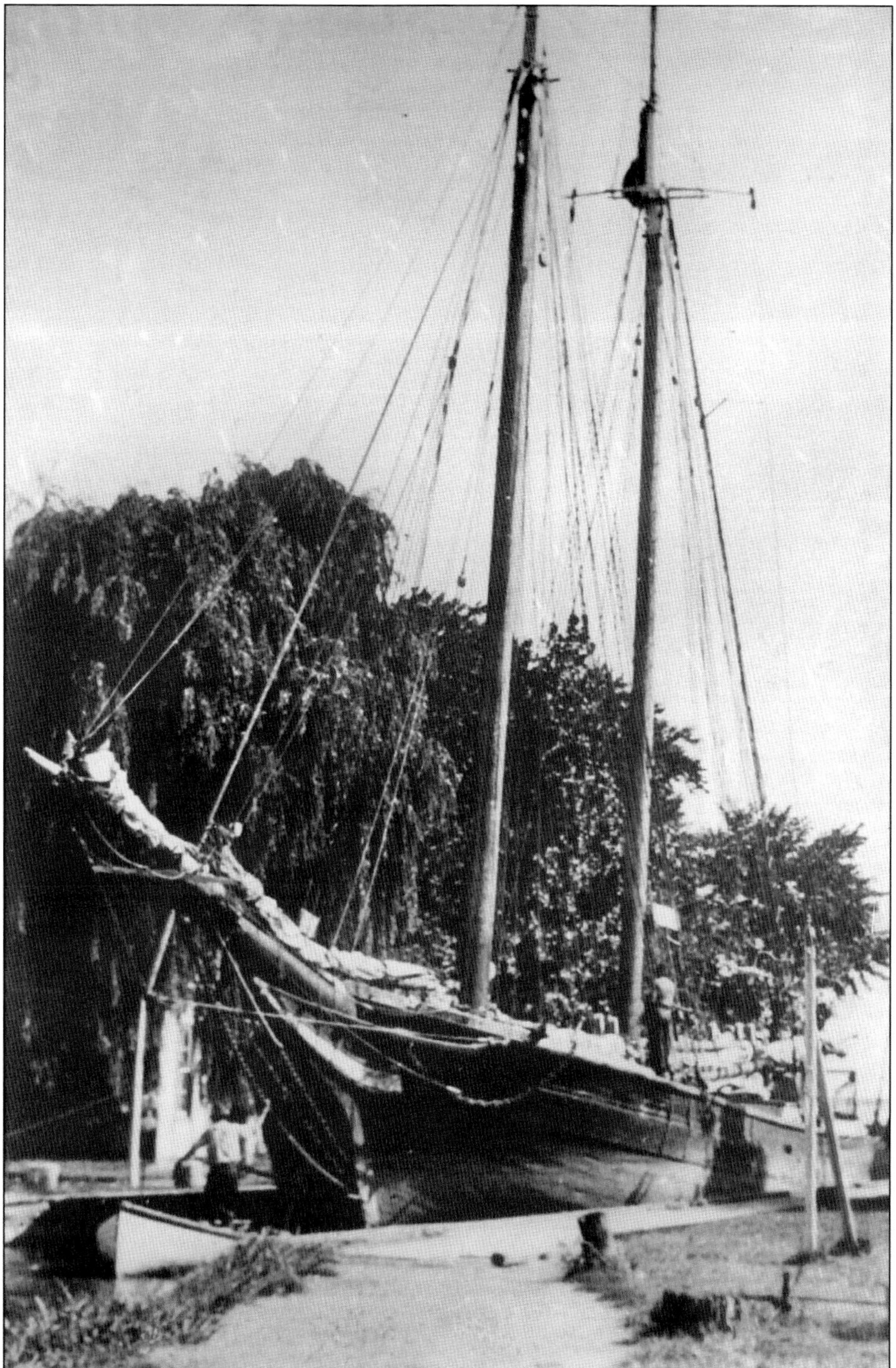

A two-masted schooner navigates the Chesapeake City lock *c.* 1900. Before the advent of steam power, sailing craft such as schooners, sloops, bugeyes, pungies, yawls, rams, and scows carried cargo and passengers through the canal to destinations on the Chesapeake, the East Coast, and beyond. (Courtesy of the C&D Canal Museum.)

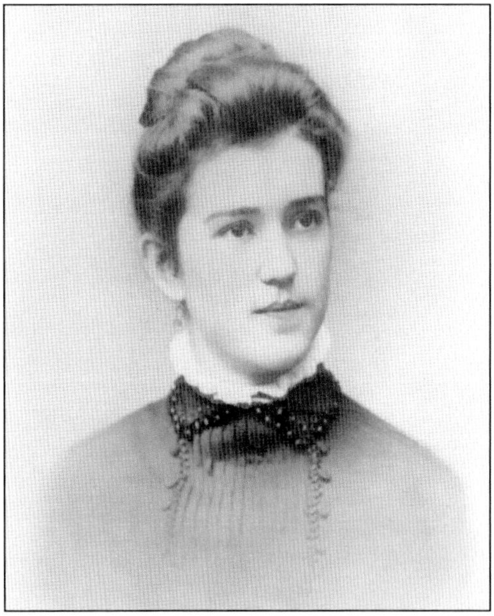

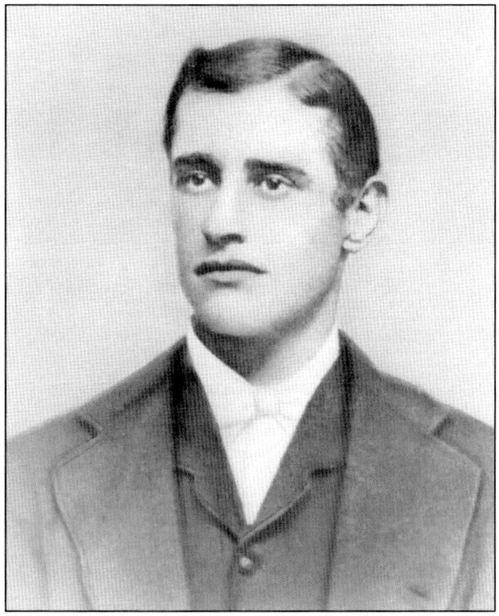

Joseph Schaefer Sr. and his wife, Winifred, (shown above) opened a grocery and ship's chandlery business in 1907 on the north side of the canal, just west of the Chesapeake City locks. Schaefer's provided launch service delivery of groceries and supplies, crews, and later pilots to ships, yachts, tugboats, and dredges. In 1935, their son John F. Schaefer opened the initial Schaefer's Restaurant. Over time, the restaurant grew to an expansive dining facility, offering the finest seafood on the Eastern Shore of Maryland. In 1966, work began to straighten the bend in the canal at Chesapeake City and the restaurant was demolished. Plans were made to build Schaefer's Canal House, and when the new restaurant was built in 1973, the business passed out of the hands of the Schaefer family. (Courtesy of Larry Ortt.)

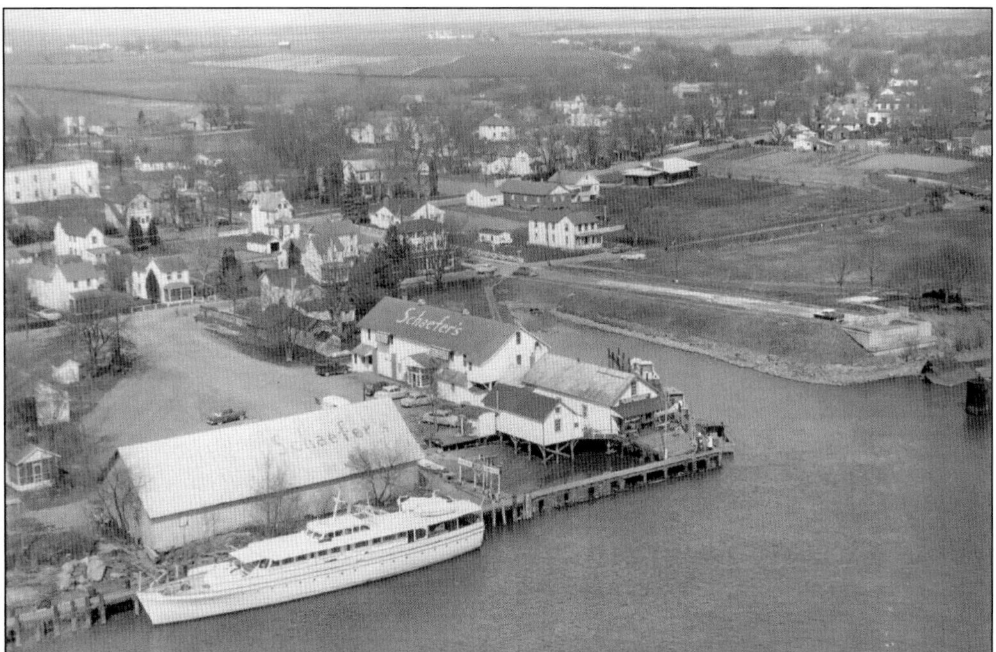

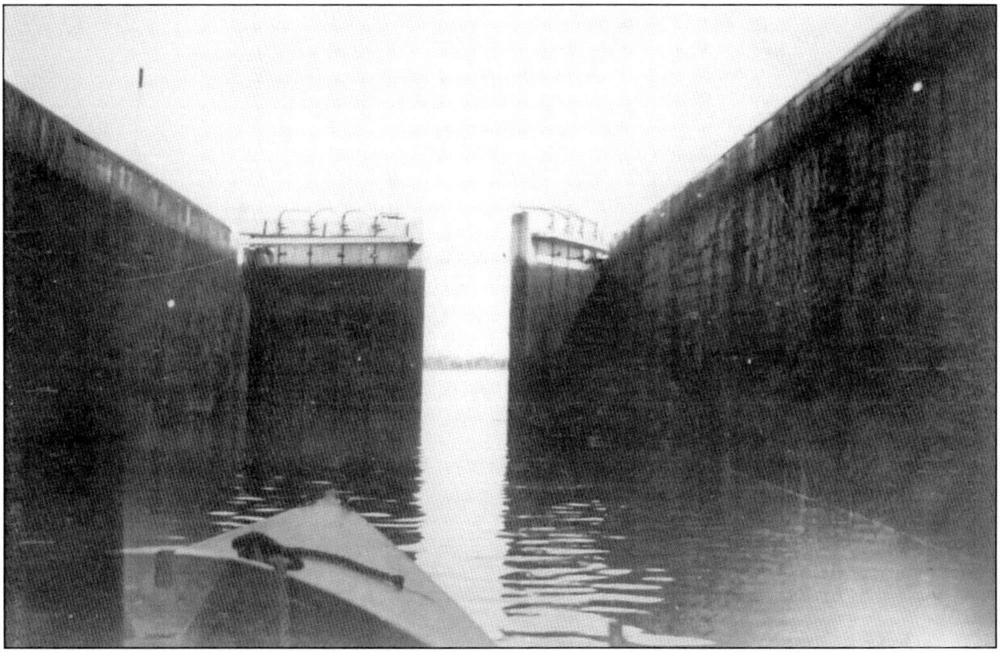

Schaefer's launch *Winifred* travels westbound c. 1915 through the Chesapeake City lock on the way to a berth at Joseph Schaefer's and Sons. (Courtesy of Larry Ortt.)

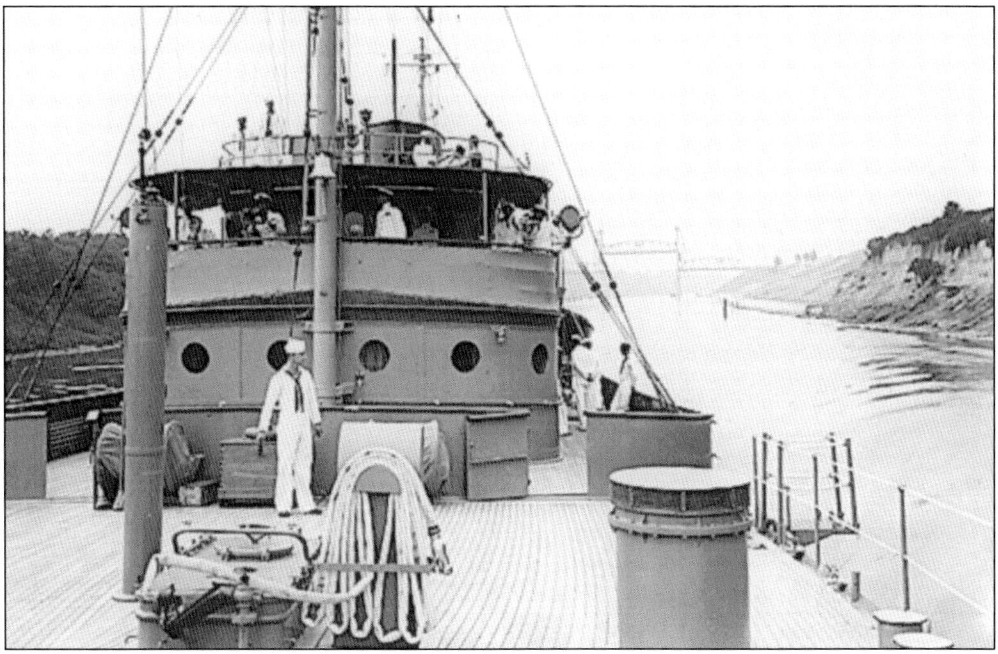

President Truman's yacht, the USS *Williamsburg*, sails up the Chesapeake and Delaware Canal on August 17, 1946, during the president's vacation cruise to Rhode Island and Bermuda after victory in World War II. The canal proved of special value during World War II when vessels were routed through the Chesapeake Bay, the canal, and the Delaware Bay to eliminate the necessity of convoying across 143 miles of submarine-infested open water from the Virginia capes to the Delaware capes. (Courtesy of the National Archives.)

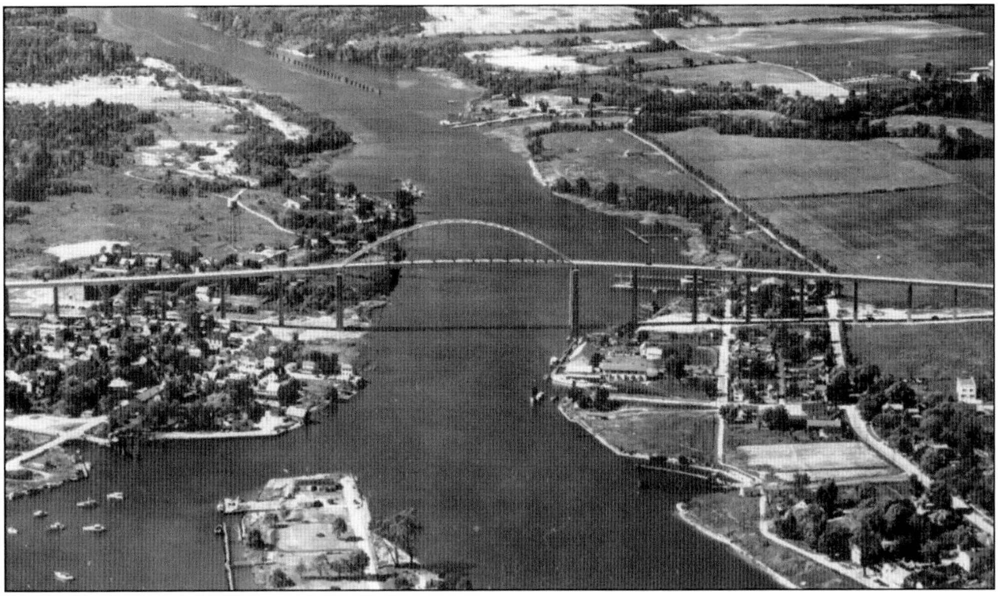

This photograph, c. 1958, shows North (right) and South Chesapeake City with the Chesapeake and Delaware Canal splitting the two towns. New bridges to accommodate highway traffic crossing the canal became necessary as deepening and widening progressed. The mechanical lift bridges at St. Georges and Chesapeake City, toppled by ship collisions, were replaced in the 1940s with high-level highway spans. Two other high-level vehicular traffic bridges, Summit Bridge in 1960 and Reedy Point Bridge in 1968, were constructed as part of the 1954 improvement authorization. (Courtesy of the U.S. Army Corps of Engineers.)

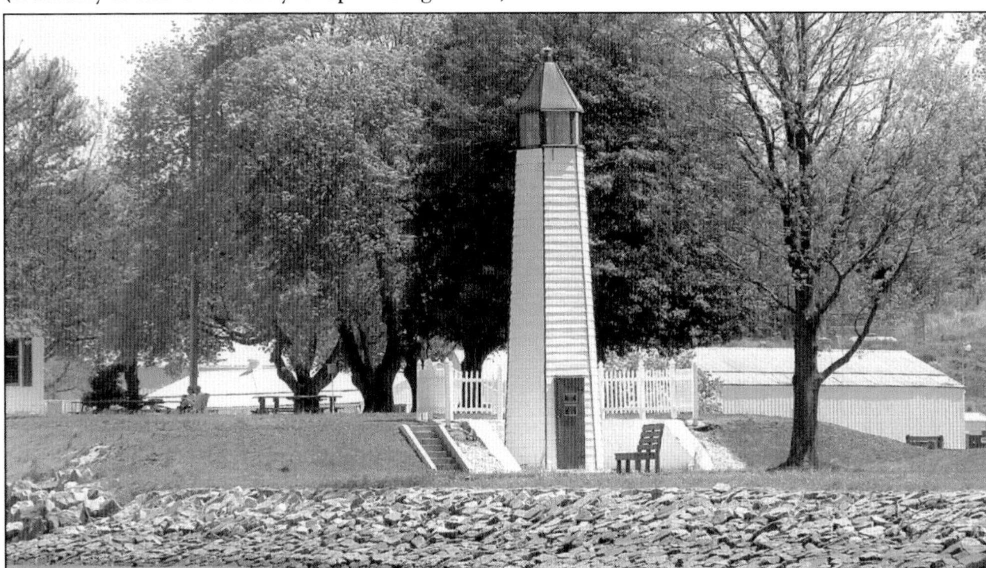

In October 1996, the U.S. Army Corps of Engineers accepted a full-size replica of the 30-foot Bethel Bridge Lighthouse. The construction was sponsored by the Chesapeake City Lions Club. The original was one of many wooden lighthouses used to warn vessels of locks and bridges in the days before the canal was made sea level. The lighthouse is located on Army Corps property, a short walk from the canal museum. (Photograph by Christopher Knauss.)

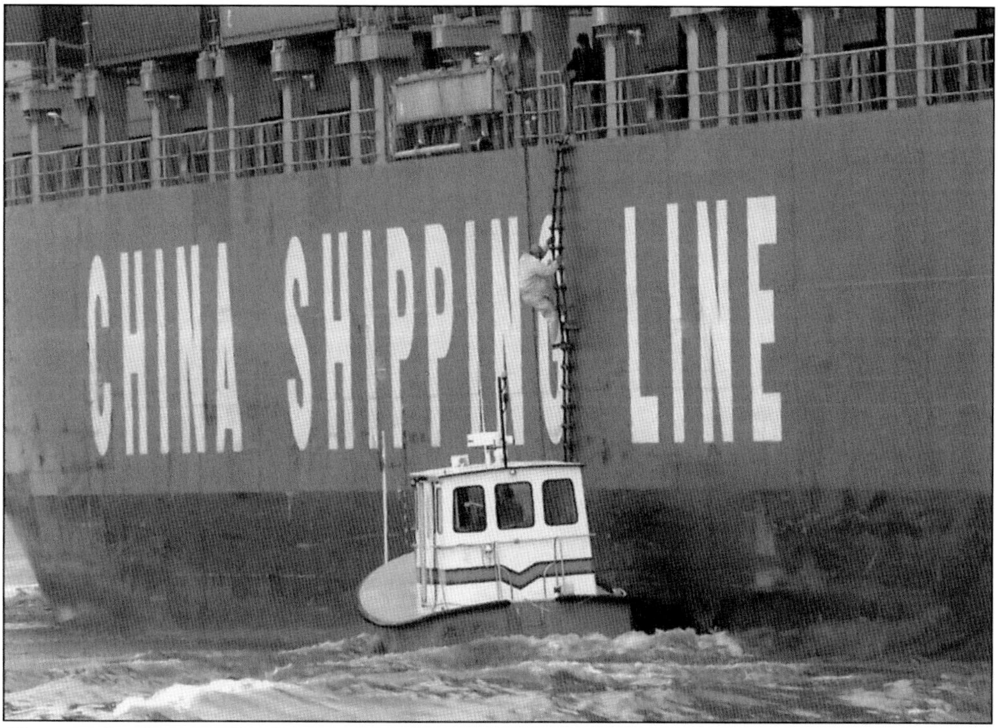

Chesapeake City marks the point in the canal where Chesapeake Bay pilots turn over their vessels to Delaware River pilots or vice versa. The pilots often board the ships by ladder, as seen here. Before the Association of Maryland Pilots was founded in 1852, small pilot schooners would race to inbound ships to offer piloting services. The use of small pilot schooners in the late 1700s led to the development of the Baltimore Clippers, the fastest vessels of their day. (Photographs by Richard LeGates.)

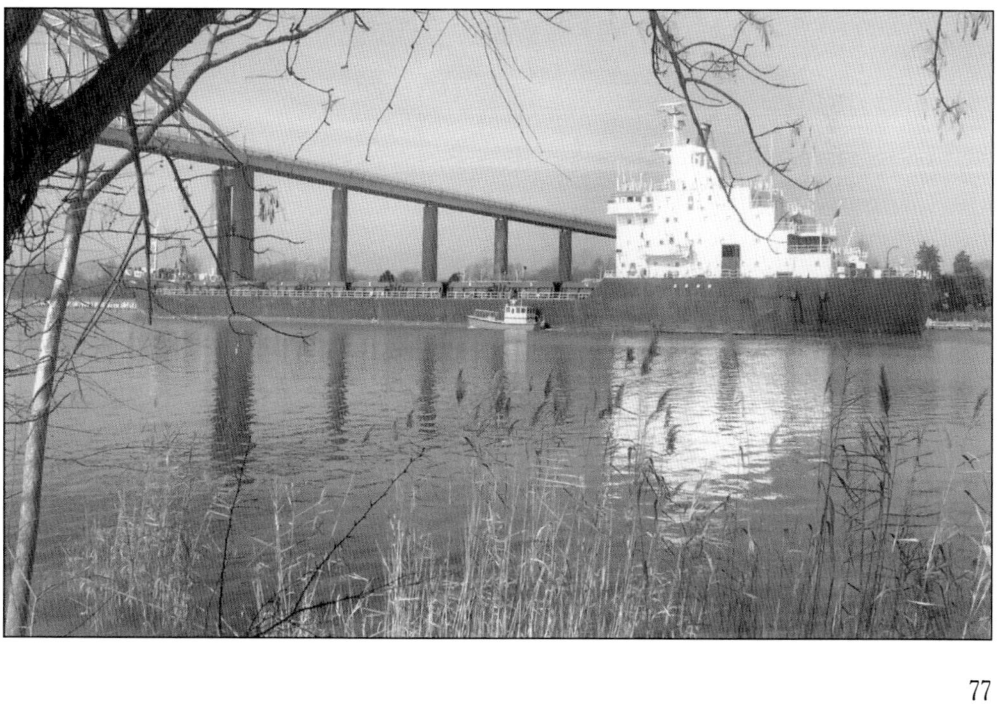

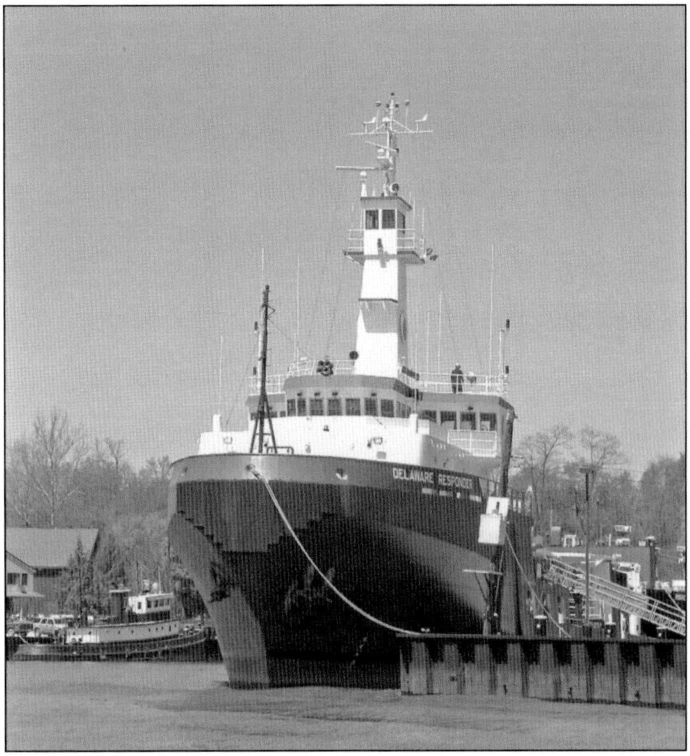

The Marine Spill Response Corporation (MSRC) and the *Delaware Responder* are located on the canal just below North Chesapeake City. MSRC was formed in 1990 to offer spill response services and mitigate damage to the environment. Its services are available to organizations, including those involved in the handling and transport of oil and other substances. (Photograph by Christopher Knauss.)

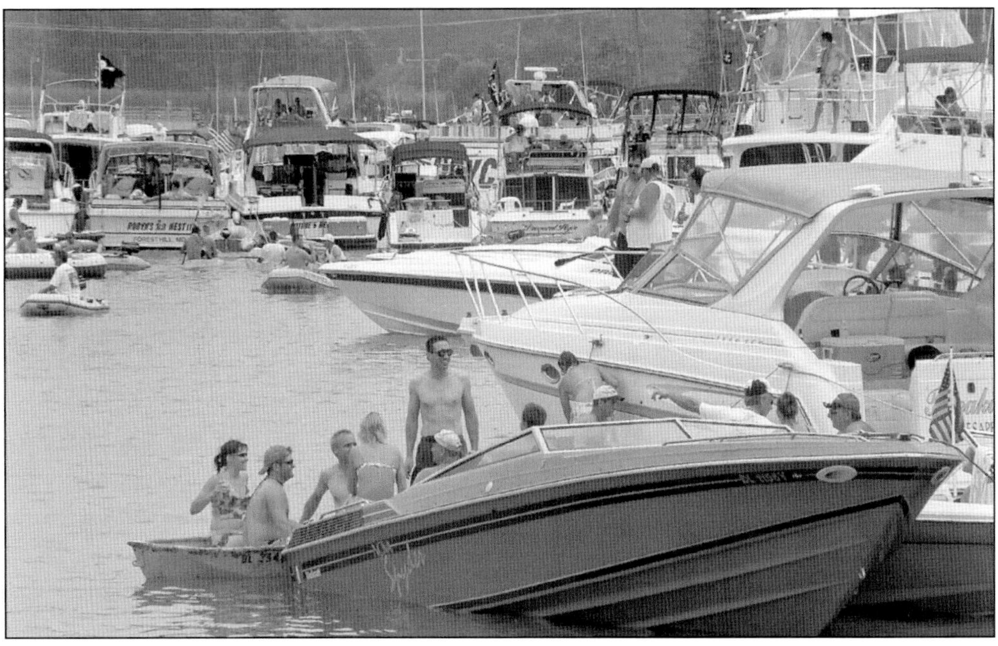

Canal Day, an annual event in South Chesapeake City since 1979, attracts boatloads of visitors. During the last weekend of June, hundreds of boats and thousands of visitors descend on the historic town to commemorate the completion of the Chesapeake and Delaware Canal. The event features street vendors, arts and crafts, games, food, and music in Pell Gardens. (Photograph by Christopher Knauss.)

Five

Waterfront Towns

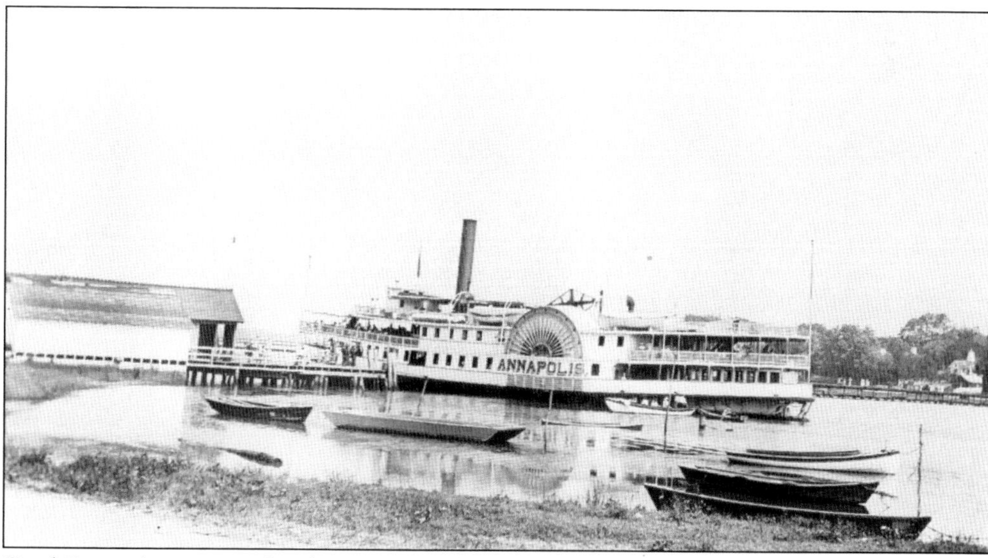

Cecil County's most populated towns evolved around the waterfront. The county's ports harbored boats loaded with products such as flour, iron, nails, wood, pork, and lumber, which sailed to cities down the bay and beyond. Ships returned with products like coal, molasses, coffee, and whiskey. Boatbuilding factories to accommodate the growing commerce also sprang up along the waterways. Eventually better inland transportation ended the necessity of the county's shipping ports, but a resurgence of the waterfront came with the growth of recreational boating. The steamboat *Annapolis*, formerly *Sassafras*, is docked at the Fredericktown wharf c. 1899. Fredericktown, on the Sassafras River, was officially created in 1736, with an initial plat plan of 60 lots. It was named after Prince Frederick, the son of King George II. Prior to that time, the place was called Pennington's Point or Happy Harbor. Located along the principal north-south road on the Eastern Shore, Fredericktown originally derived most of its income from travelers. (Courtesy of the Mariners' Museum.)

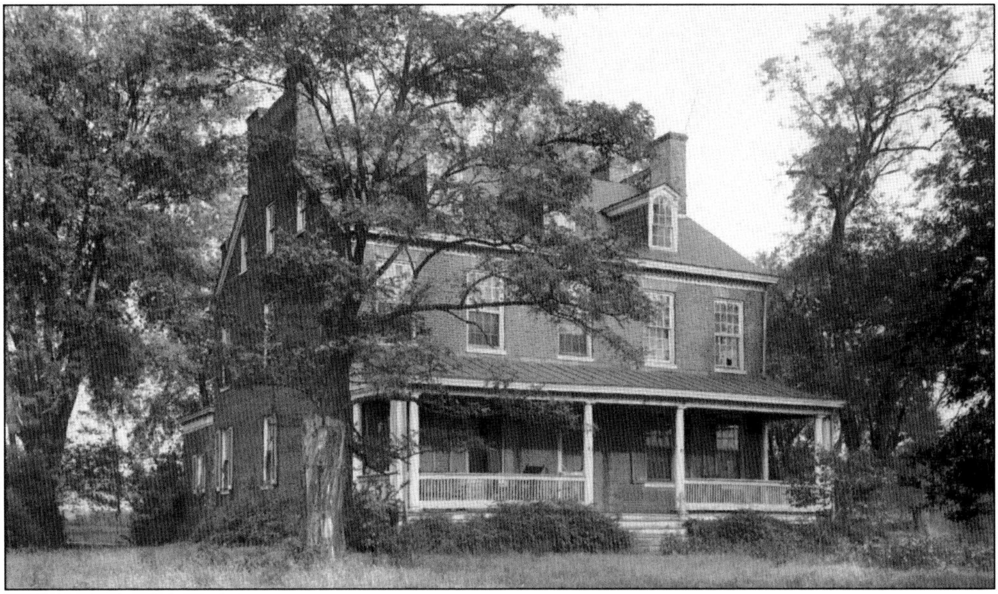

Frenchtown Landing House, shown *c.* 1936, is believed to have been a hotel. While the building and the town no longer exist, Frenchtown on the Elk River was an important travel route during the 18th and 19th centuries. Goods bound for Philadelphia from Baltimore were most economically transported by cargo boats to Frenchtown and from there taken by wagons, carts, and later railroad to New Castle and then on to Philadelphia. (Courtesy of the Library of Congress.)

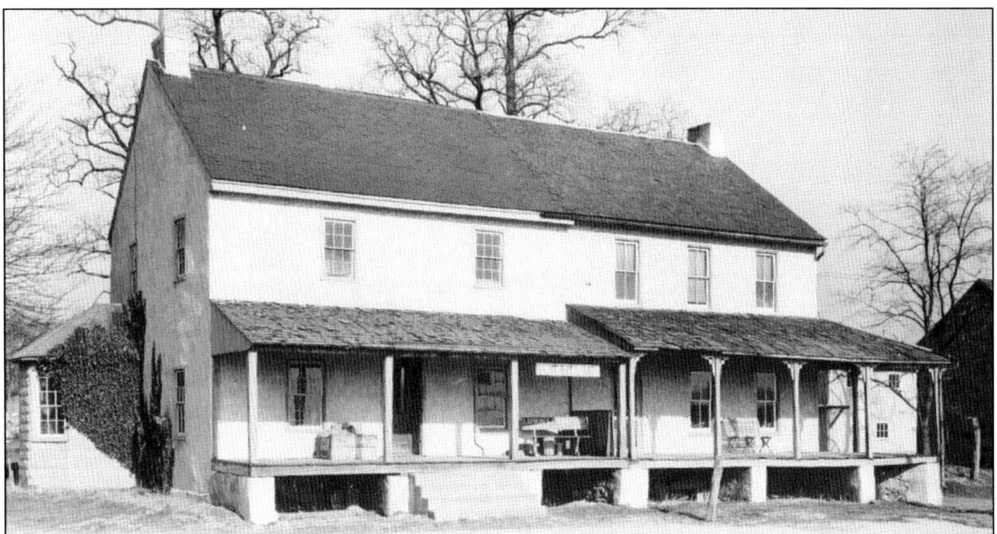

The town of Blue Ball in Cecil County does not have a major waterway, but it does contain the Blue Ball Tavern with a fictional and nonfictional maritime history. Blue Ball Tavern was established about 1710 by Andrew Job, who secured it from William Penn. Job's son Thomas married Elizabeth Maxwell, niece of Daniel Defoe, who wrote the famous shipwreck adventure novel *Robinson Crusoe*. Elizabeth paid for her passage to America from England by bargaining with the captain of the ship to sell her upon her arrival. During the 17th century, indentured servants constituted three-quarters of all European immigrants to the Chesapeake region. (Courtesy of the Library of Congress.)

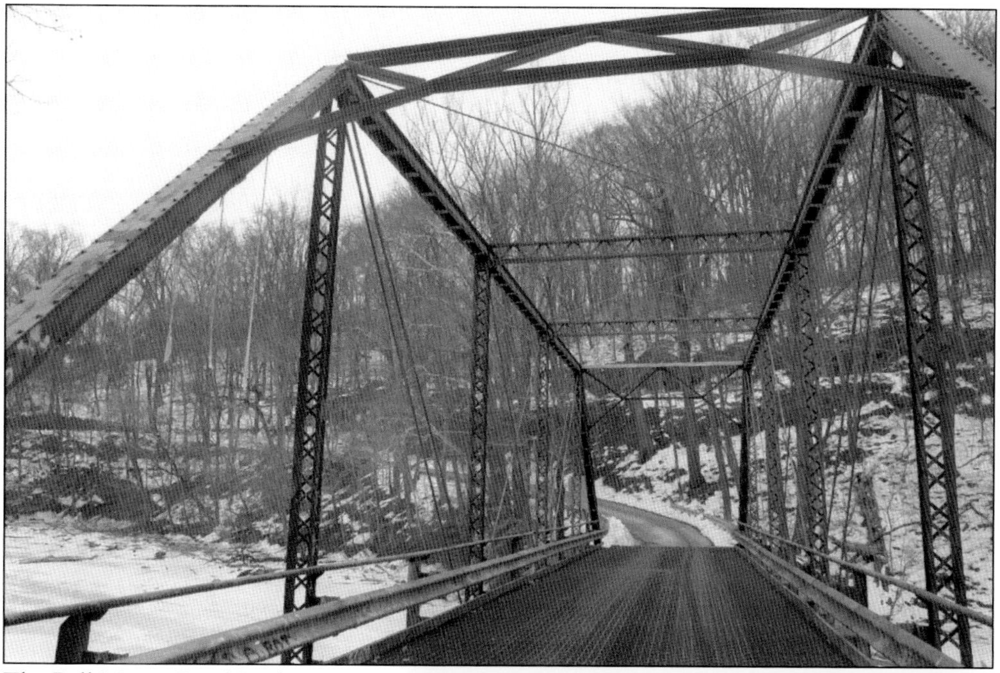

The Bell Manor Road Bridge, built in 1885, still crosses the lower Conowingo Creek near Pilottown in northwestern Cecil County. Pilottown was named for the Susquehanna riverboat pilots who maintained residence there so they could be close to the pilot station. Conowingo Creek originates in Pennsylvania and flows south, entering Fulton Township just above the birthplace of Robert Fulton. Fulton, at right, designed the first commercially successful steamboat in the world. On August 7, 1807, his *Clermont* went from New York City to Albany, a 150-mile trip, taking 32 hours at an average speed of about five miles per hour. (Above, photograph by Christopher Knauss; at right, courtesy of the Library of Congress.)

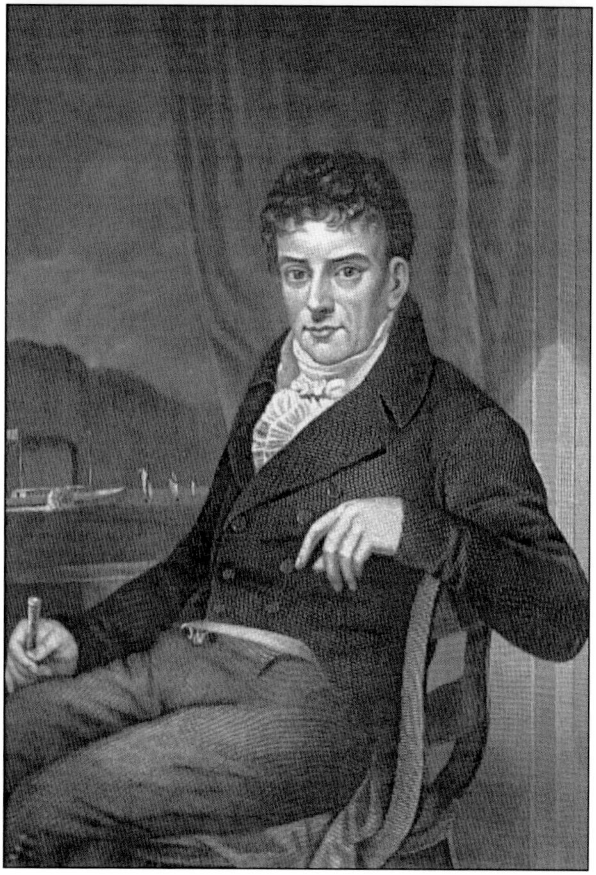

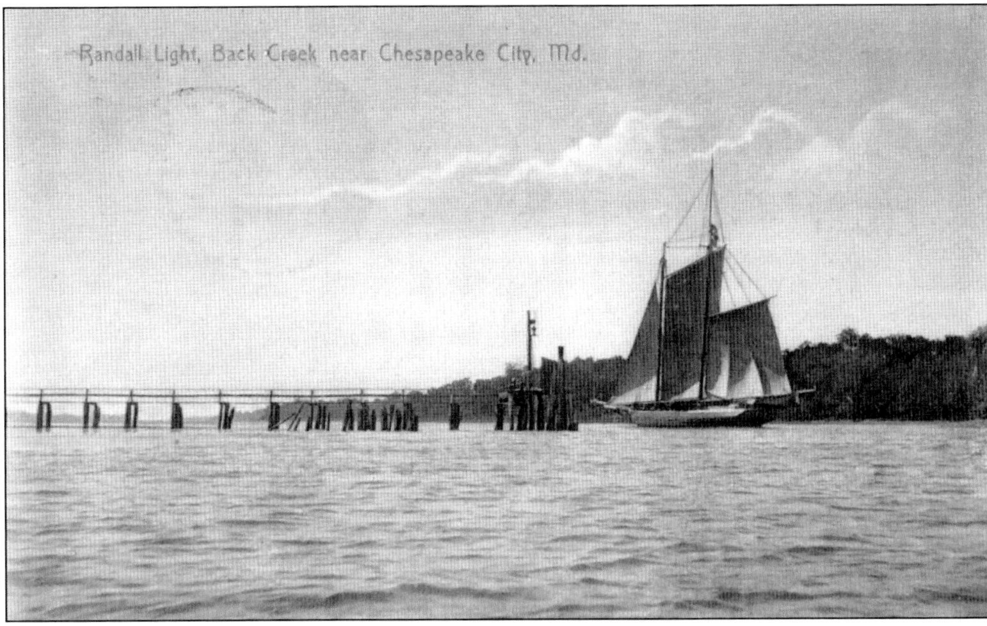

A schooner sails west past Randall's Light as depicted in this postcard c. 1907. The Randalia area was originally another part of Augustine Herrman's holdings. Randalia derives its name from John Randall, a surveyor for the C&D Canal. Before the widening of Back Creek, boats often found it difficult navigating Sandy Point, which led to the need of Randall Light. The kerosene-fueled light was kept lit through the night by a light keeper. (Courtesy of Jack Manning.)

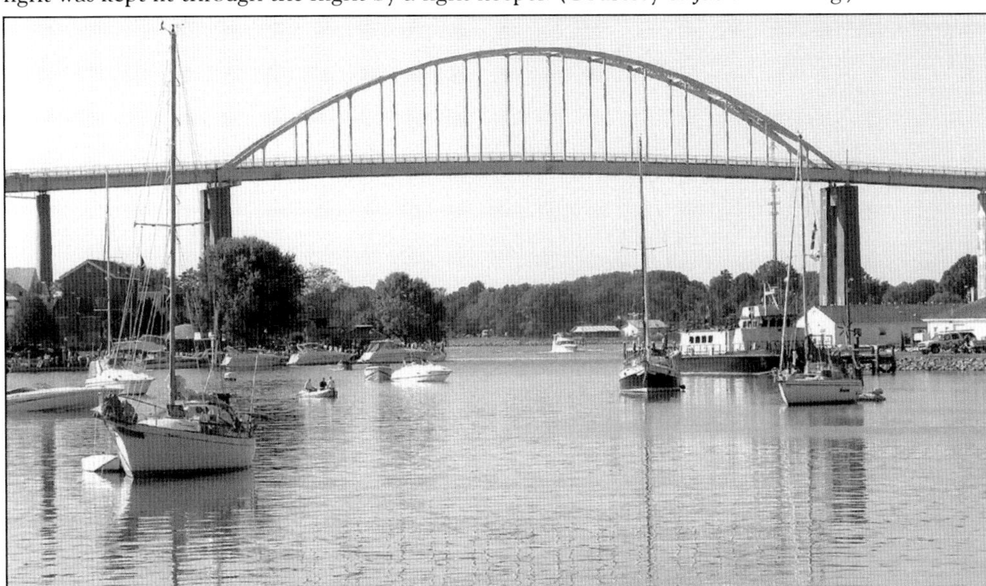

Boats are anchored in the mooring basin in South Chesapeake City c. 2004. Once known as "Bohemia Village," Chesapeake City happened as a result of the C&D Canal. When the canal opened in 1829 and ship traffic increased, the town sprang up along its banks. By 1839, the town was named, and in 1849, it became incorporated. Today an arched bridge 135 feet above the water spans the canal and connects the north and south sides of town. (Photograph by Christopher Knauss.)

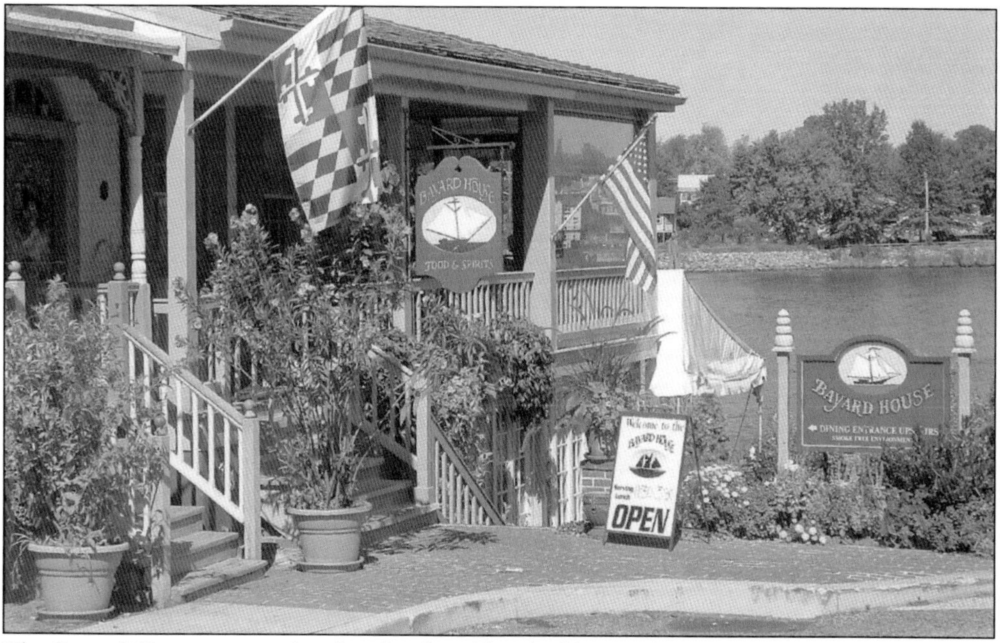

The Bayard House is considered to be the oldest building in historic South Chesapeake City. Samuel Bayard built the original manor in early the 1780s. Five years after the completion of the C&D Canal in 1829, the Bayard House was converted into a tavern and inn called Chick's Tavern. Today the fully restored restaurant stands on the banks of the canal and is a favorite eating spot for locals and travelers on land and on the canal. (Photograph by Christopher Knauss.)

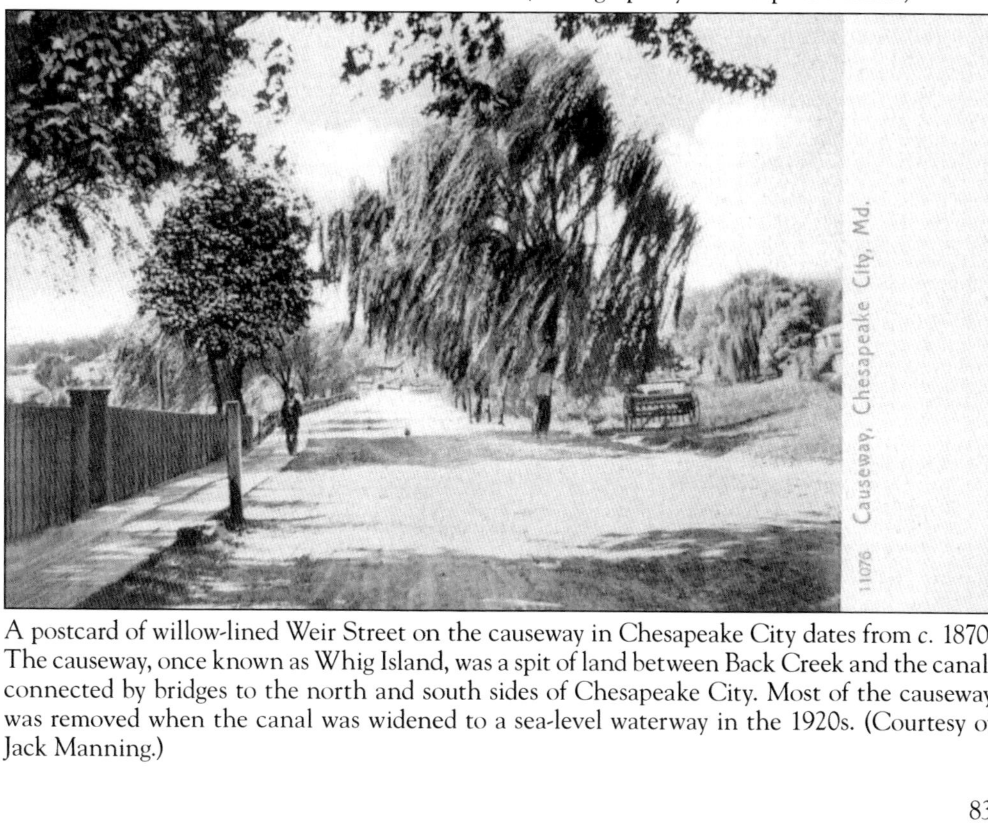

A postcard of willow-lined Weir Street on the causeway in Chesapeake City dates from c. 1870. The causeway, once known as Whig Island, was a spit of land between Back Creek and the canal, connected by bridges to the north and south sides of Chesapeake City. Most of the causeway was removed when the canal was widened to a sea-level waterway in the 1920s. (Courtesy of Jack Manning.)

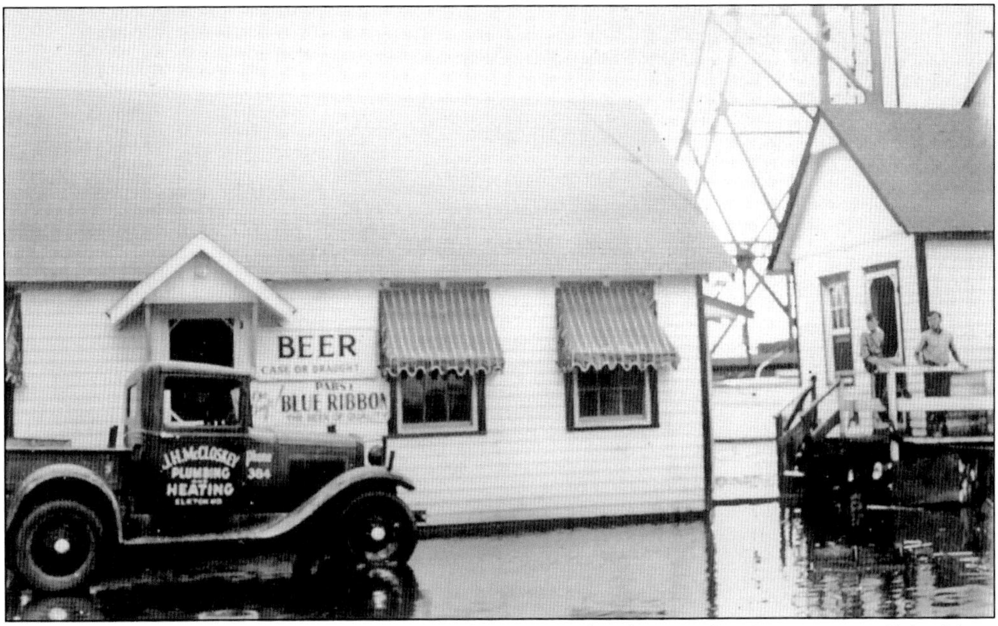

In 1935, John F. Schaefer opened a beer garden in North Chesapeake City in a small building constructed behind the second store. This actually was the initial Schaefer's Restaurant, as hard-boiled eggs and crab cakes prepared by Winifred Schaefer were available at the bar. (Courtesy of Larry Ortt.)

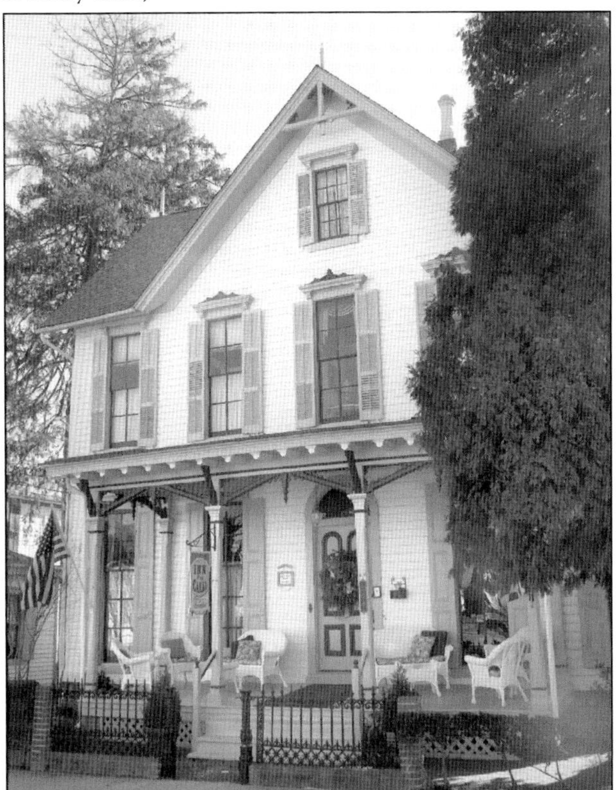
The Brady-Rees House in South Chesapeake City was built about 1868 by Henry H. Brady, who had a monopoly on the mules that towed barges through the Chesapeake and Delaware Canal in the 1800s. Today the house on Bohemia Avenue is known as the Inn at the Canal bed-and-breakfast. The entire South Chesapeake City Historic District, which includes 100 buildings on 150 acres, was added to the National Register of Historic Places in 1974. (Photograph by Christopher Knauss.)

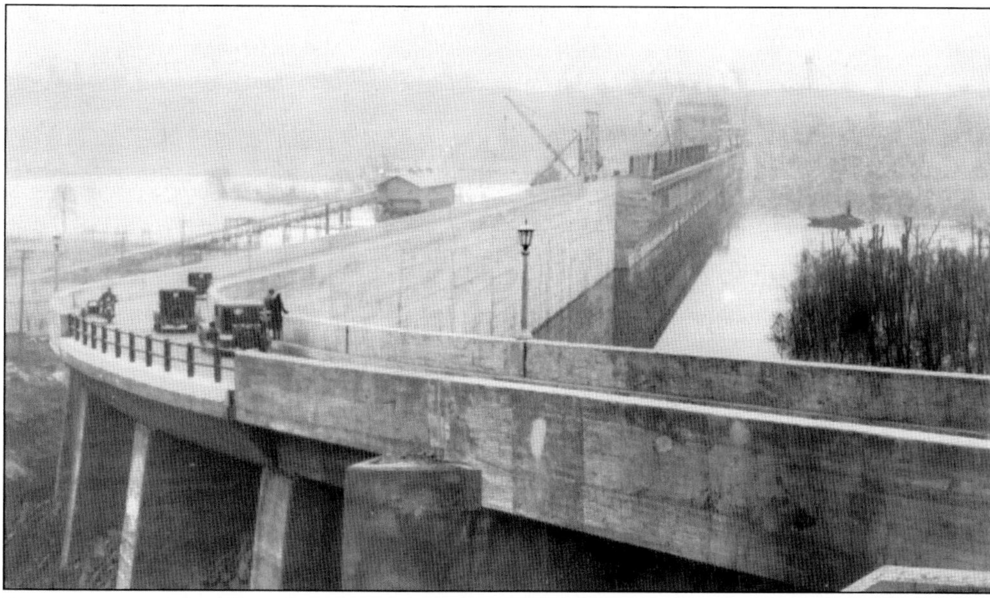

Construction of the $52 million Conowingo Dam and Hydroelectric Plant, which uses the power of the Susquehanna River to produce electricity, began in 1926. During construction, some 3,800 workers lived in camps around the dam. (Courtesy of the Historical Society of Cecil County.)

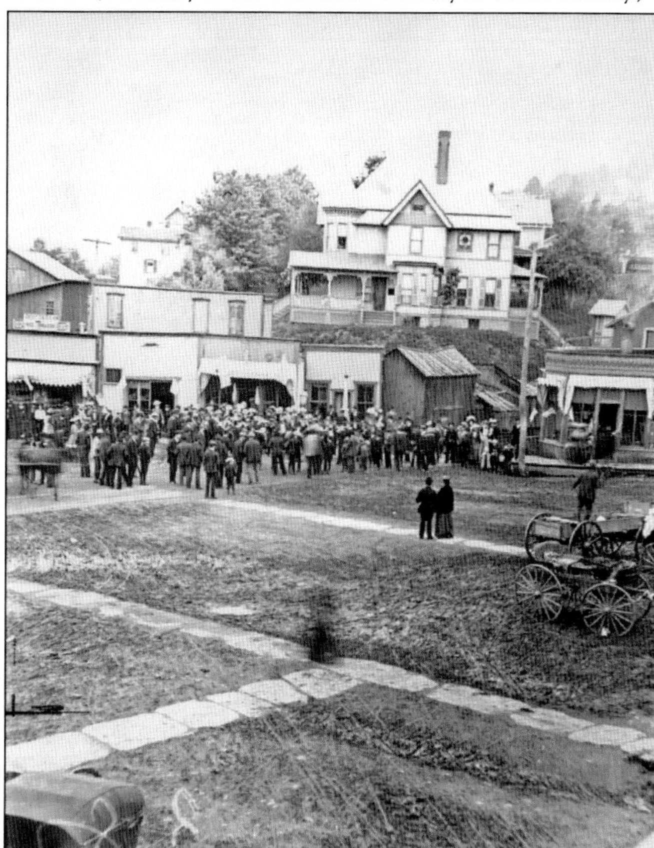

The building of a mile-long channel around the falls in southern Pennsylvania happened between 1793 and 1797. The channel eventually became part of the Susquehanna and Tidewater Canal. The old village of Conowingo was born on this site. This civic event in the village was held before the Conowingo Dam began commercial operation in 1928. The dam formed a 9,000-acre lake, spreading across land and over rooftops of the remaining village of 30 to 40 buildings, submerging old Conowingo forever. (Courtesy of the Historical Society of Cecil County.)

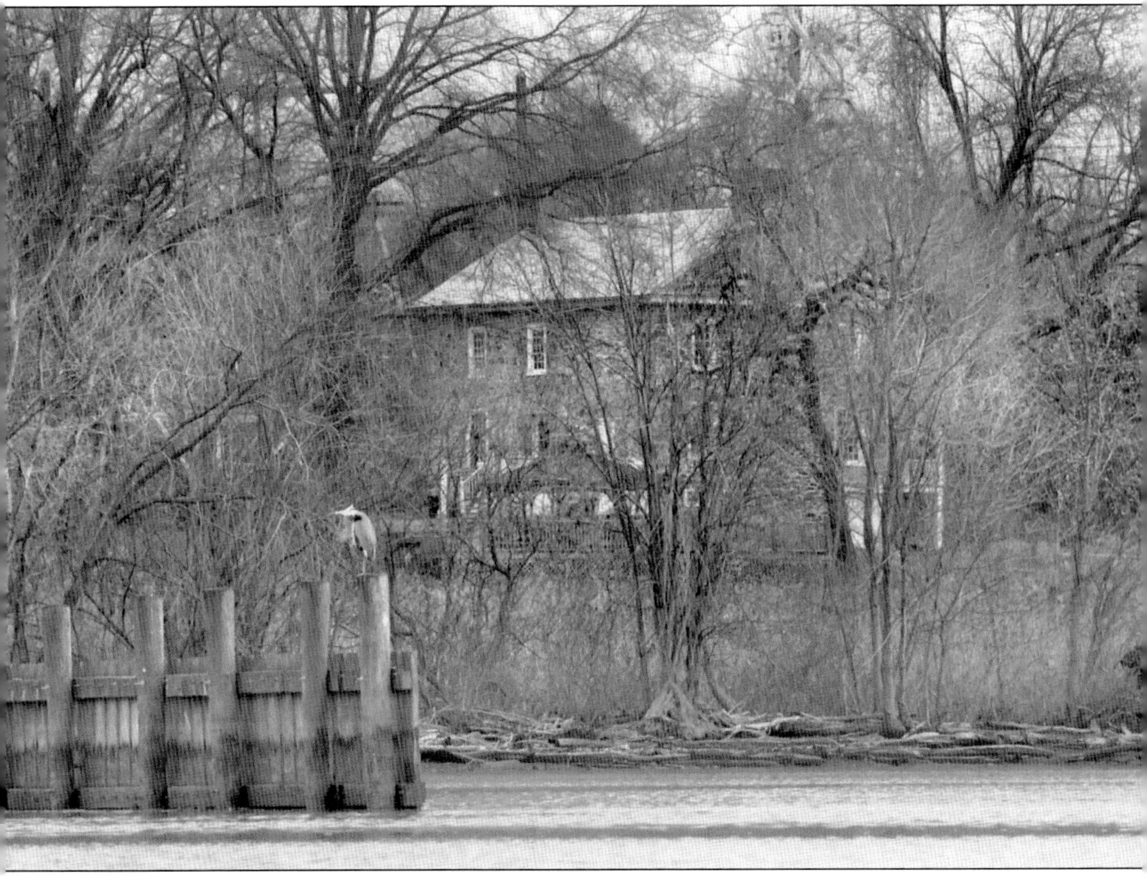

Rodgers Tavern, along the banks of the Susquehanna in Perryville, continued to be run as a tavern by Elizabeth Rodgers and other tavern keepers until at least 1886. As bridges and railroads superseded ferries and carriages, the Lower Ferry route diminished in use and the tavern declined. The Philadelphia, Baltimore and Washington Railroad bought the property, and the building entered a period of neglect and deterioration. In 1956, the Society for the Preservation of Maryland Antiquities bought the building and the Friends of Rodgers Tavern was organized to preserve and restore it to its former state. (Photograph by Christopher Knauss.)

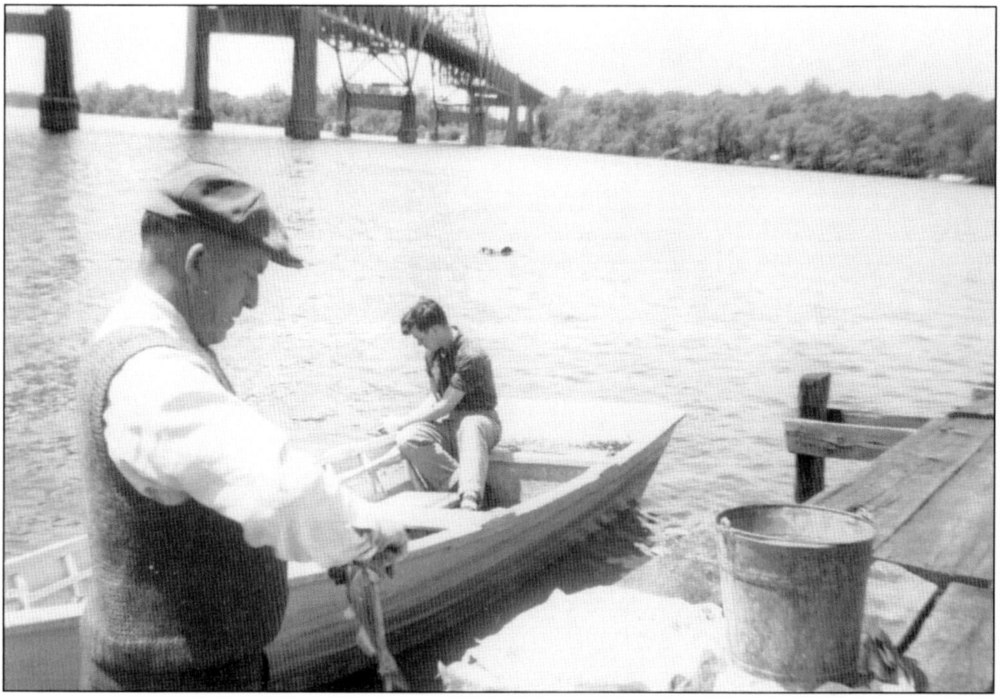

Leslie Owens Jr. of Perryville, left, and Tom McClune, a visiting relative, return from a fishing outing in a bushwhack boat on the Susquehanna c. 1940. Muscle power was often used to get to favorite fishing holes in the area. In the background is the Thomas J. Hatem Memorial Bridge (Route 40) and Garrett Island, which was named after John W. Garrett, former president of the B&O Railroad. (Courtesy of Barbara Brown.)

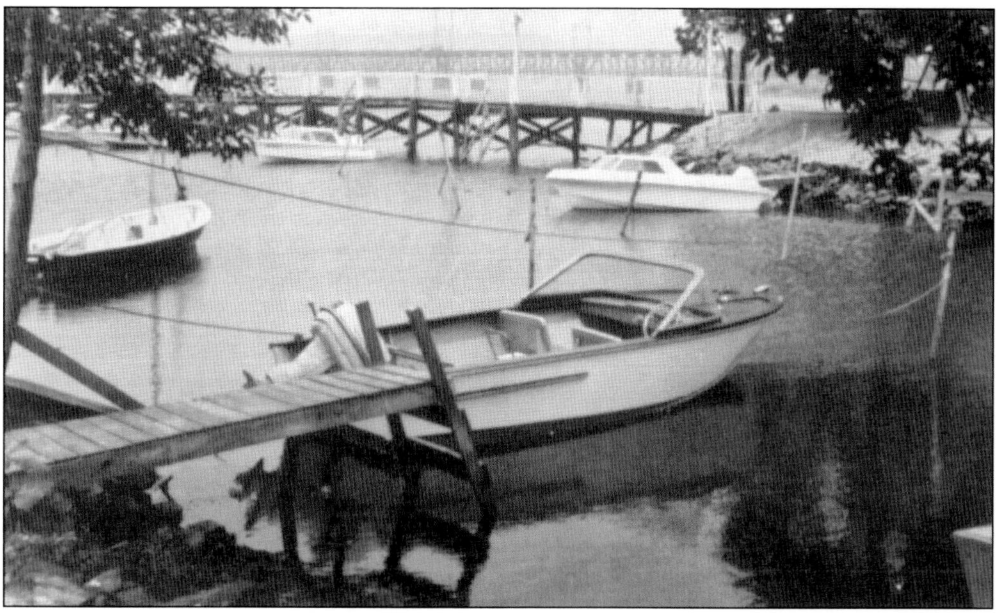

Before incorporation in 1882, Perryville was known as Lower Ferry (c. 1695) and Susquehanna (c. 1700s) and finally was named Perryville after Mary Perry, the wife of John Bateman. (Courtesy of the Historical Society of Cecil County.)

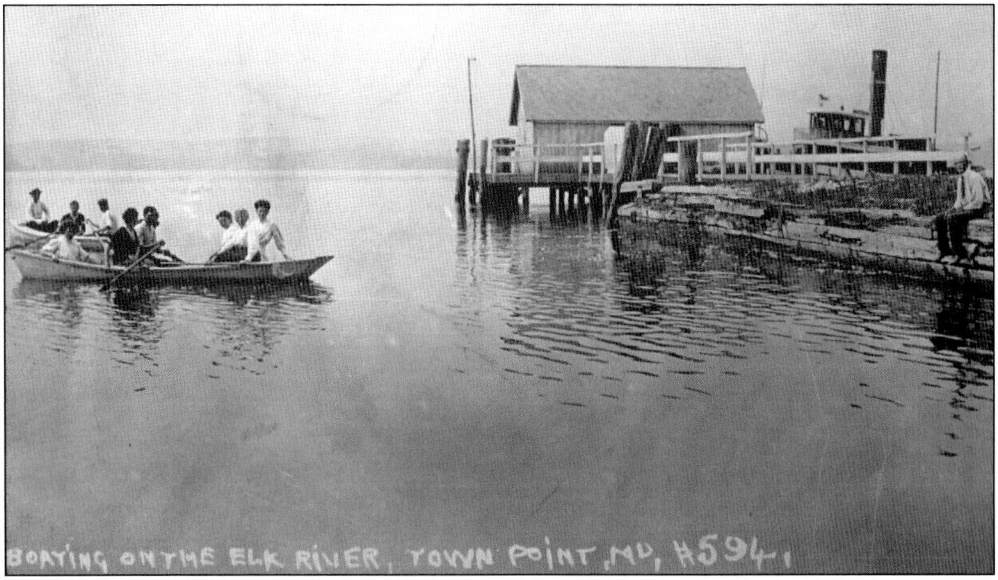

In Cecil County, there are two places named Town Point. One is the actual point of land projecting into the Elk River, which is the location of this *c.* 1909 postcard. The other is the village of Town Point, about 2 miles inland between the Elk and the Bohemia Rivers. (Courtesy of the Maryland State Archives.)

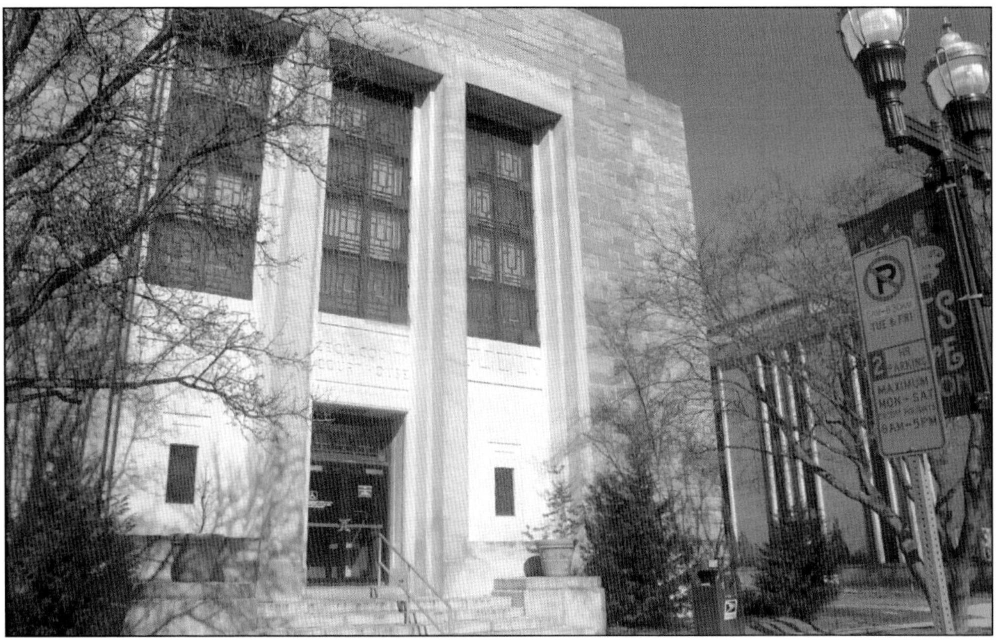

When the first settlers traveled to court, they hoisted sail aboard their boat and hoped the wind was favorable. The county's first courthouse was built at Ordinary Point on the north side of the Sassafras River prior to 1679. In 1719, it was moved to Court House Point, an important ferry location between north and south Cecil County on the Elk River. Court was moved to Charlestown in 1782. Charlestown's prosperity was short-lived, surpassed by a village known as Head of Elk, where the court was moved in 1787. The village was incorporated under the name of Elkton, where the courthouse stands today. (Photograph by Christopher Knauss.)

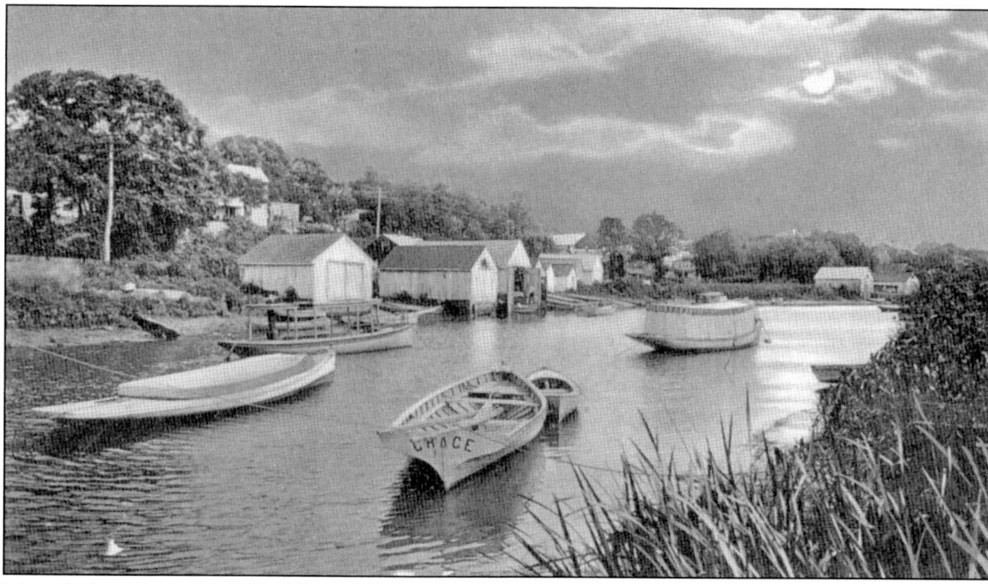

Moonlight illuminates Big Elk Creek on this 1¢ postcard. Elktonians often made voyages down the winding stream for diversion. In the early 1900s, Memorial Day was a big day on the Elk River and many boats were seen plying its waters. Crafts were available for hire, and customers traveled down the Elk to nearby resorts. Powerboats with names like *Jeanette*, *Spray*, and *Ono* transported passengers on cruises each summer. (Courtesy of the Historical Society of Cecil County.)

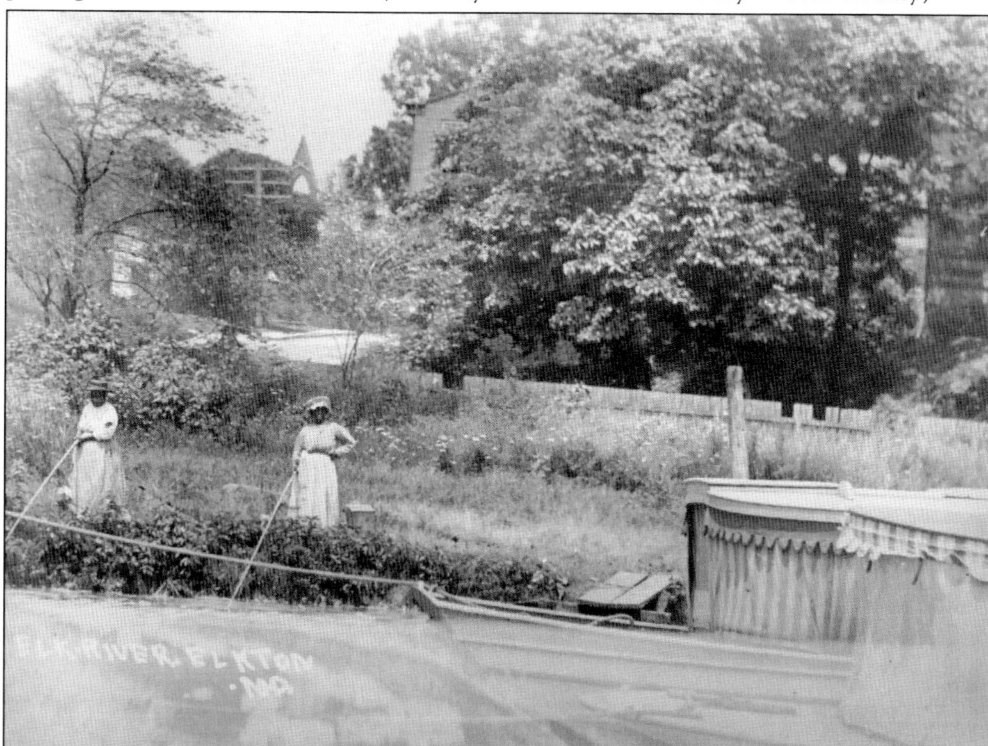

Two women fish on the Elk River in this postcard c. 1900. Several canopied skiffs, a common craft of the era, appear in the foreground at right. (Courtesy of the Maryland State Archives.)

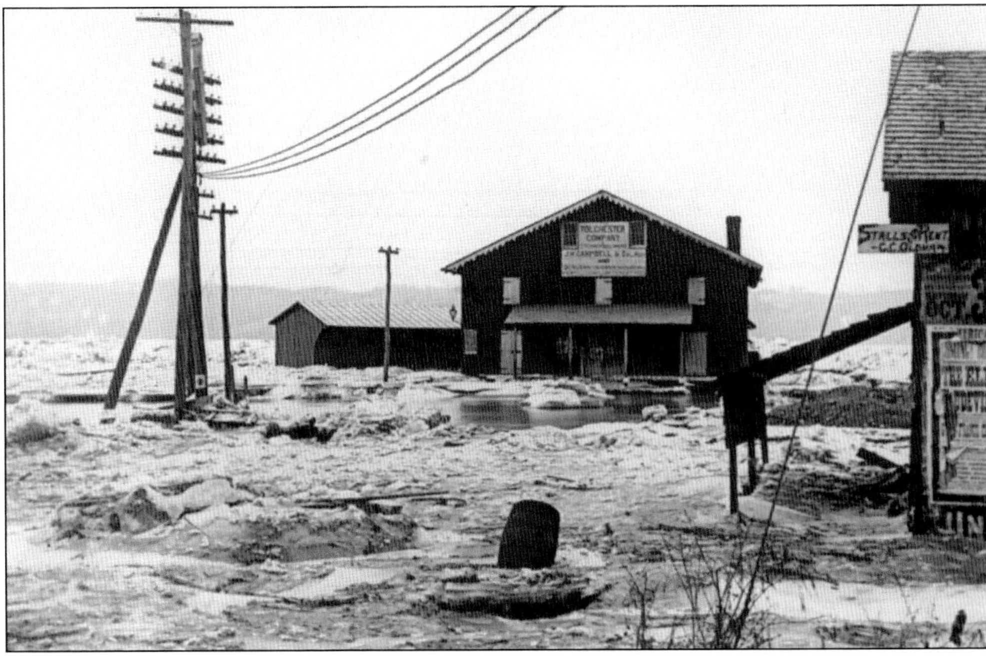

The Susquehanna River, prior to the construction of the Conowingo Dam, was frequently plagued by ice gorges that jammed piles of ice and caused floodwaters to intrude into the streets of Port Deposit. In this photograph, Campbell's steamboat wharf is shown inundated by ice chunks. The most destructive ice gorge in the history of Port Deposit came on January 23, 1910. The gorge destroyed homes, streets, and most of the town's records. (Courtesy of the Historical Society of Cecil County.)

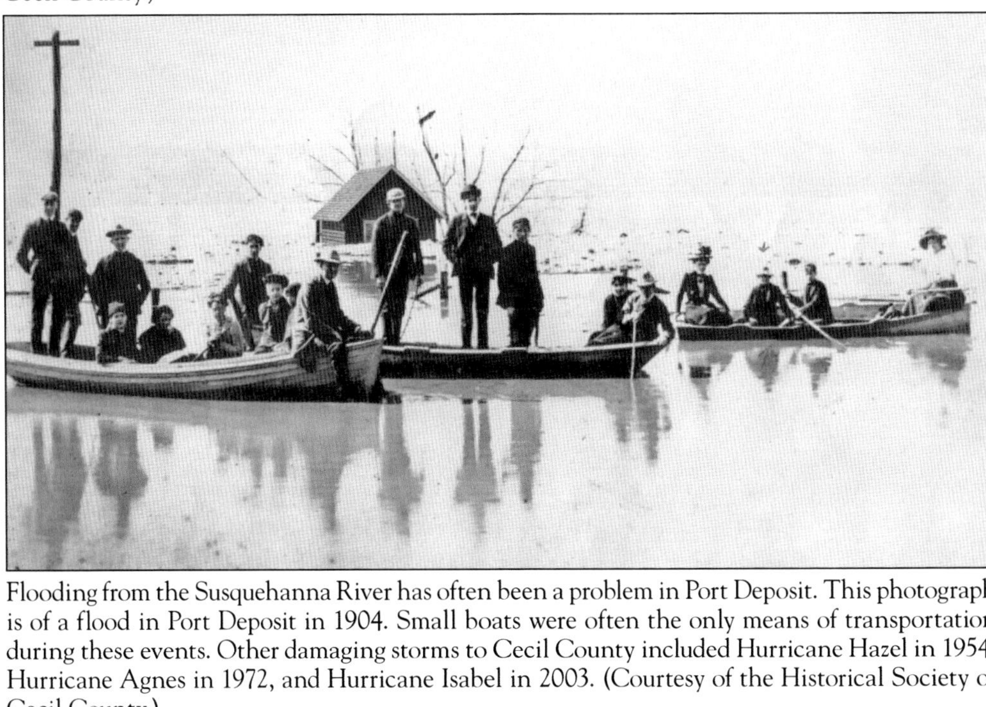

Flooding from the Susquehanna River has often been a problem in Port Deposit. This photograph is of a flood in Port Deposit in 1904. Small boats were often the only means of transportation during these events. Other damaging storms to Cecil County included Hurricane Hazel in 1954, Hurricane Agnes in 1972, and Hurricane Isabel in 2003. (Courtesy of the Historical Society of Cecil County.)

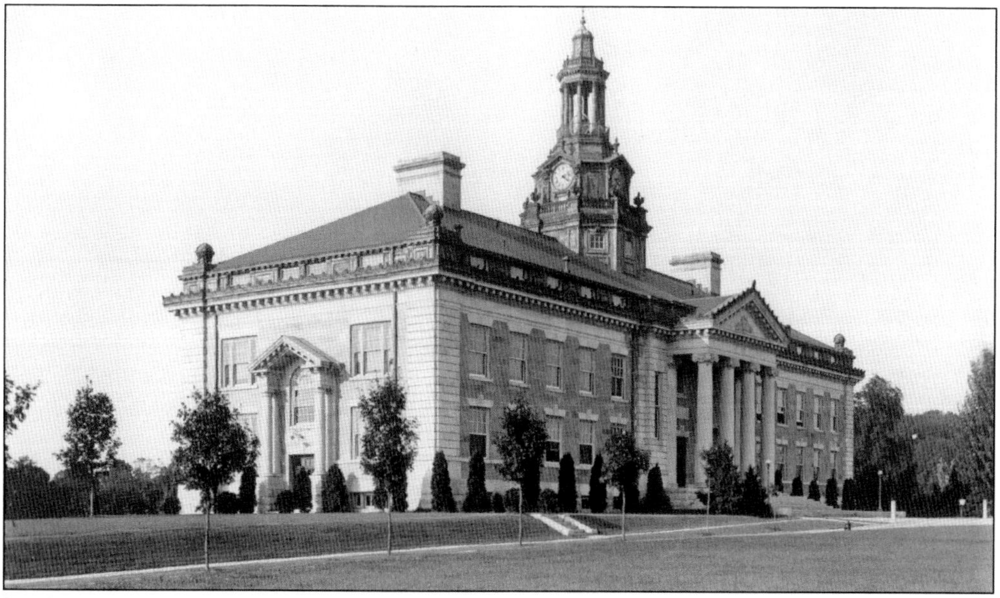

Jacob Tome came to Cecil County along the Susquehanna River in 1833 on a raft from York County, Pennsylvania. When he arrived in Port Deposit, he was penniless but ambitious. Tome formed a partnership with men of greater means and entered the lumber business. He eventually expanded his business holdings as far away as the Great Lakes and became one of the wealthiest men in the country. Tome used part of his wealth to establish Jacob Tome Institute in Port Deposit. Shown here is the Memorial Hall at Tome Institute. (Courtesy of the Historical Society of Cecil County.)

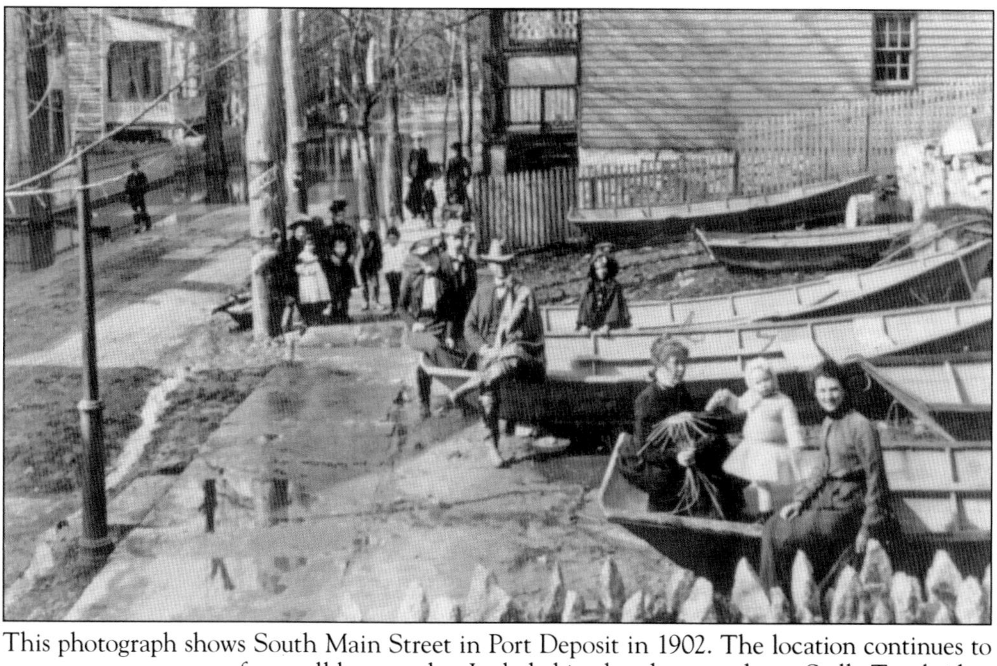

This photograph shows South Main Street in Port Deposit in 1902. The location continues to serve as a storage area for small boats today. Included in the photograph are Stella Trowbridge, Cecil Trowbridge, Frank Benson, Phil Bond, Margaret Benson, and Mrs. Frank Benson. (Courtesy of the Historical Society of Cecil County.)

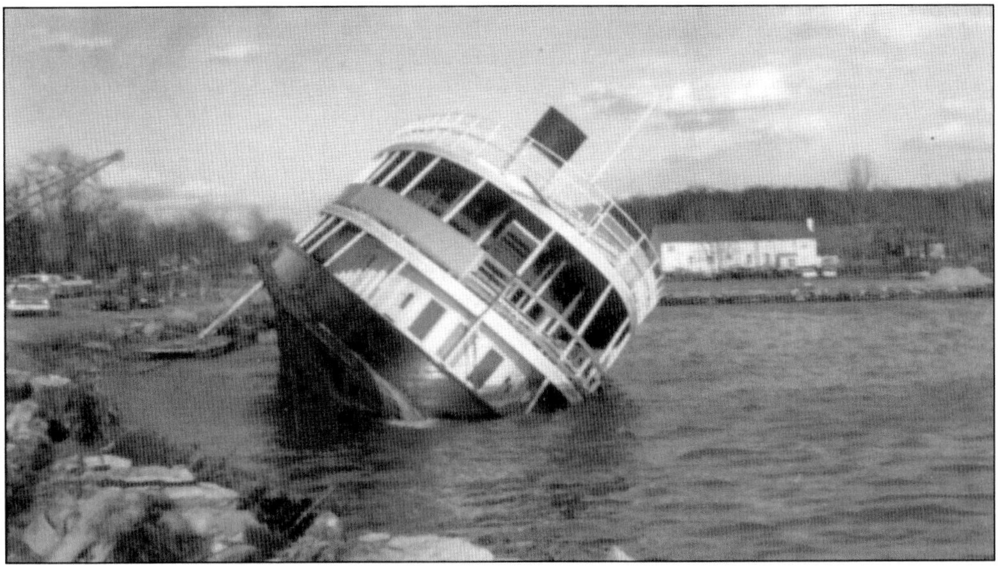

The 192-foot, 782-ton *Chauncey* M. *DePew* excursion boat was left aground by tide changes in March 1971 in North East harbor. John Cooke Jr., of Oldfield Point Road, south of Elkton, was responsible for bringing the boat to North East. He purchased the boat from the Bermuda government and launched his trip to Cecil County in June 12, 1970. Cook's largest previous craft had been a 16-foot runabout. After lying nearly two and a half years in the mud at North East, the *Chauncey* was freed after being bought by Feeney E. Repoley, a Baltimore truck driver. (Courtesy of Jack Manning.)

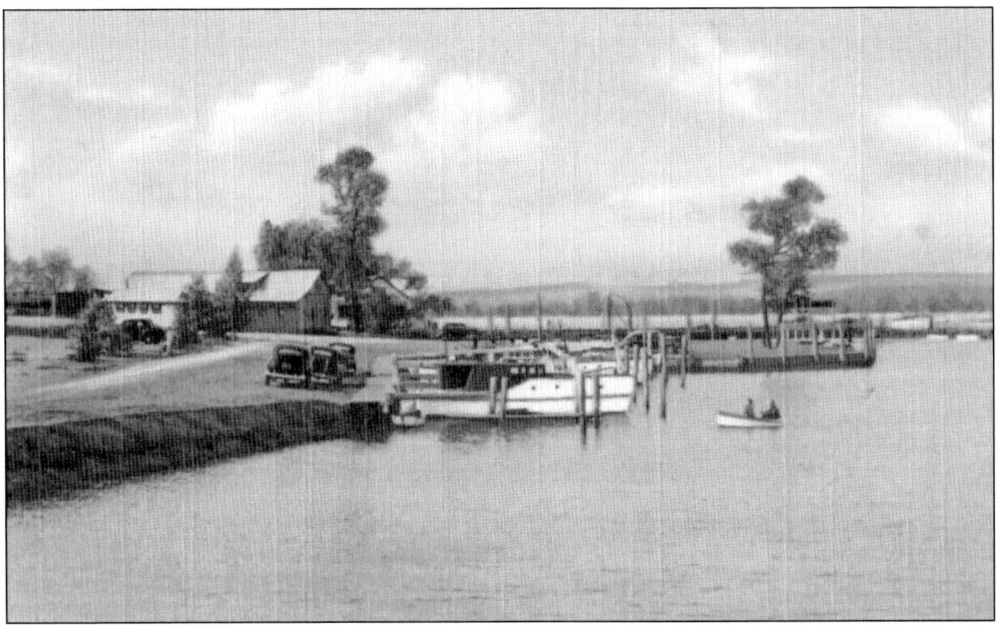

This vintage postcard portrays McDaniel Yacht Basin, established on the Northeast River in 1929. The marina provided boaters from around the region with storage slips, service, and supplies. The operation continues today with 200 slips and storage for over 400 boats on land. McDaniel also serves as a dealer for Carver Yachts, Jeanneau Prestige Yachts, and Larson Boats. (Courtesy of the Historical Society of Cecil County.)

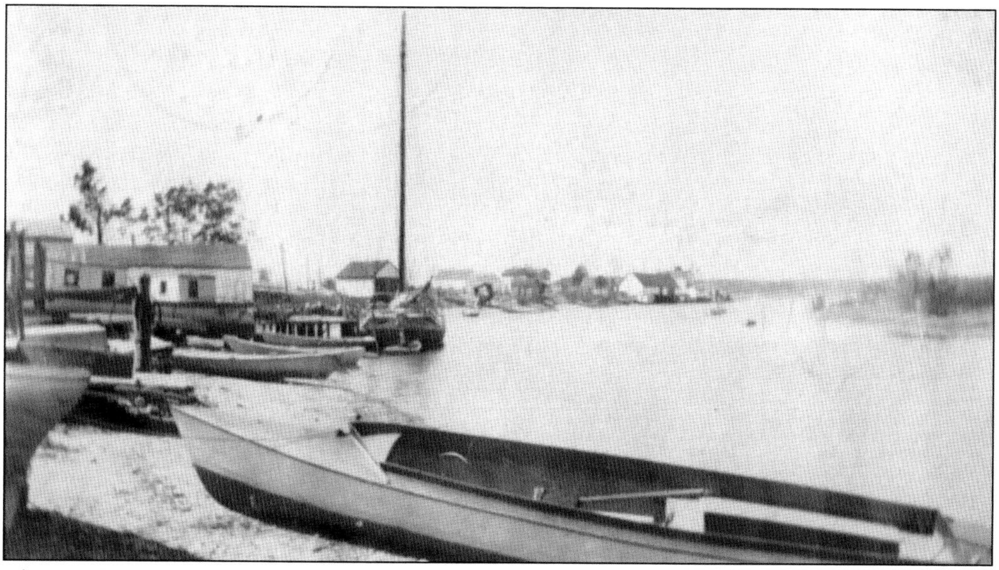

The Northeast River played a large role in the early years of the town North East. Mills were built along its shores, farms prospered, and local fishermen found the area filled with stock. Though North East was settled prior to 1700, it didn't become incorporated until 1850. One of its churches, St. Mary Anne's Episcopal Church, dates back to the early 1700s and maintains one of the oldest graveyards in the state. Today revitalized North East is a tourist destination for visitors drawn to the area by regional foods, antique and collectible shopping, history, and boating. (Courtesy of the Historical Society of Cecil County.)

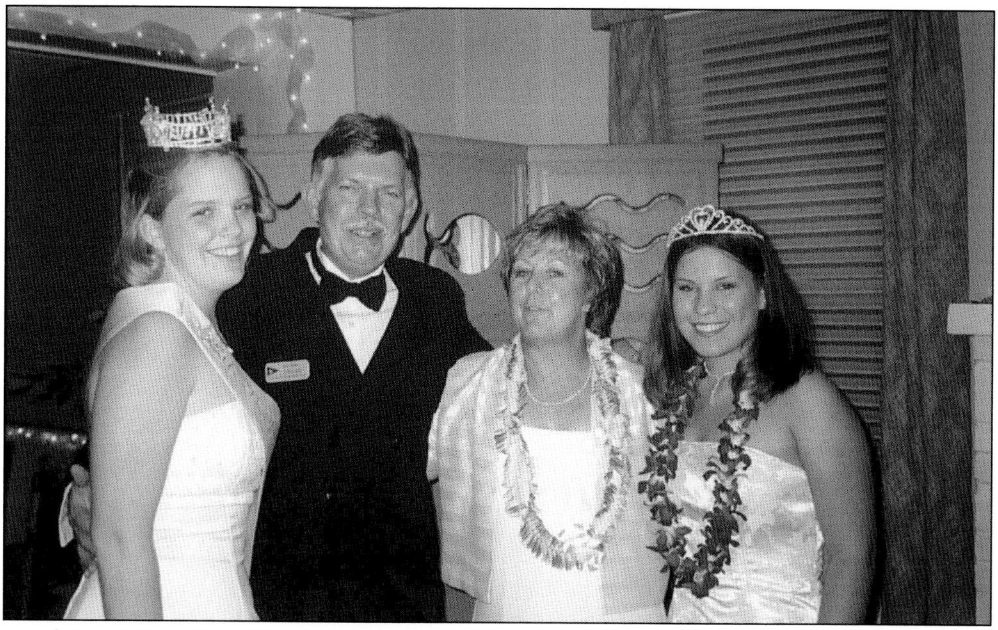

North East River Yacht Club commodore Bill Roos poses with First Lady Lyla Roos along with Queen of the Chesapeake Bay Bridget Smith, left, and NERYC Princess Lavern Roos during season-opening festivities in May 2003. The North East River Yacht Club has been a landmark in Cecil County since 1930 and remains one of the oldest and most respected boating and dining social clubs on the bay. (Courtesy of *Mariner* magazine.)

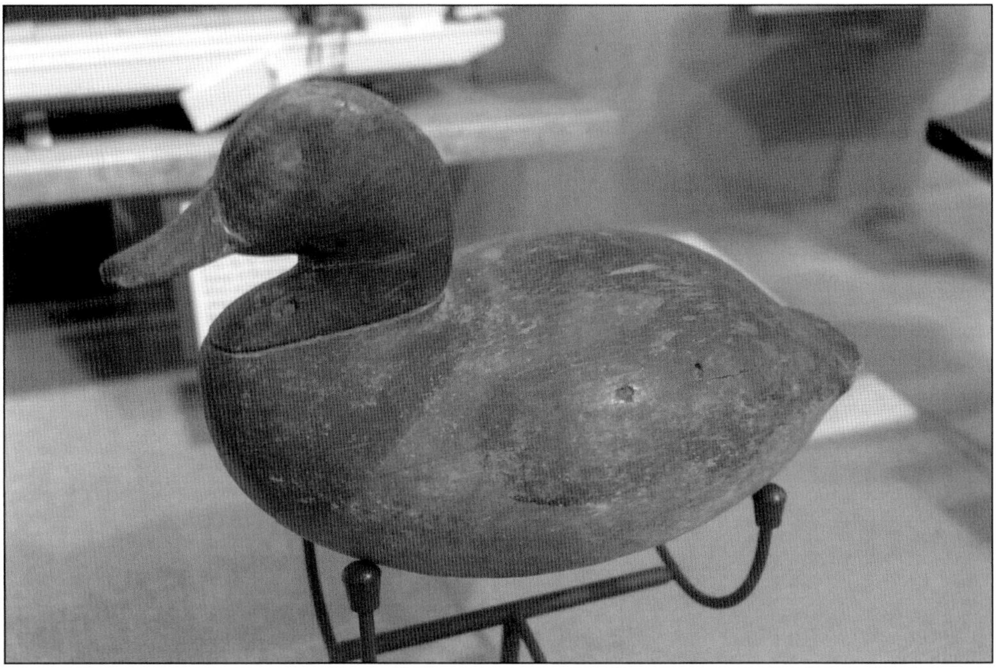

Cecil County decoy carvers such as John Graham and William Heverin, both of Charlestown, helped shape the evolution of working decoys. This scaup decoy, attributed to Graham, is exhibited at the Chesapeake Bay Maritime Museum in St. Michaels. Decoys have evolved over the years from a crude tool to lure ducks into range for market hunters into a fine art form, popular throughout the country. The town of Charlestown was known for its gunning opportunities and decoy making. Heverin, pictured below, was a fisherman and hunter by trade and carved thousands of decoys over 50 years. (Above, photograph by Christopher Knauss; below, courtesy of Jack Manning.)

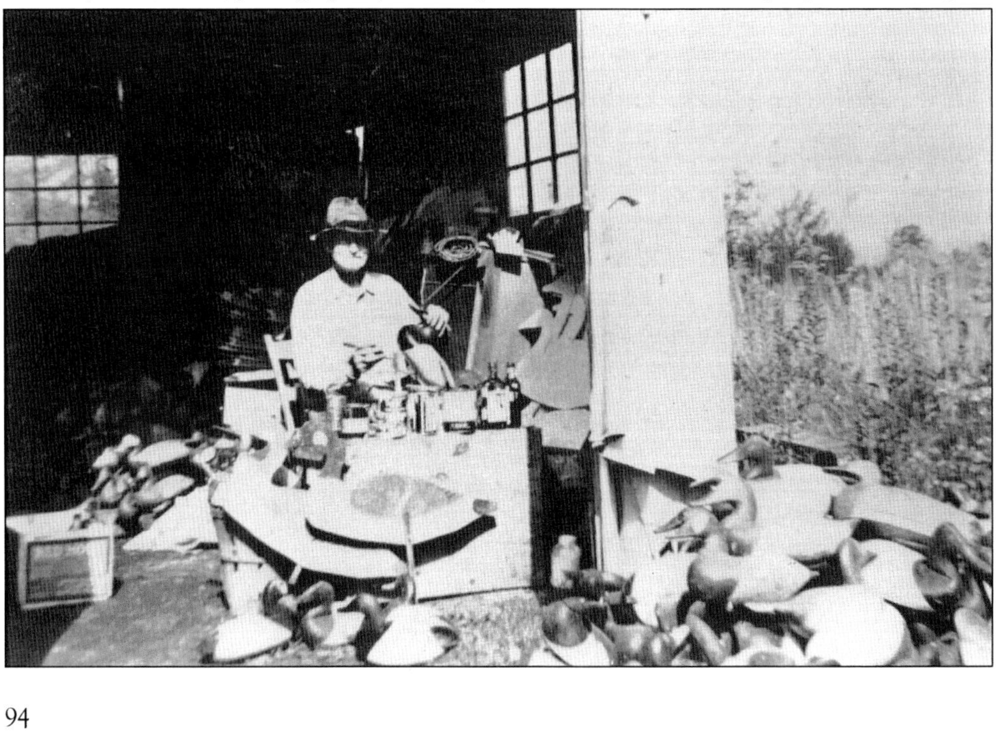

Harry Heisler of Charlestown tends to his gill net c. 1975 on the shores of the Northeast River. In 1838, gill nets were introduced to commercial fishing and revolutionized the industry on the Susquehanna and the Chesapeake Bay. Heisler was an avid hunter and fisherman, harvesting species such as striped bass and herring, which he smoked in a small smokehouse. Charlestown today is a small, water-oriented municipality with a population of about 1,000 people, four marinas, a general store, two restaurants, an elementary school, and a post office. (Courtesy of Jack Manning.)

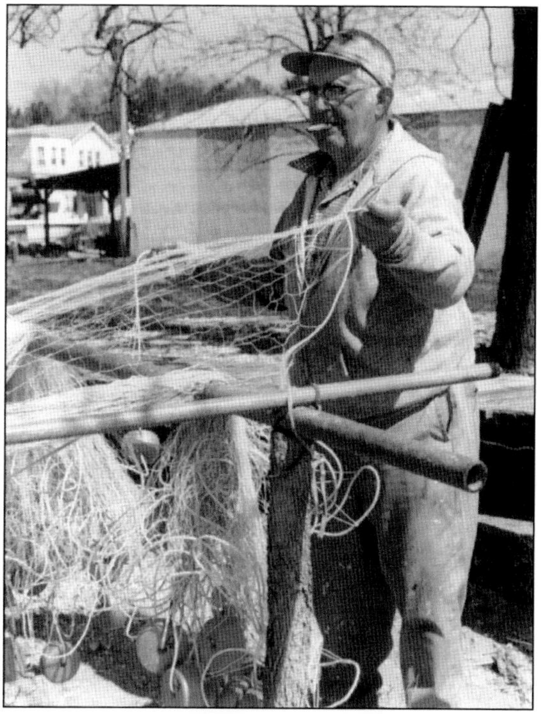

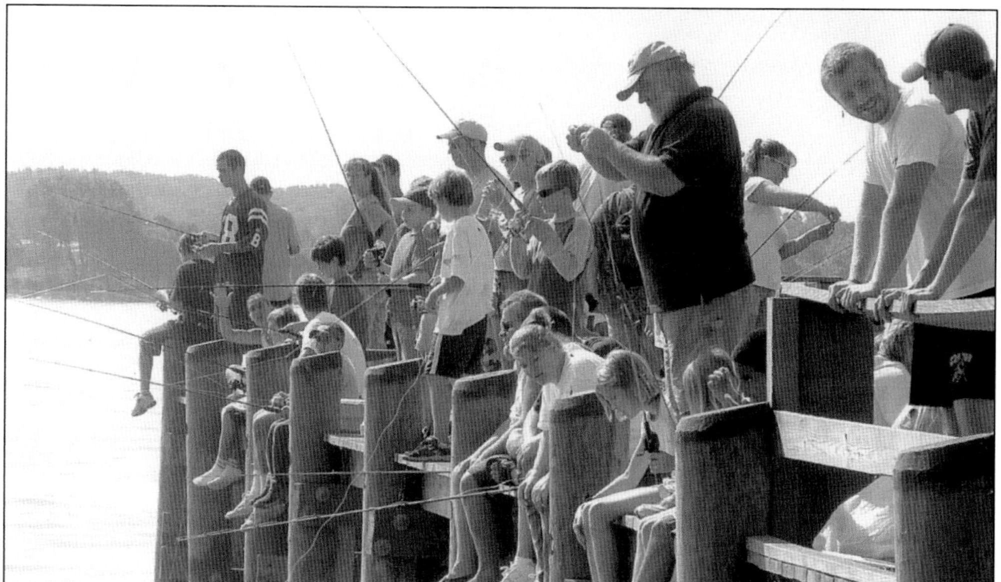

In 1742, the Maryland Assembly directed that "a place called Long Point on the west side of North East River in Cecil County be the location of a new town and that it be named Charles Town in honor of the Right Honourable Charles, Lord Baron of Baltimore." A public wharf and a three-story warehouse were built. An inspector was appointed to ensure only flour of superior quality was sold. The original 18th-century wharf is no longer standing, but the town has built a reproduction of the wharf at the end of a stone pier, placed over the remains of the original cribbing. The pier, a state free-fishing area, hosts an annual kids fishing tournament each September during Riverfest. (Photograph by Christopher Knauss.)

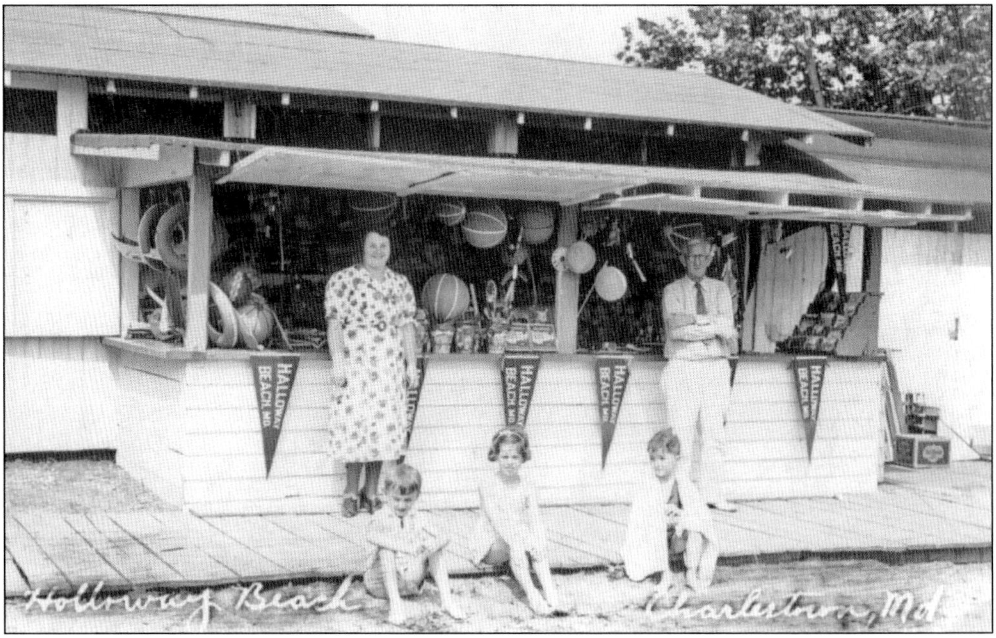

In the 1920s, Charlestown's Holloway Beach on the Northeast River became a popular summer getaway. Vacationers came to enjoy the nettle-free water and stay in cottages along the shoreline. The lady standing is Geneva Barnes of Charlestown. (Above, courtesy of the Historical Society of Cecil County; below, courtesy of Jack Manning.)

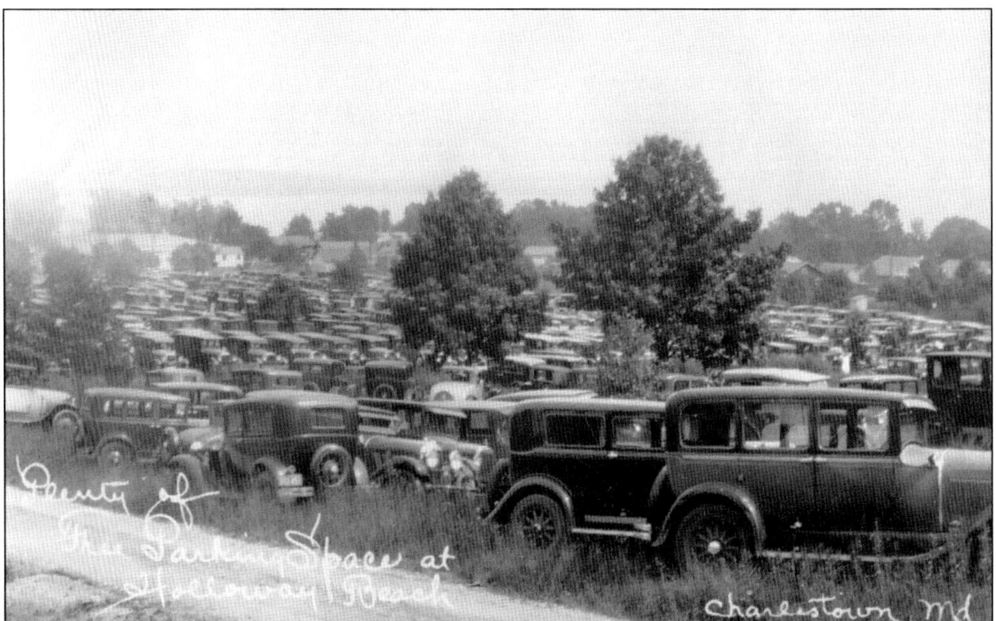

Six

LETTING OFF STEAM

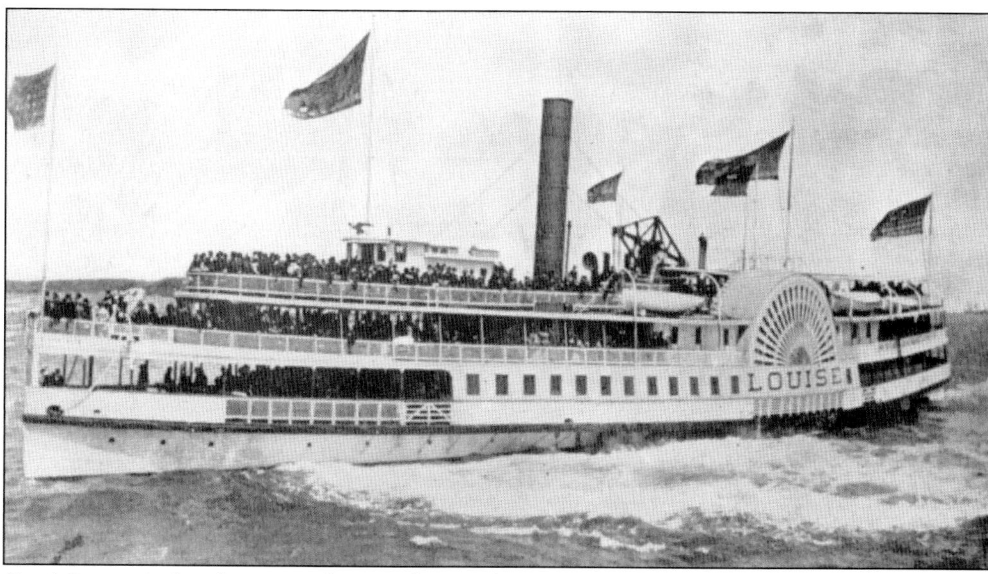

Cecil County's abundant waterfront and natural resources have made it a favorite place to "let off steam" since the beginning of settlement. Fishing, hunting, paddling, and sailing were necessities of survival but also enjoyable pursuits that often led to friendly competitions. In the late 1800s to mid-1900s, steamboats departed from Cecil's wharves to transport fun-loving vacationers to beaches and resorts along the bay. Getting there in style was a big part of the fun. Steamboat numbers on the bay reached their peak in the first decade of the 20th century and steadily declined until the end of the era in the 1960s. The steamboats *Louise*, *Annapolis*, and *Emma Giles* made regular runs on the Susquehanna and Sassafras Rivers. The side-wheeler *Louise*, with a capacity of 2,500 passengers, carried five million passengers in 40 years of service. Today boaters flock to the waters of the county to enjoy the nautical scene and ease their minds of daily burdens. (Courtesy of the Historical Society of Cecil County.)

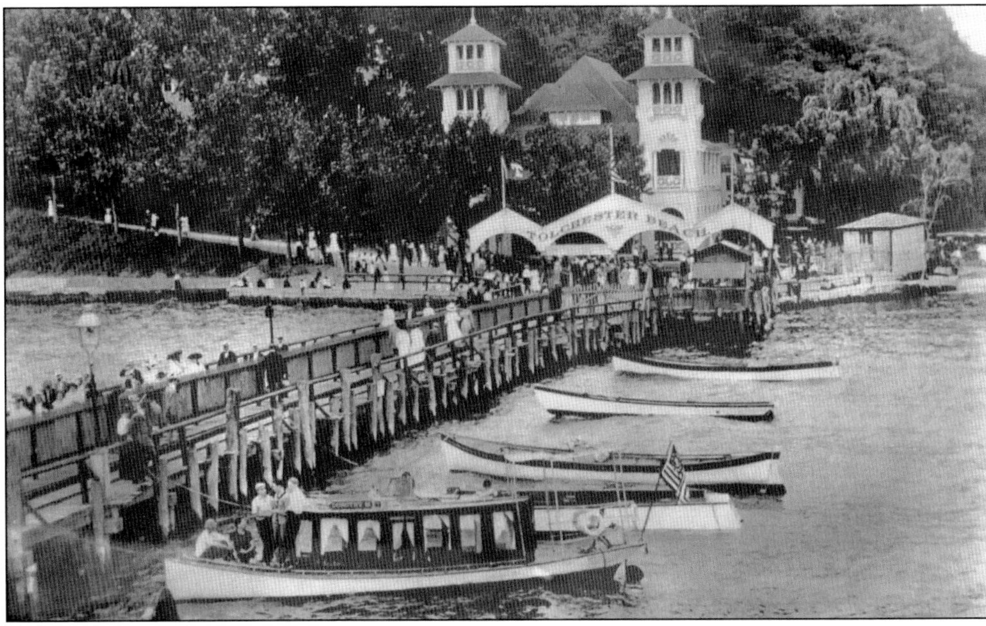

In 1887, the Tolchester Beach Improvement Company formed to develop a resort at Tolchester Beach on the Kent County side of the Sassafras River. Small passenger boats and large steamers scheduled transportation service to the resort from ports in Cecil County and throughout the upper Chesapeake. The park began with just a few concessions, picnic grounds, and a merry-go-round and grew to become one of the largest and most popular resorts on the bay. Activities included games of skill and chance, a bowling alley, a roller-skating rink, rides on a roller coaster and a carousel, and even harness racing. The resort also featured bathhouses, a restaurant, and a hotel. Passengers disembark from the steamer *Louise* during a visit to the resort in the postcard below. (Courtesy of Tolchester Beach Revisited Museum.)

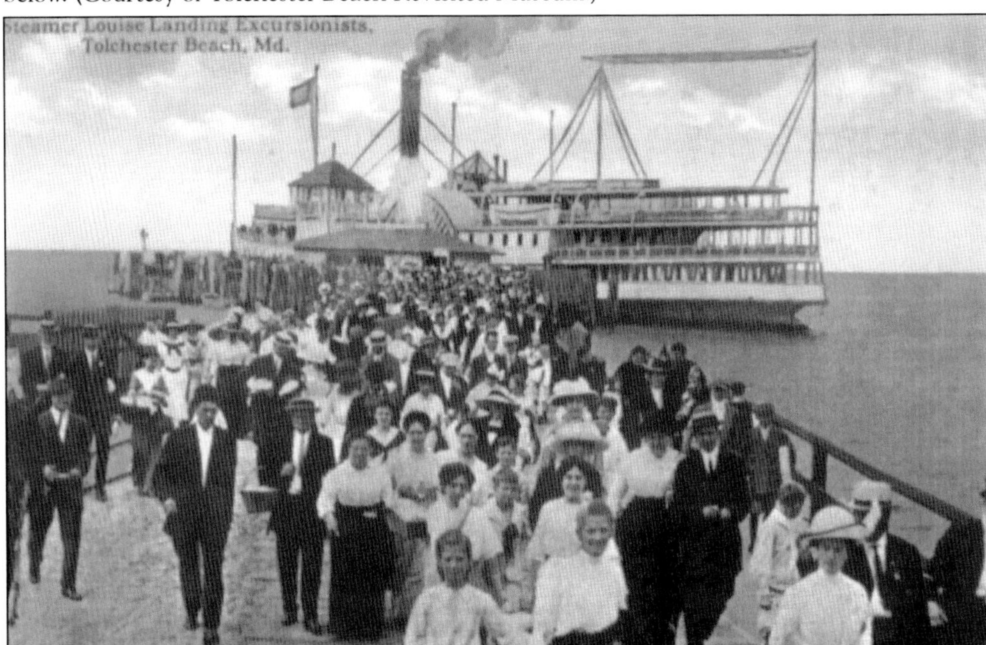

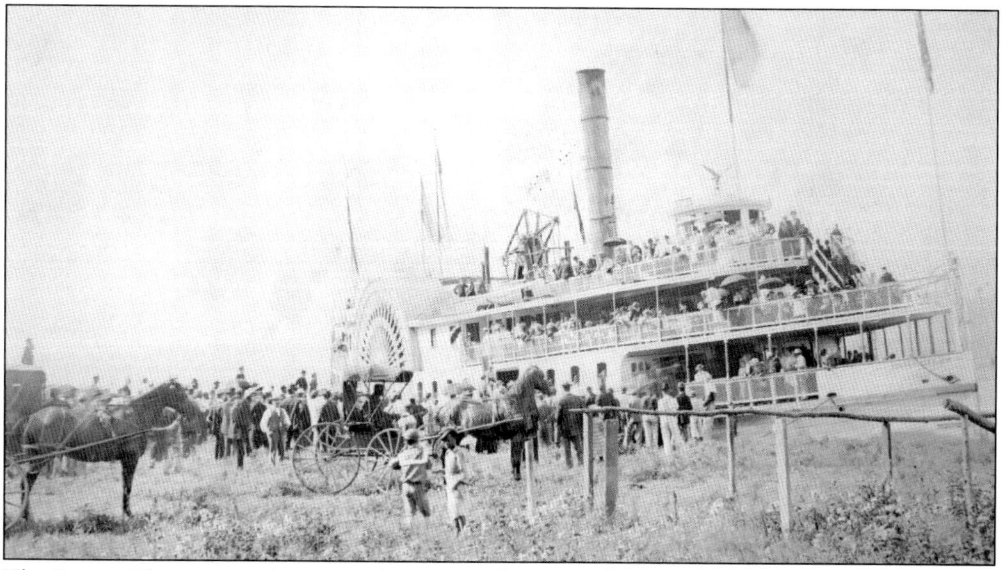

The *Emma Giles* prepares for a special excursion departing from Port Deposit *c.* 1895. A steamboat of the Tolchester line, *Emma Giles* also made scheduled runs on the Susquehanna and Sassafras. A *Cecil Democrat* advertisement from August 19, 1905, states: "Special Excursion to Great Kent, Queen Anne's and Cecil Co. Fair at Tolchester, Thursday August 31, 1905. Steamer *Emma Giles* leaves Fredericktown." (Courtesy of the Port Deposit Heritage Corporation.)

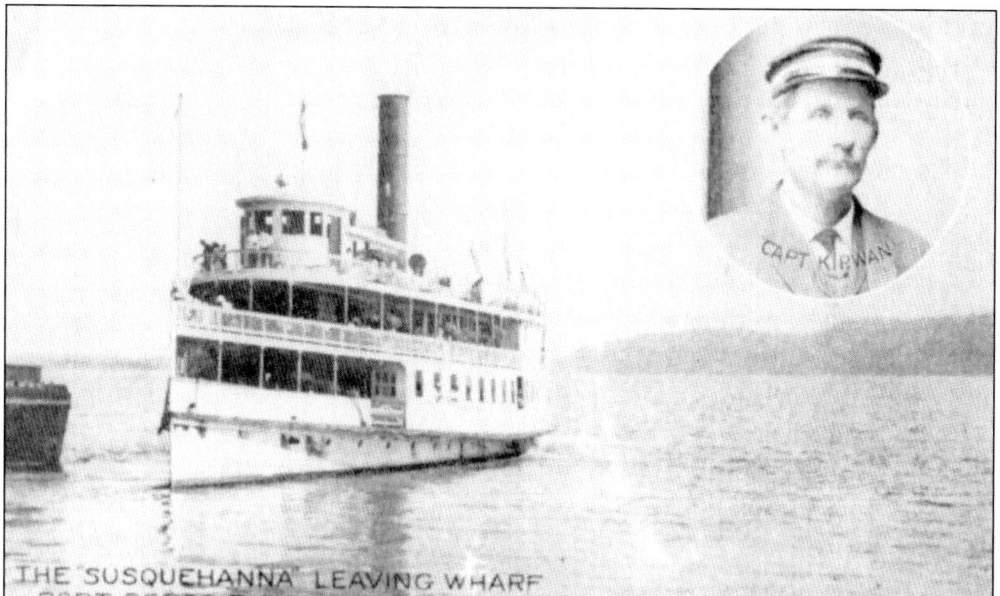

This postcard shows the *Susquehanna* leaving Campbell's Wharf in Port Deposit. The *Susquehanna* ran the circuit between Betterton, Port Deposit, and Havre de Grace under the direction of Capt. John Kirwan. The propeller-driven steam vessel was built by Charles Reeder of Baltimore for the Tolchester Beach Improvement Company in 1898. The steamer was owned by the Tolchester Steamboat Company, which eventually closed in 1936 and was taken over by Tolchester Lines, Inc. The company's excursion service to Tolchester Beach remained in operation through the early 1960s. Service from Port Deposit ended during the Great Depression. (Courtesy of Jack Manning.)

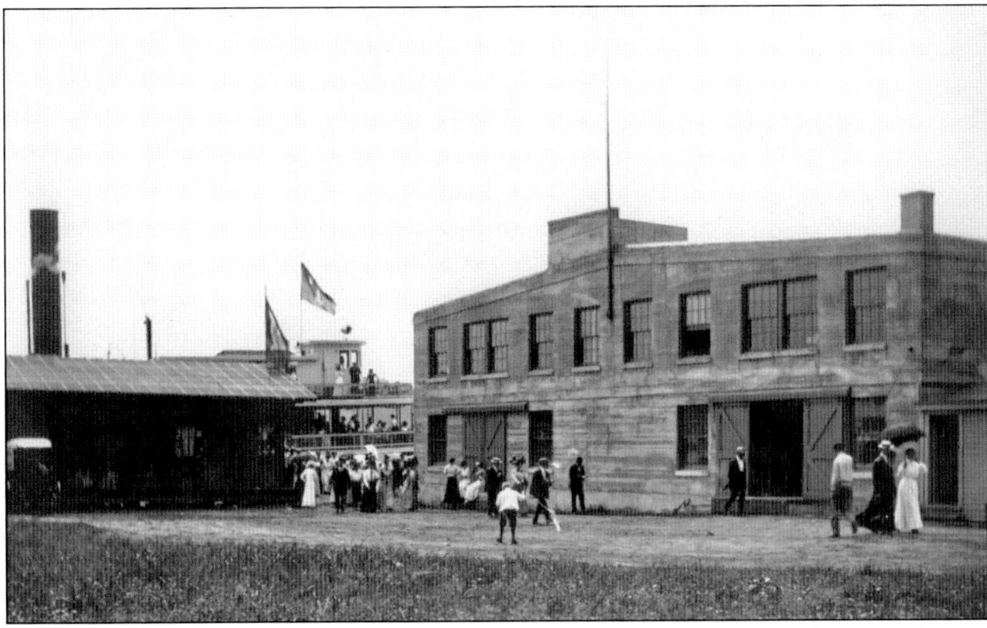

The *Susquehanna* steamer, built in 1898, transported resort-goers to and from Port Deposit, taking on passengers at Campbell's Wharf *c.* 1905. (Courtesy of the Historical Society of Cecil County.)

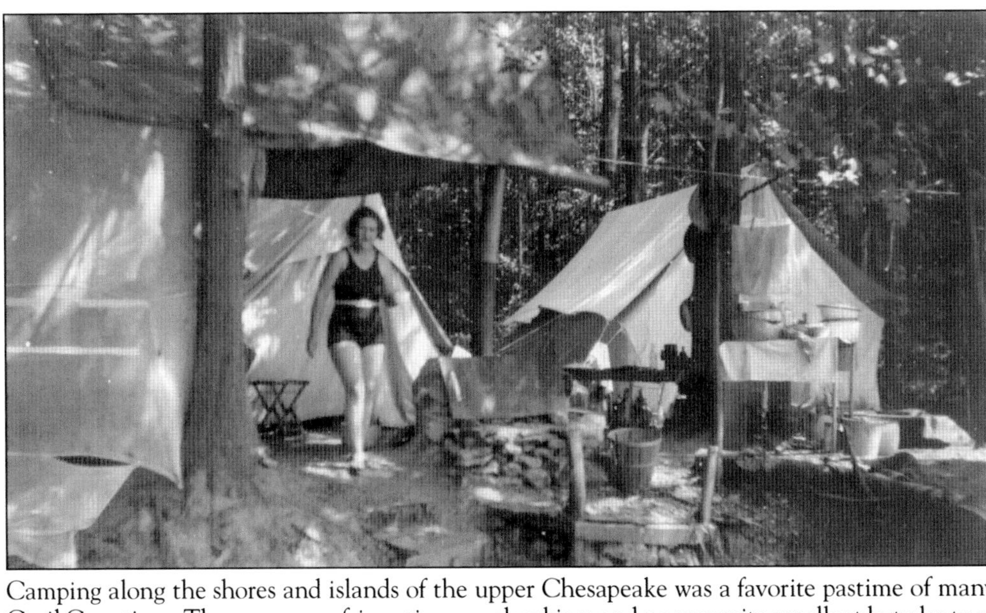

Camping along the shores and islands of the upper Chesapeake was a favorite pastime of many Cecil Countians. There was no refrigeration, no plumbing, and no mosquito repellent but plenty of time to enjoy the peace and quiet of the outdoors. The men of the group delivered the passengers and supplies by rowboat. Campers would often spend weeks and months enjoying the wilderness, fishing and bathing in the nettle-free upper Chesapeake. (Courtesy of Barbara Brown.)

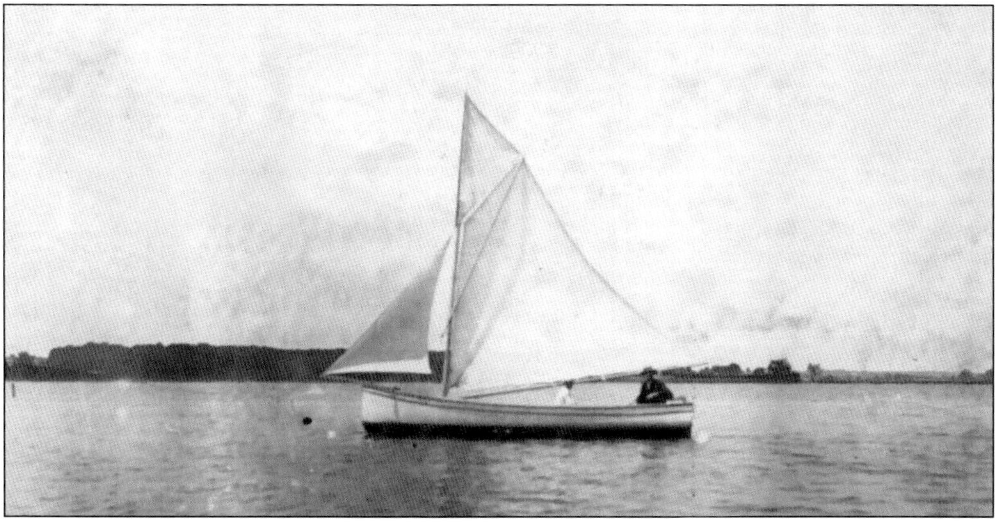

Ever since European settlers came to Cecil County, sailing served as a means of transportation as well as a tranquil and pleasant pastime to enjoy the beauty of the waterways. In this early-1900s photograph, John Wesley Williams and Walter Williams of Port Deposit enjoy a cruise on the Susquehanna in a V-bottom sailing skiff. John Williams's wife was a seamstress who made the sails. (Courtesy of the Port Deposit Heritage Corporation.)

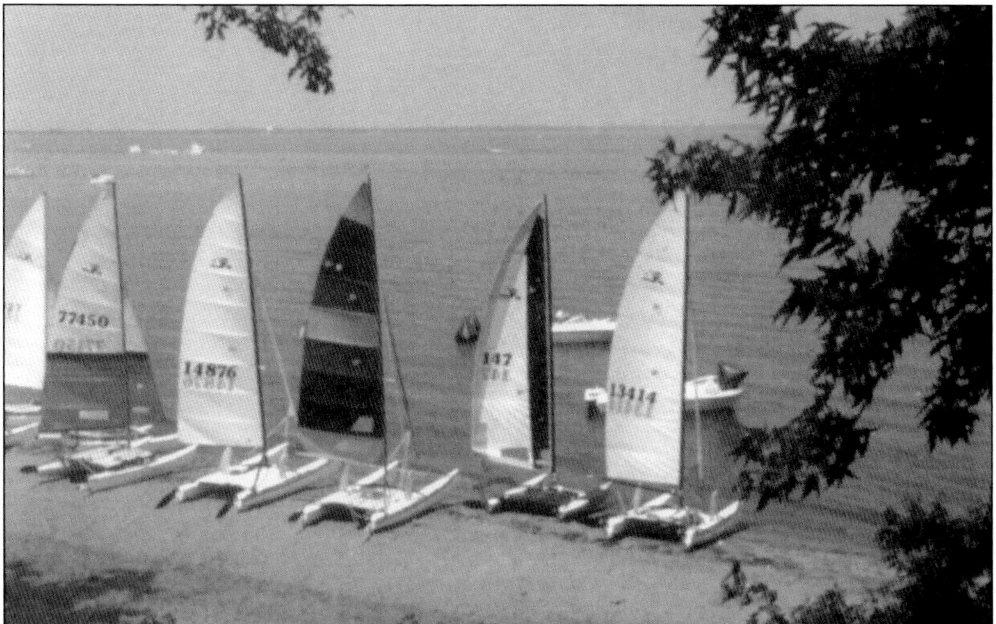

Catamarans on the beach at Elk Neck State Park are ready for a day of sailing on the Chesapeake Bay. (Courtesy of the Historical Society of Cecil County.)

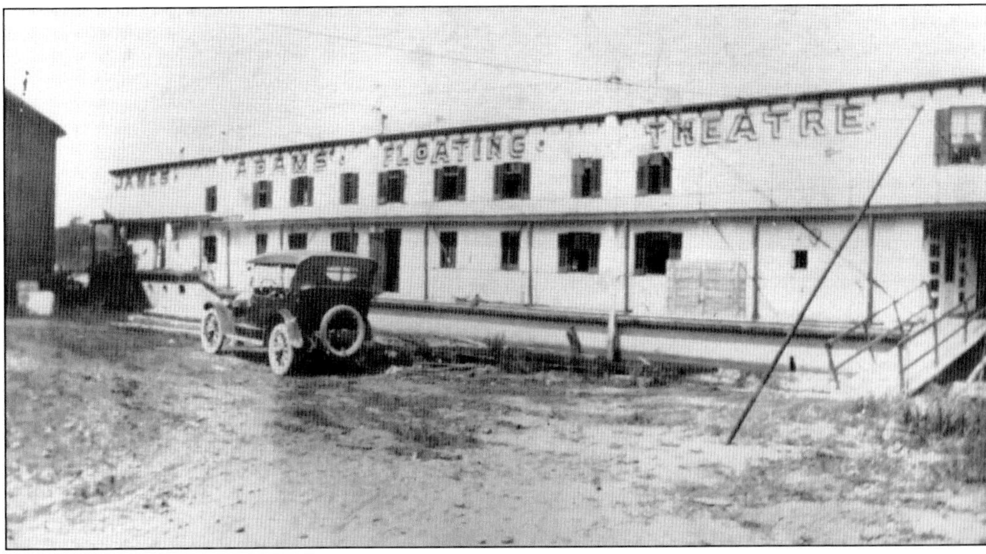

The James Adams Floating Theatre, shown here docked in North East, traveled the waters of the Chesapeake Bay from 1914 to 1941, towed by the powerboats *Elk* and *Trouper*. It could seat 700 people and had 8 dressing rooms and a 19-foot-wide stage. The Floating Theatre became a cultural resource for people in metropolitan, rural, and small coastal towns. It was the only showboat Edna Ferber visited to do research for her novel *Show Boat*, which inspired the Broadway hit of the same name and several film versions. The theater was owned by James Adams and his wife, who built a home in Chesapeake City on Mount Nebo. (Courtesy of the Historical Society of Cecil County.)

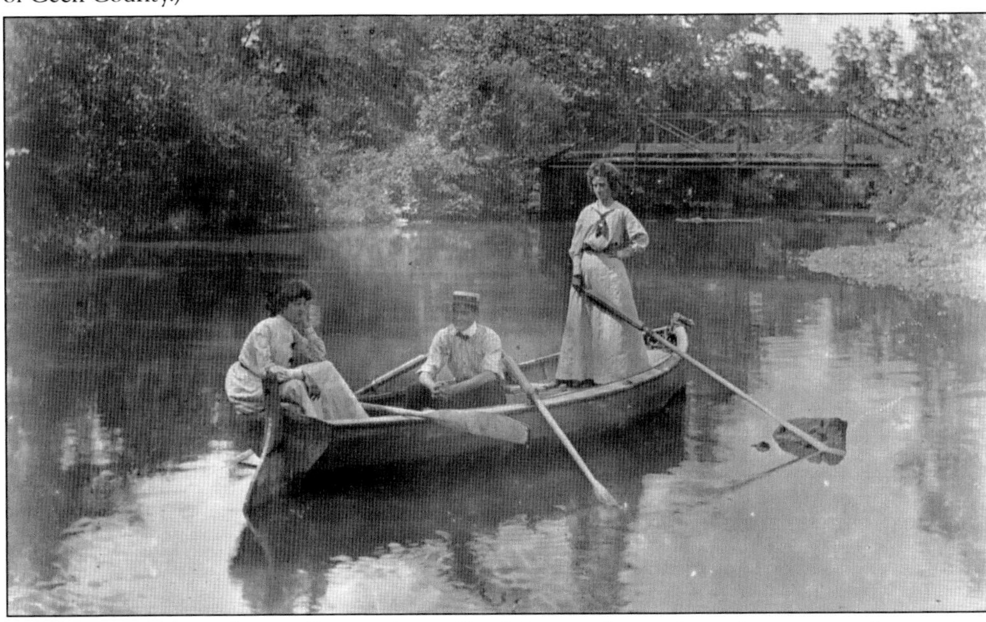

Paddling trips along the smaller creeks in Cecil County have always been a popular pastime. In the late 19th and early 20th centuries, fashionable women's clothing styles shed some of the extravagances of previous decades. Unfussy, tailored clothes were worn for outdoor activities and traveling. In the 1890s, the bow tie returned to popularity for men and flat straw boaters hats were worn for yachting and beach-going. (Courtesy of the Historical Society of Cecil County.)

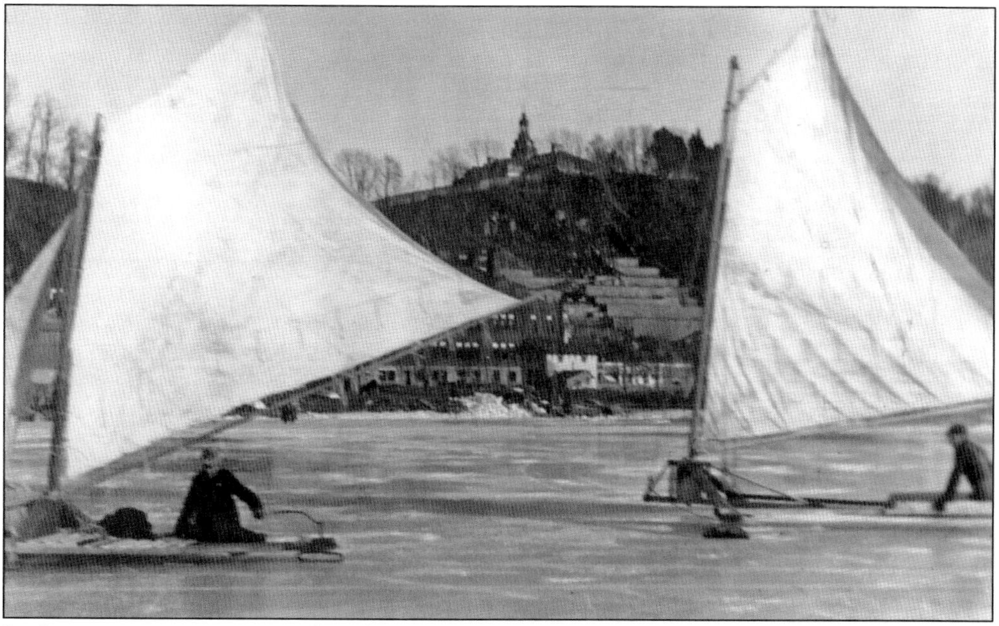

Ice boaters enjoy crisp air and cool breezes while gliding across the frozen Susquehanna River in 1905. In an interesting side note, in 1852, ice on the Susquehanna was so thick that railroad tracks were laid across the frozen river, and for 40 days, more than 1,300 loaded freight cars crossed the river safely between Perryville and Havre de Grace. (Courtesy of the Historical Society of Cecil County.)

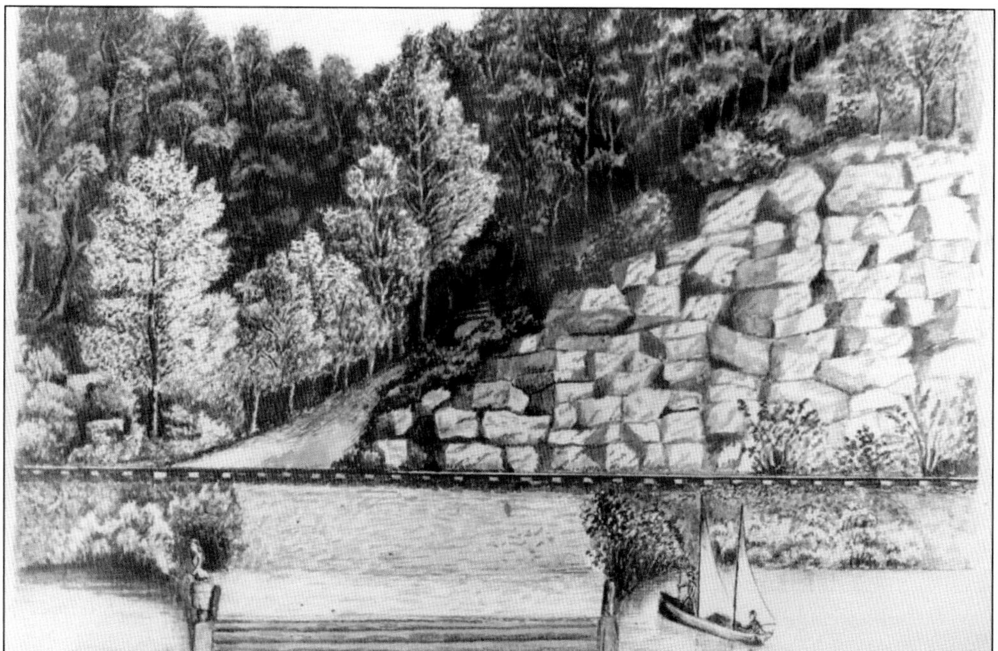

City dwellers seeking a sabbatical or a scenic location for summer vacation often visited Happy Valley in Port Deposit through the early part of the 20th century, many arriving by boat. The resort's spring was said to exude feelings of well-being. (Courtesy of the Port Deposit Heritage Corporation.)

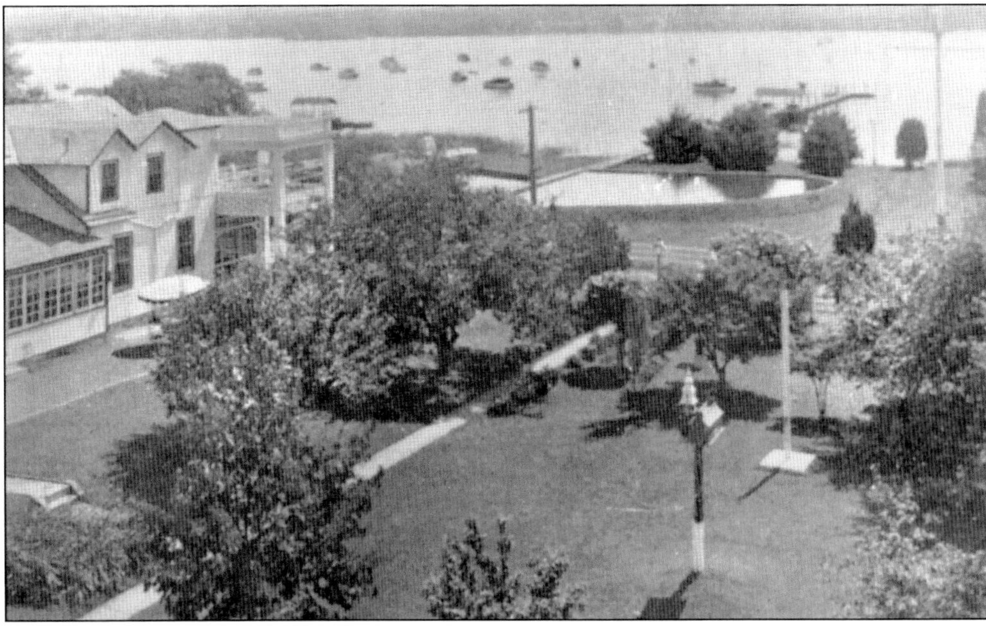

In the late 1800s, the Wellwood Club in Charlestown on the Northeast River was a private hunting and fishing club. The club was established as "an organization of optimists and humanitarians in the broadest sense. Its purpose is to promote the 'happy' habit; to reduce the friction of life to a minimum and increase the pleasure of existence to the maximum; to discourage strife and promote good fellowship." Later the Wellwood became a private country and yacht club. Members and visitors to the Wellwood included Presidents Theodore Roosevelt and Calvin Coolidge. (Courtesy of the Historical Society of Cecil County.)

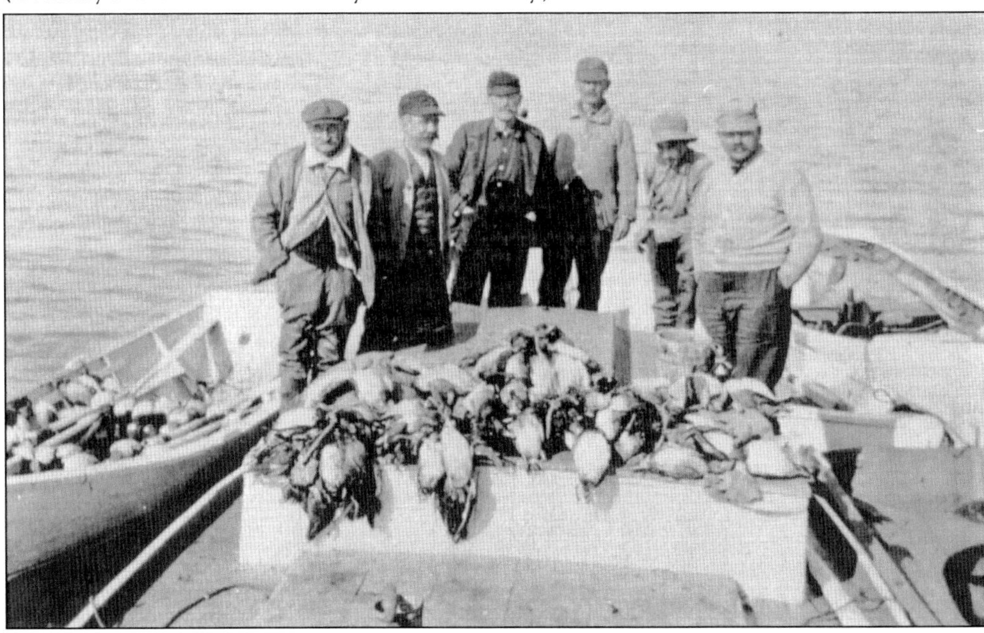

From left to right, Perry K. Barnes, George W. Barnes, Bob Gibson, Will Heverin, Harry Heverin, and Harry Barnes pose with their waterfowl harvest in this photograph from the early 1900s. (Courtesy of Jack Manning.)

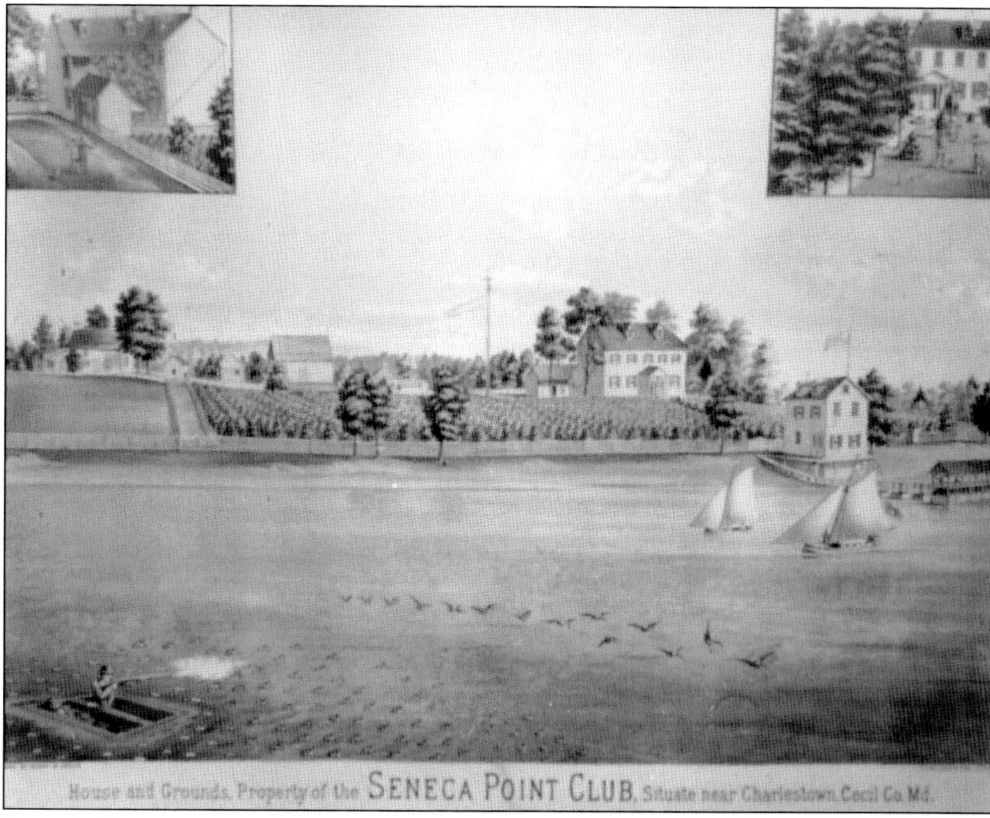

From the beginning, Cecil County's waters hosted large numbers of migratory waterfowl. In the early 20th century, wealthy individuals assembled tracts of riverfront land for purchase or lease to establish private gunning clubs. Cecil County drew hunters from around the bay as well as cities like Philadelphia, Baltimore, and New York, hoping to take part in the robust sport. The reproduction of a postcard above features hunters firing from a sinkbox at ducks fooled by a decoy spread. At right is a schedule of fares typical for the day. (Above, courtesy of the Historical Society of Cecil County; at right, photograph by Christopher Knauss at the Chesapeake Bay Maritime Museum.)

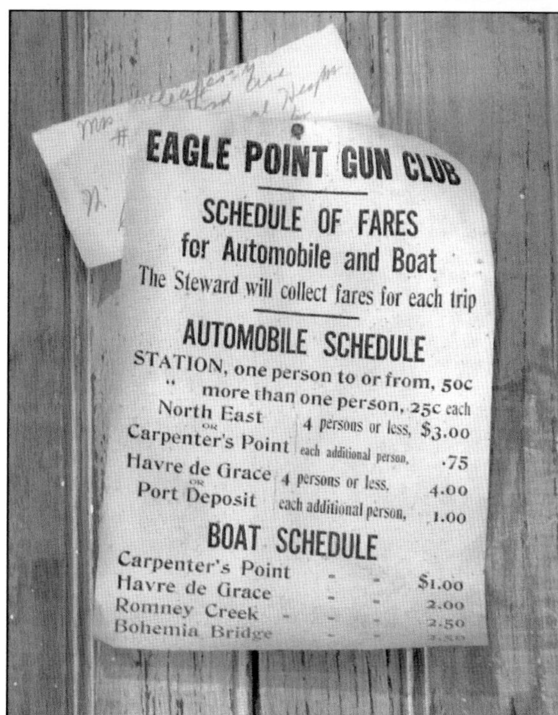

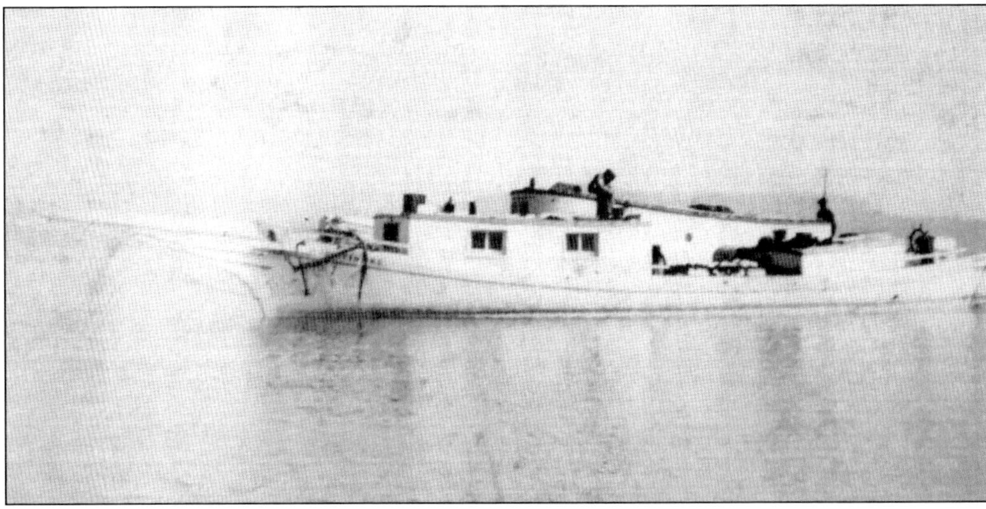

This bugeye, owned by Harry Barnes, was converted to a sport gunning boat in the early 1900s. Barnes also owned several sinkboxes that he used to entertain hunters. The rig was placed at "The Knoll" at Carpenter's Point and the Wild Duck Cove area. A bugeye was a two-masted sailing vessel used for dredging oysters. Bugeyes, which came into existence around 1875, descended from the log canoe when the time for a larger boat was needed. The schooners of the day were too large and the canoe was too small. Harry Barnes, right, poses with a sport gunner below. Notice the bottles of champagne to the left, as clients tended to party and have a good time during hunting trips. (Courtesy of Jack Manning.)

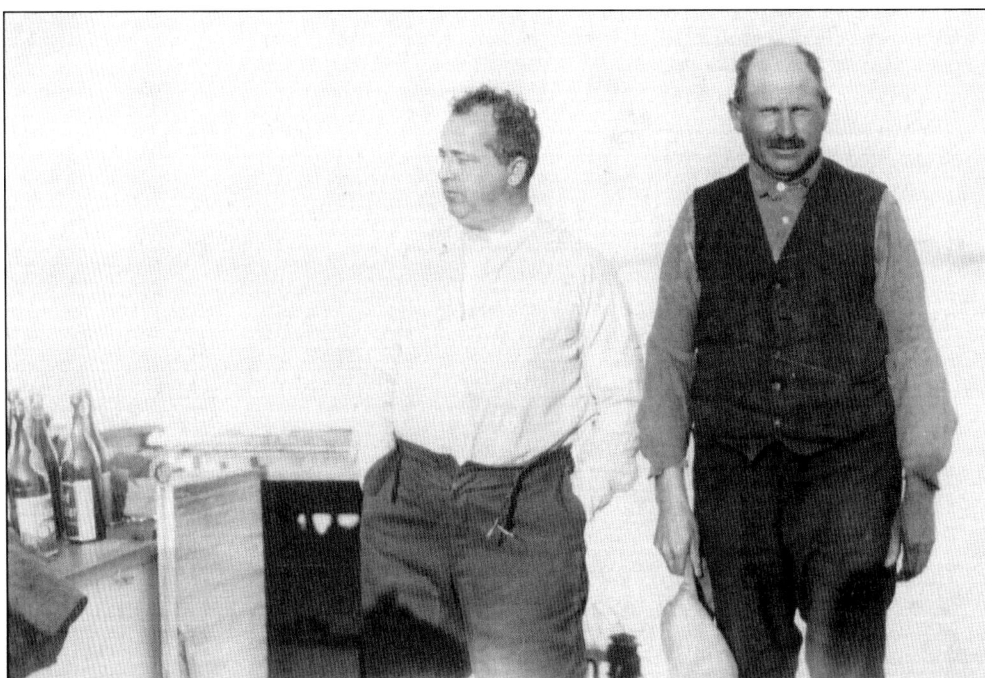

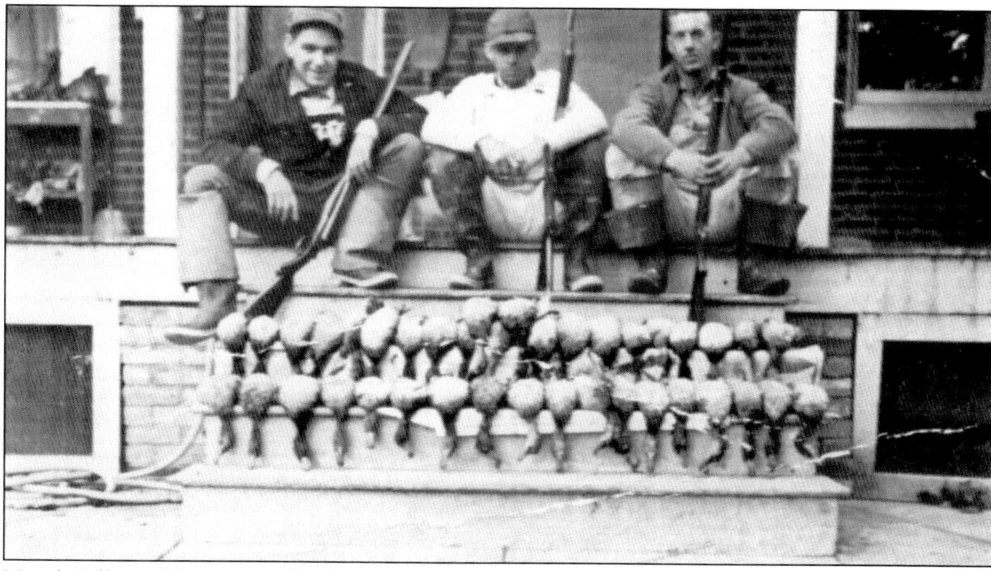

Virgil Gilbert, Herman Walbeck, and Sam Reeder display the spoils of their recreational hunt on the steps of a Beech Street home in North East c. 1940. Cecil County is the site of the famed Susquehanna Flats, a hunting mecca that has attracted many famous people, including J. P. Morgan and Grover Cleveland. Wildfowl hunting was once primarily a commercial activity that supported the communities around the bay. In 1918, the Migratory Bird Treaty Act ended market hunting for waterfowl. Today recreational hunting continues on the Flats, with seasons and bag limits managed by the U.S. Fish and Wildlife Service. (Courtesy of Jack Manning.)

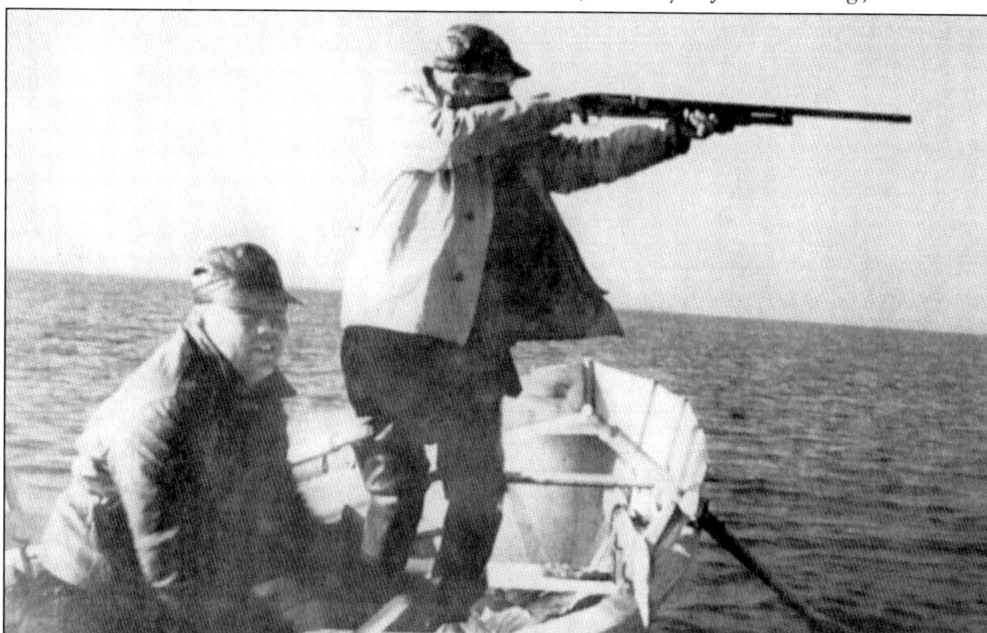

Arnette Armour sculls a bushwhack skiff as his father fires at waterfowl on the Northeast River. A bushwhack boat was used because it offered a low profile in which one or two hunters could surprise large groups of ducks rafting on the water. A hole in the transom allowed for sculling of the boat as the hunters crouched low. (Courtesy of Jack Manning.)

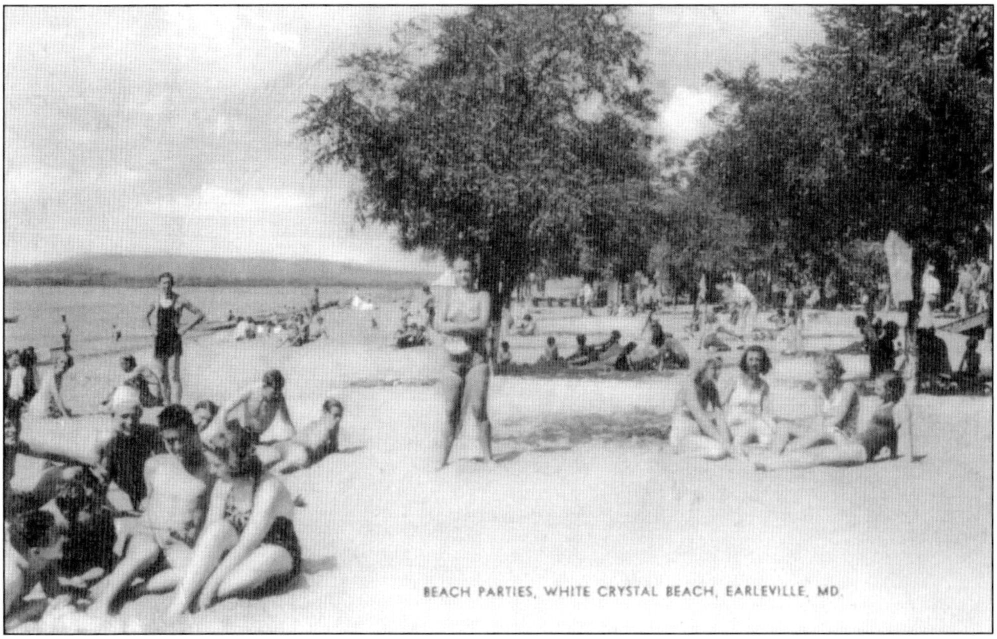

White Crystal Beach, shown c. 1950, became one of many places along the waterfront in Cecil County where vacationers enjoyed summer fun, participating in beach activity during the day and dancing and nightlife during the evening. The sandy beach along the Elk River remains open to the public with picnic tables, a concession stand, and a view of Turkey Point. Other favorite Cecil County vacation destinations included Port Herman Beach, Town Point Beach, Red Point Beach, and Holloway Beach, presented in the postcard below. (Courtesy of the Historical Society of Cecil County.)

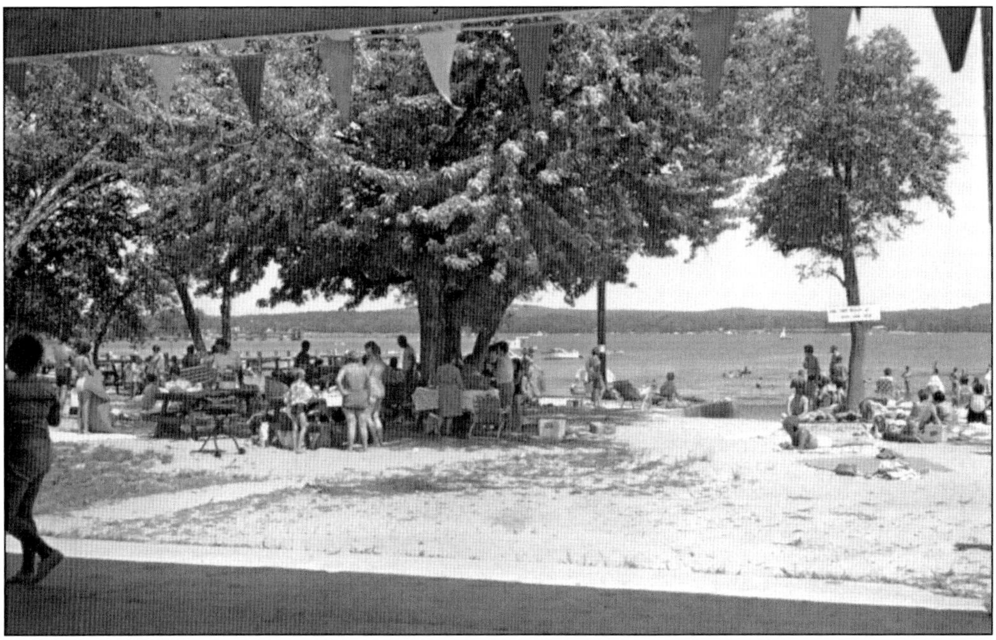

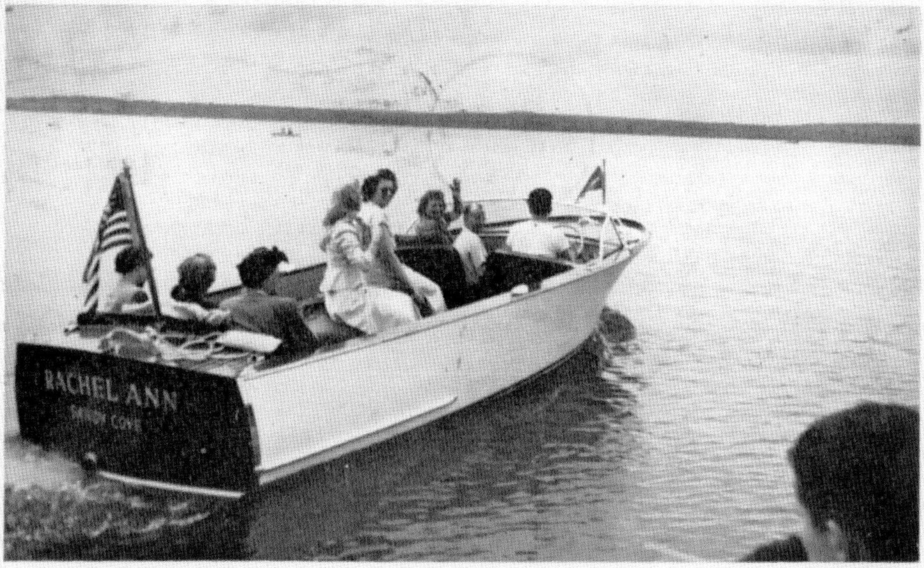

"THE SPEEDBOAT" Morning Cheer Bible Conference, Sandy Cove, North East, Maryland

Recreational boaters enjoy a cruise courtesy of Sandy Cove Ministries in this postcard c. 1949. During the Great Depression of the 1930s, Dr. George Palmer, pastor of Haddon Heights Baptist Church in Haddon Heights, New Jersey, hosted one of the earliest Christian radio broadcasts. During this time, when businesses and banks were failing, his daily *Morning Cheer* broadcast attracted many listeners. The Sandy Cove site on the Northeast River was acquired for a summer tent revival and camp meeting facility. The pier and boathouse appear in the postcard below. (Courtesy of Jack Manning.)

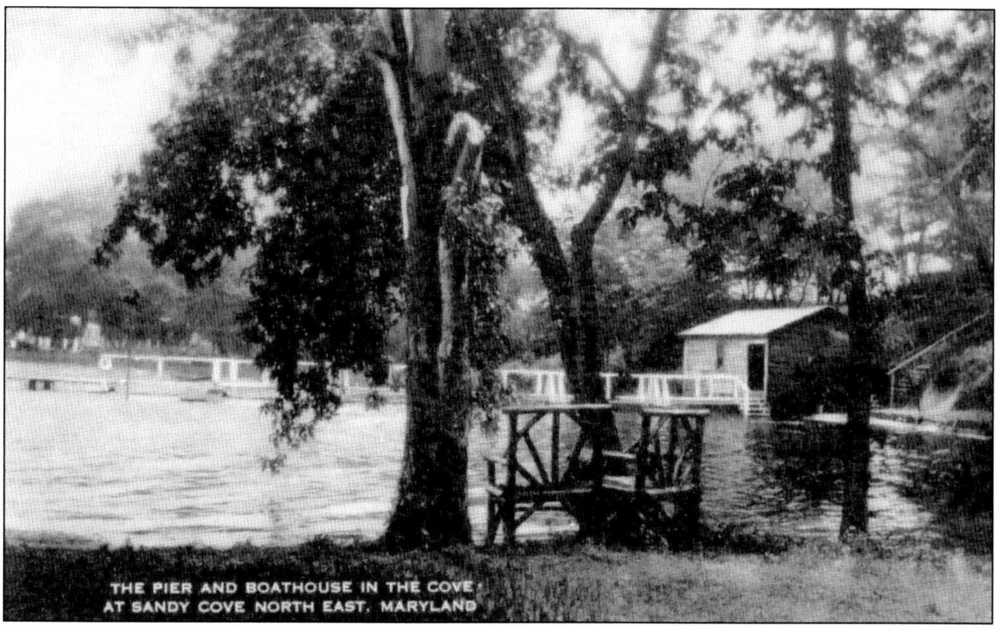

THE PIER AND BOATHOUSE IN THE COVE AT SANDY COVE NORTH EAST, MARYLAND

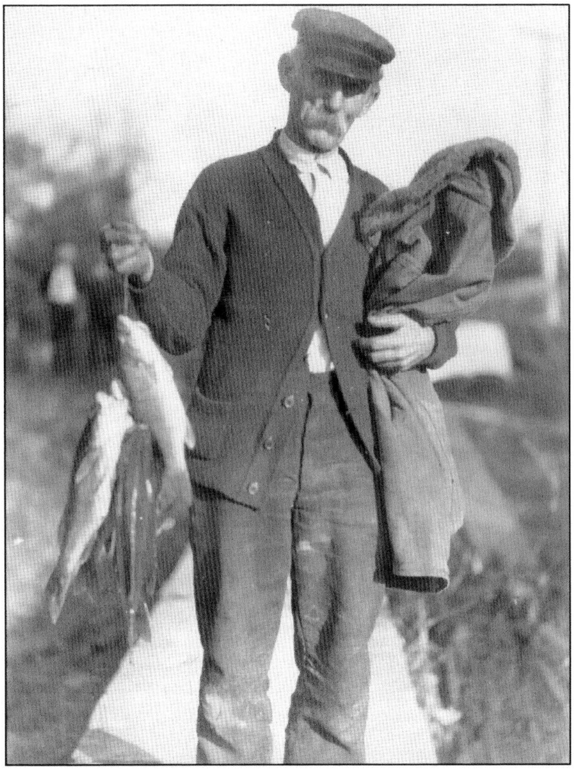

Leslie Owens Sr. of Perryville displays fresh bass taken from the lower Susquehanna *c.* 1915. During times of economic depression, fishing was not only a recreational activity for citizens of Cecil County, but also a means to procure healthy and fine-eating table fare. (Courtesy of Barbara Brown.)

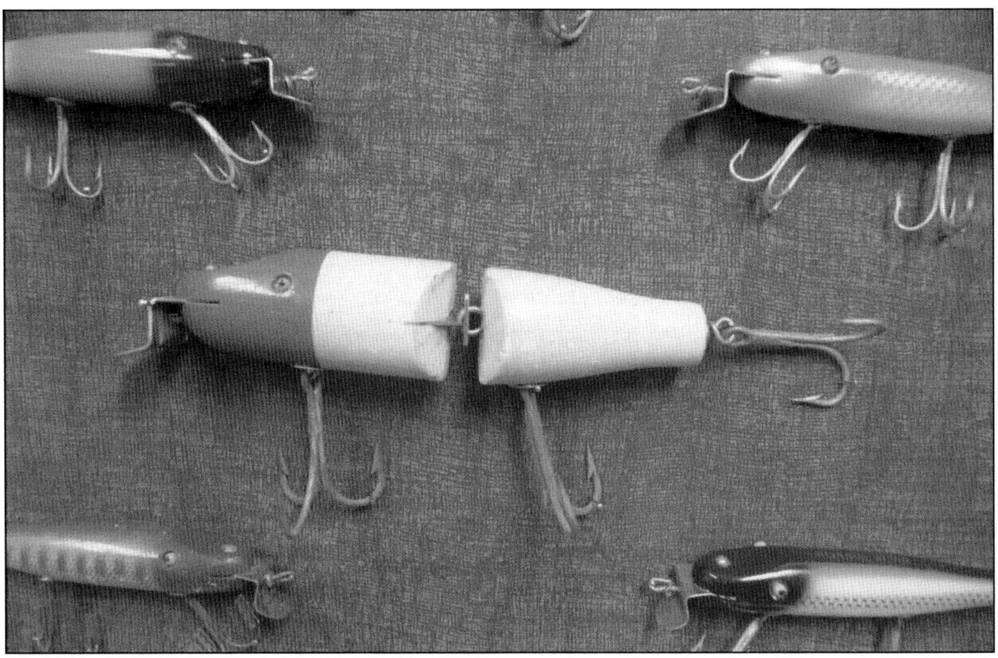

Creek Chub Bait Company's Striper Pikie, *c.* 1935, with an improved lip, is an example of lures trolled behind boats by recreational anglers in Cecil County tributaries and the main body of the Chesapeake Bay. The head was red, the body white, and the action of the lure mimicked baitfish prominent in the area. (Courtesy of Antiquated Anglers.)

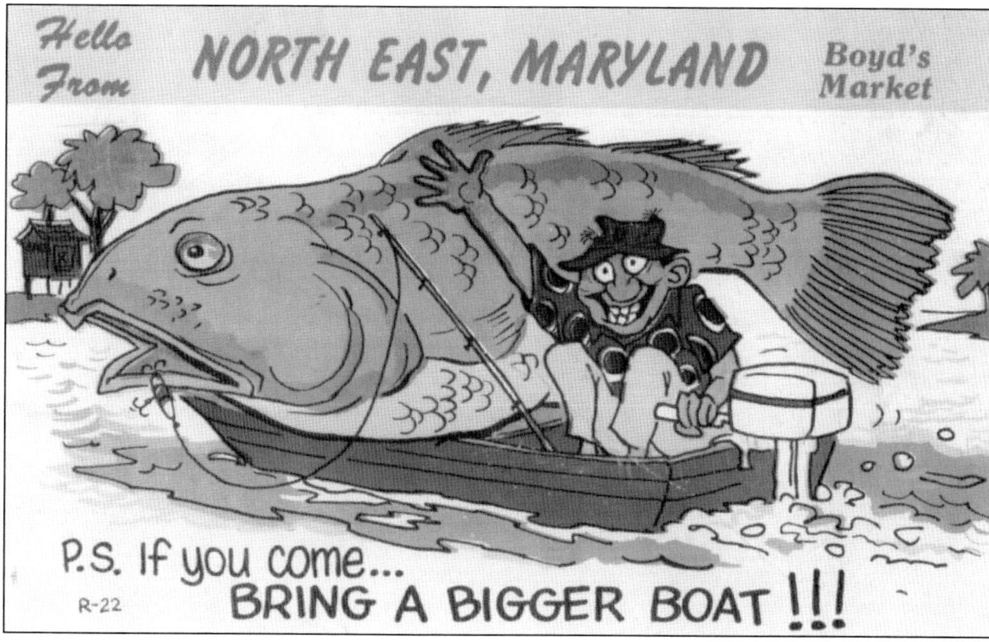

Cecil County has always been known for its fishing, with shad biting in the spring and perch, striped bass, and largemouth bass biting much of the year. These postcards presented tourists with a means to inform friends and relatives of their activities while on vacation. (Courtesy of Jack Manning.)

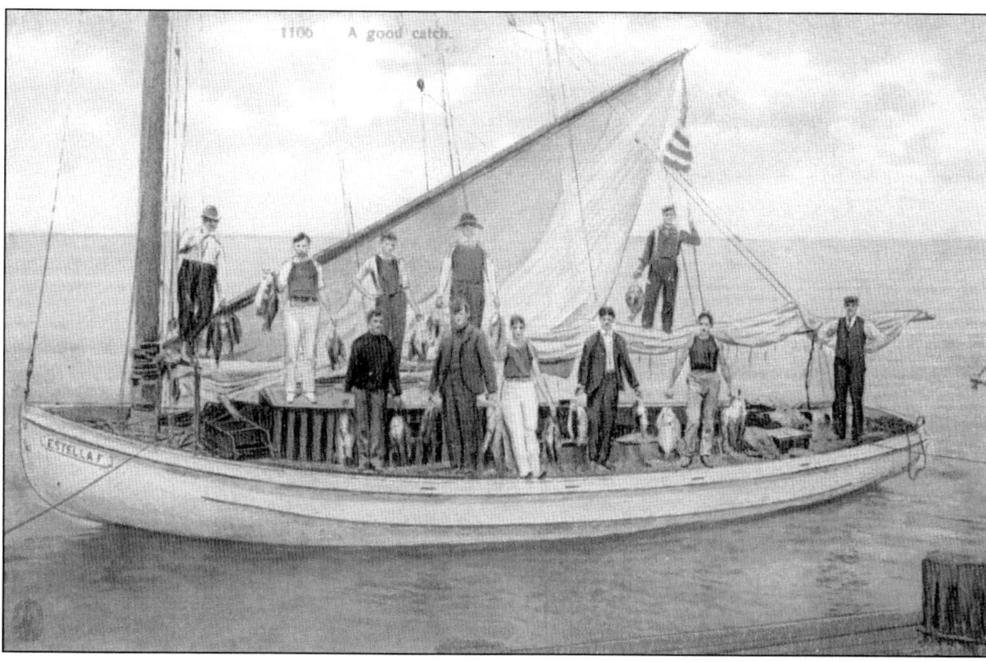

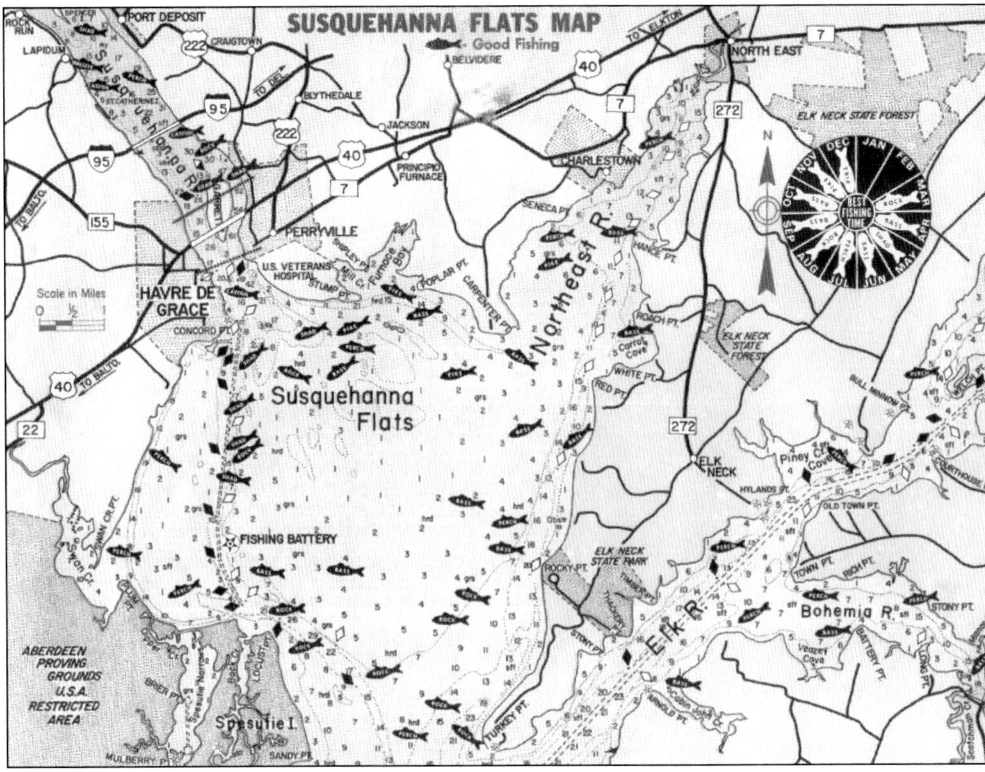

This map, which appeared in the 1969 *Fishing in Maryland* magazine, displays fishing opportunities available to anglers in the upper Chesapeake. Articles in that year's magazine included "Big Bass at the Northeast River and the Flats" and "Don't Horse that White Shad." (Courtesy of *Fishing in Maryland* magazine.)

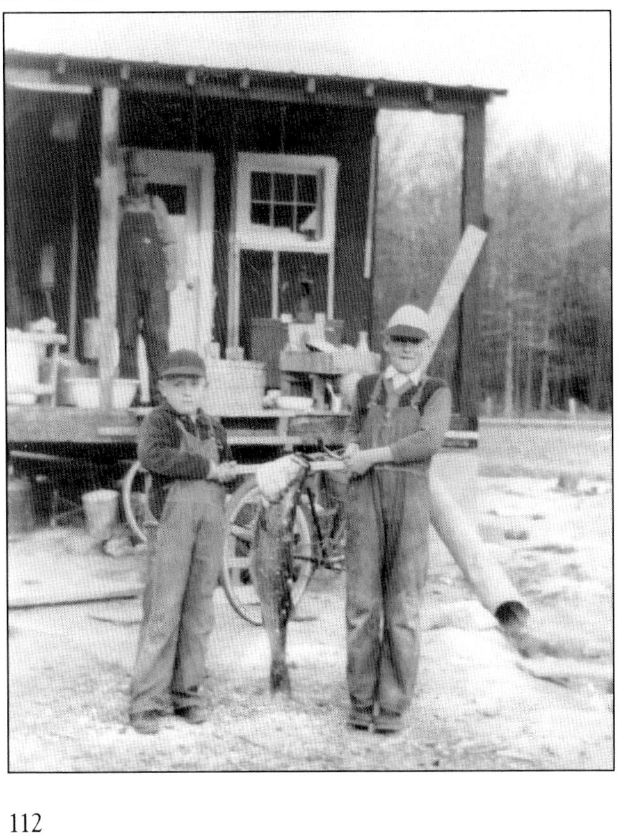
Edward, left, and Ellis Howell pose with their large striped bass caught from upper bay waters c. 1939. In the background is their father, Harry, on the porch of their home on Otts Chapel Road. Edward eventually became the owner of Edward P. Howell, Inc., a construction company on Pulaski Highway. (Courtesy of Martha Harris.)

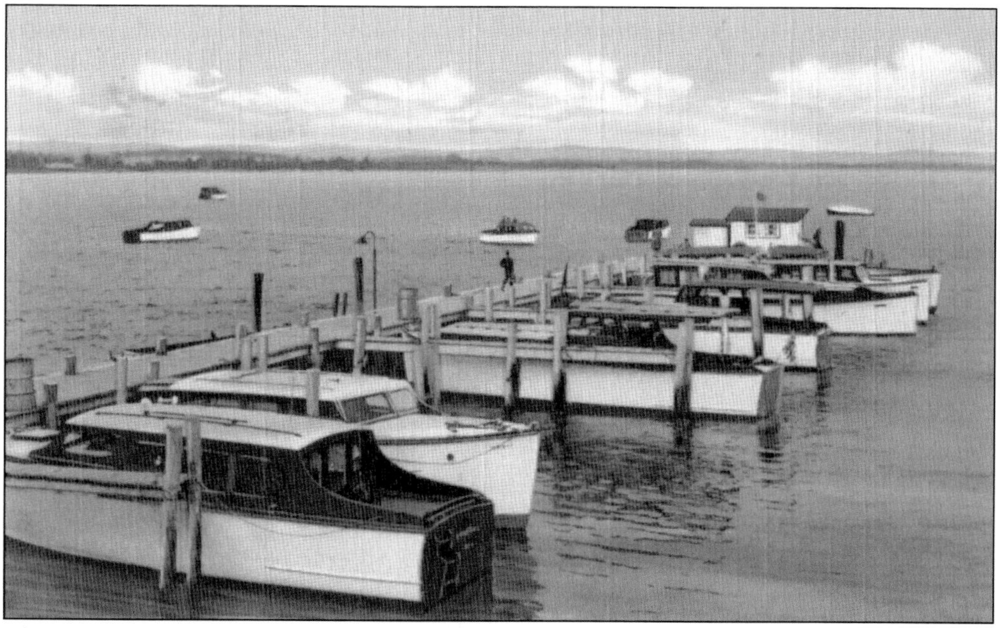

This postcard depicts a mid-20th-century scene at Bay Boat Works at Hances Point near North East. The surge of powerboating after World War II boosted boating's popularity as a family activity. Developments in hull and motor design produced craft for virtually every purse and purpose. (Courtesy of the Historical Society of Cecil County.)

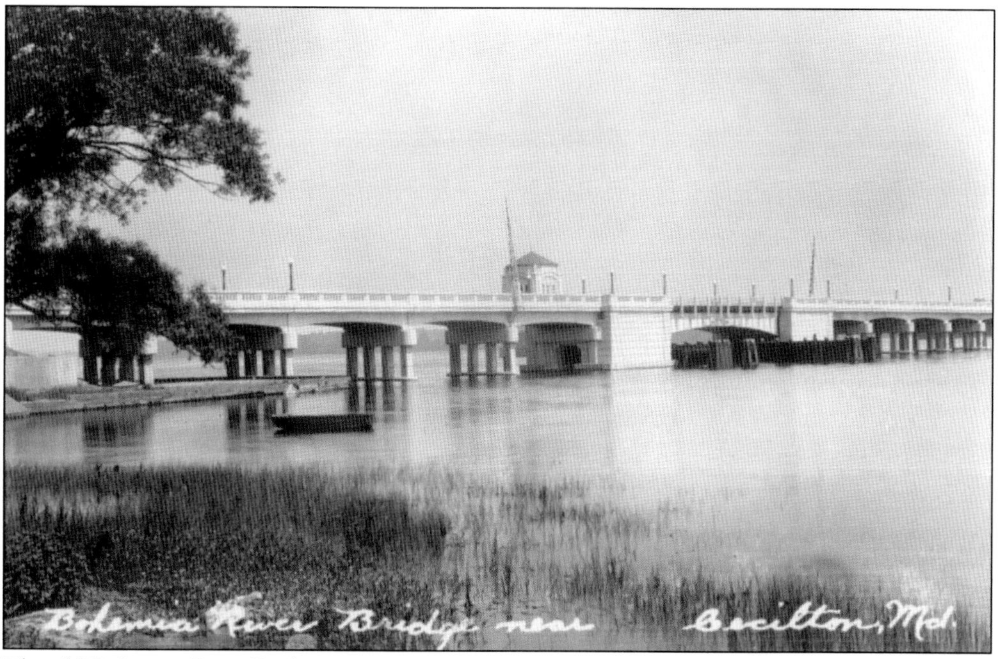

The old Bohemia River Bridge at Route 213 was a favorite location for fishermen, as reported in the 1969 *Fishing in Maryland* magazine. White perch moved into the area in mid-March with the best fishing in April and May. Catfish and striped bass could also be caught. Launching ramps and boat rentals were available at Scotchman Creek Bridge. (Courtesy of the Historical Society of Cecil County.)

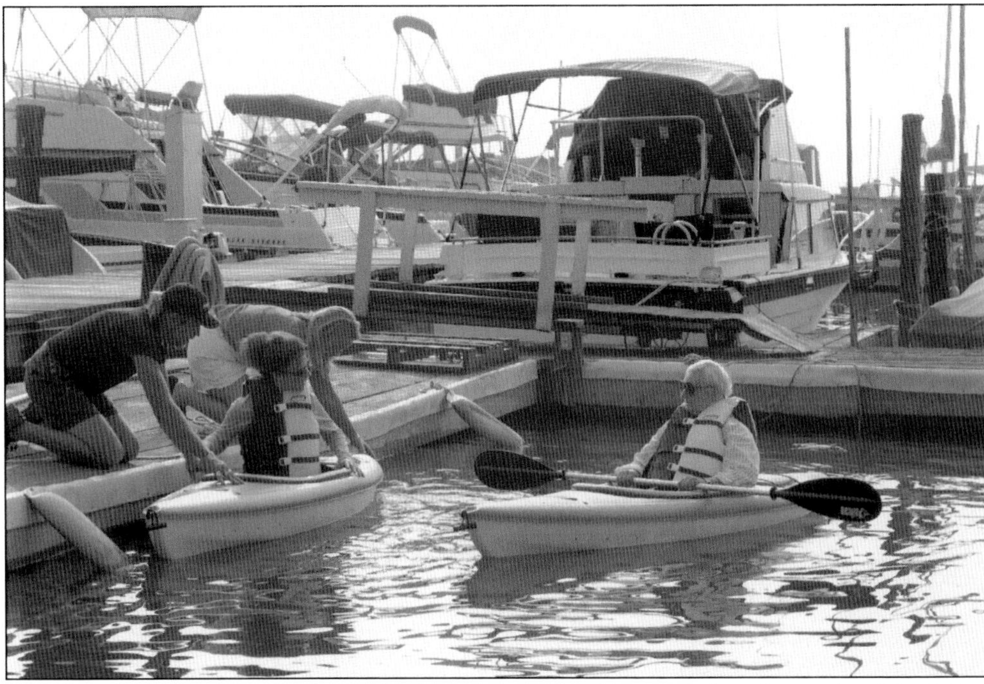

Lois Ashworth and Helen Vinick embark on the inaugural launch of kayak rentals at North East River Marina during the marina's grand opening on September 9, 2006. Helping launch the boats are Greg Newswanger and Amy DeSimone. (Courtesy of *Mariner* magazine.)

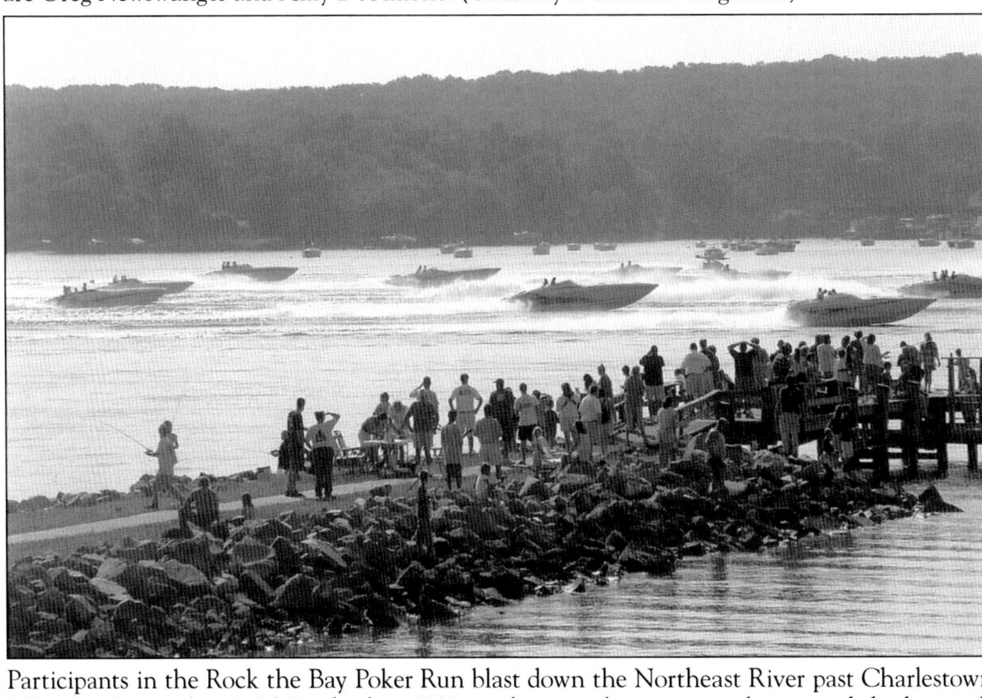

Participants in the Rock the Bay Poker Run blast down the Northeast River past Charlestown Wharf in September 2005. In the late 1990s, poker runs became popular around the bay with boaters traveling to card stops at pick-up points located on the waterways to try their luck at five-card stud for fun and charities. (Photograph by Christopher Knauss.)

Seven

MODERN MOMENTS

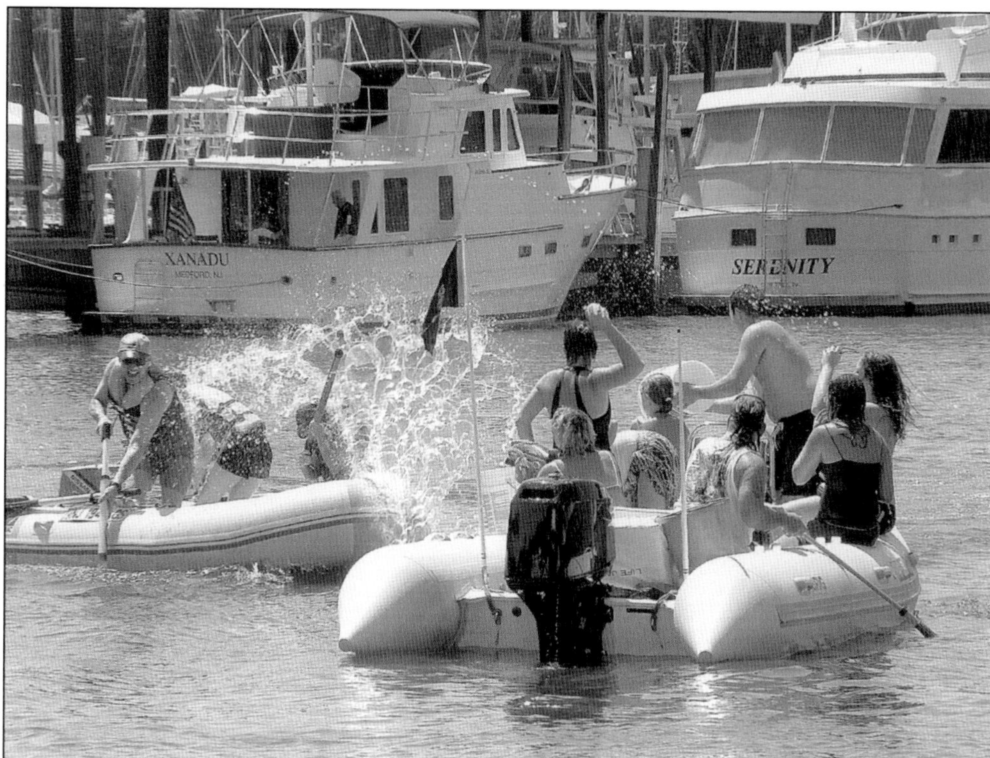

Today's maritime scene in Cecil County revolves around the warm-weather visitors interested in recreational boating and fishing and the marinas and companies that service their needs. Weekends include sailing regattas, powerboat poker runs, raft-ups, rendezvous, fishing tournaments, Jet Ski races, tubing and wakeboarding, kayaking, cruising, and partying. Developers and realtors try to meet the demand for waterfront property, and marina staffers work hard to ensure boating continues to be an enjoyable family activity. Here dinghy poker-runners battle for supremacy during a fierce battle on the Sassafras River on August 5, 2006. The Sassafras River Yacht Club hosted the fun event, which benefited the Alzheimer's Association. The big winners were Linda Slade and Carolyn Eachus, who drew a flush, ace high. (Courtesy of *Mariner* magazine.)

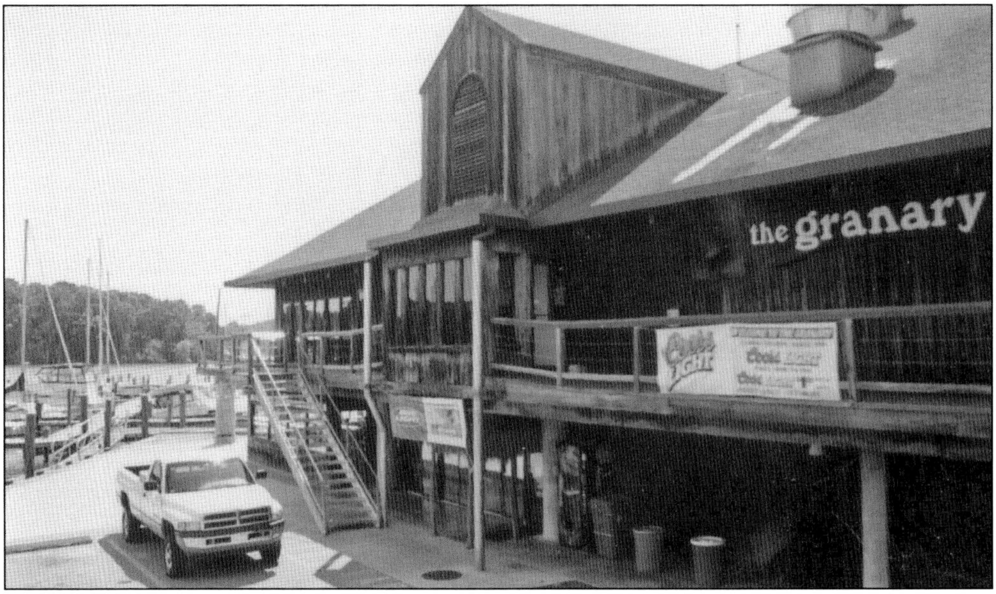

The Granary Restaurant and Marina on the Sassafras River in Fredericktown is a converted grain warehouse dating back to the 1820s. Two of the old grain bins now serve as dining areas with hand-hewn beams and preserved floorboards. The exact date of construction is unknown, but 1887 documents show that Ben Walmsley purchased the building for the storage of corn and grain for shipment to Baltimore. The restaurant site was also the location of Fort Duffy, built in 1812 as a defense against the British. (Photograph by Christopher Knauss.)

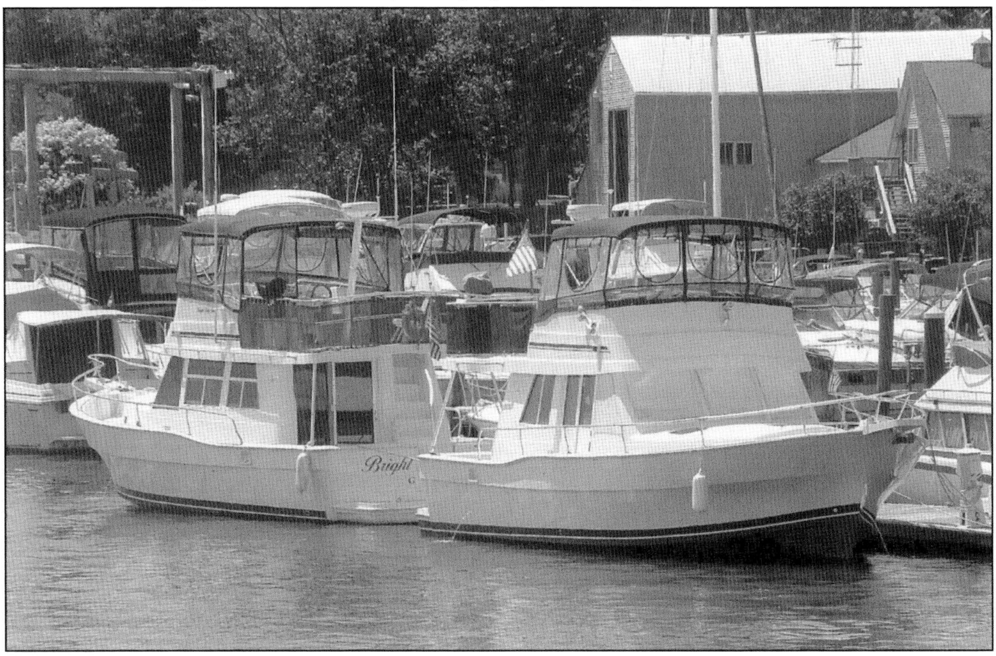

Mainship trawlers are docked stern-to-stern at the Sassafras River Harbor Marina during an owner's club rendezvous in August 2006. Owner's club gatherings are another way boaters congregate to swap sea stories, make friends, and learn different ways to maintain their craft. (Courtesy of *Mariner* magazine.)

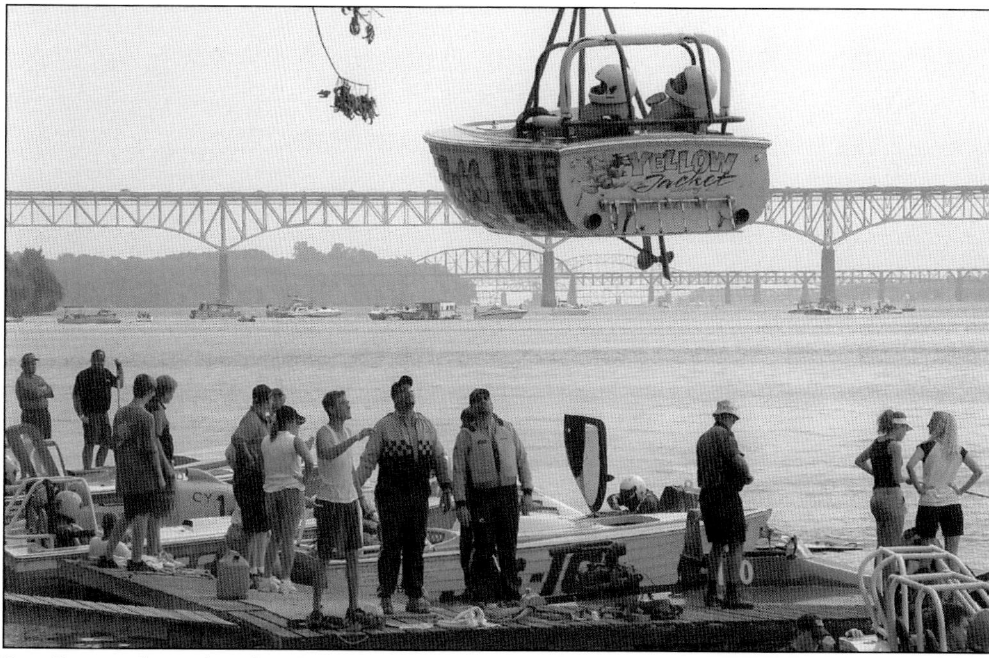

Port Deposit hosted its first Ragin' on the River powerboat races at Marina Park on Labor Day weekend in 2004. American Power Boat Association racers visited from all over the United States and Canada to compete in the event. A portion the race proceeds for this annual two-day race is donated to the Boys and Girls Club of Cecil County. (Photograph by Christopher Knauss.)

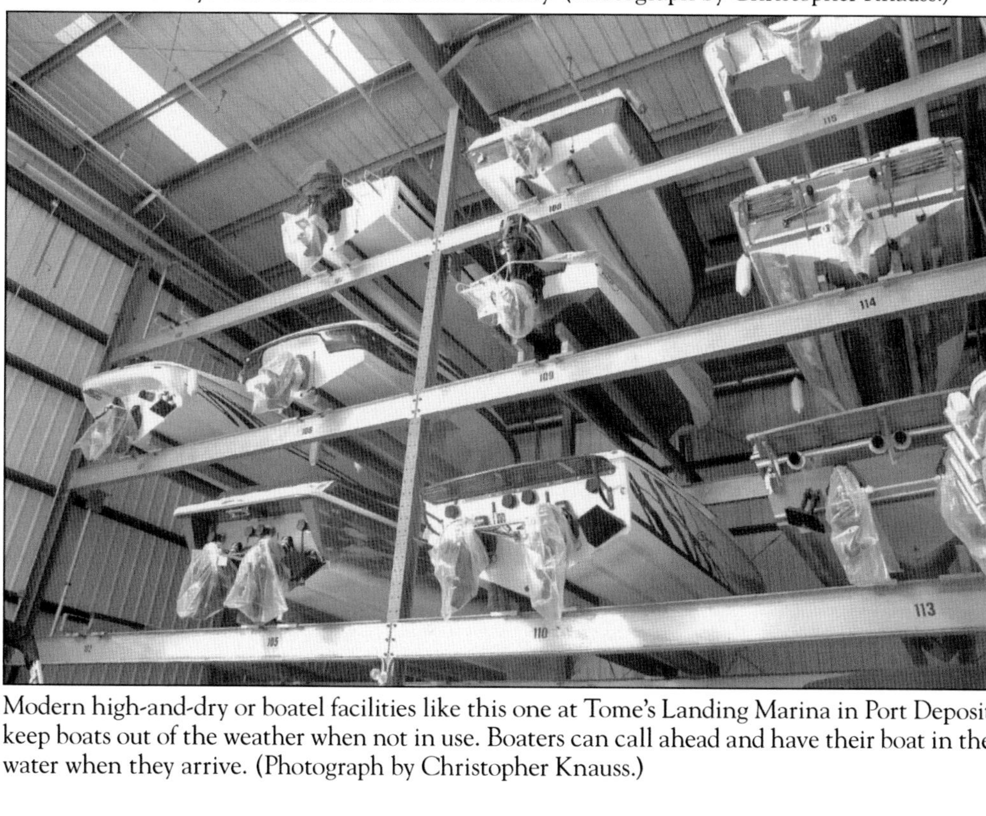

Modern high-and-dry or boatel facilities like this one at Tome's Landing Marina in Port Deposit keep boats out of the weather when not in use. Boaters can call ahead and have their boat in the water when they arrive. (Photograph by Christopher Knauss.)

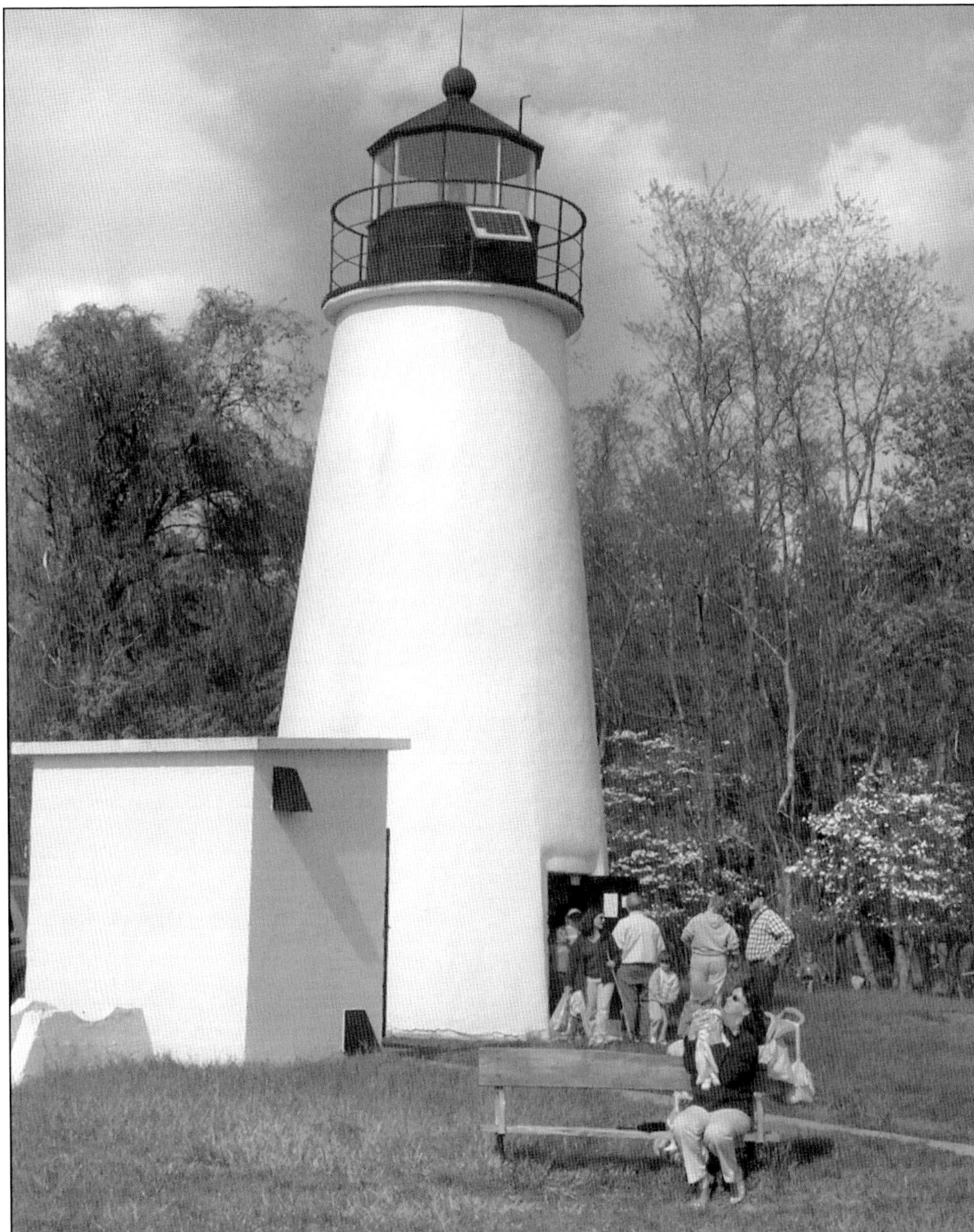

Hiking is a popular activity at Elk Neck State Park, thanks to the spectacular views of the water from the bluffs of the peninsula. The Turkey Point Lighthouse Trail is the most popular hike, featuring an easy, wide trail with a few gentle hills. The round-trip distance is 3.2 miles. The lighthouse stands on cliffs that rise 100 feet above the waves of the Chesapeake, presenting breathtaking views. Now completely automated, shown here in 2005, the lighthouse remains in operation and has been important to navigation since 1833. (Photograph by Christopher Knauss.)

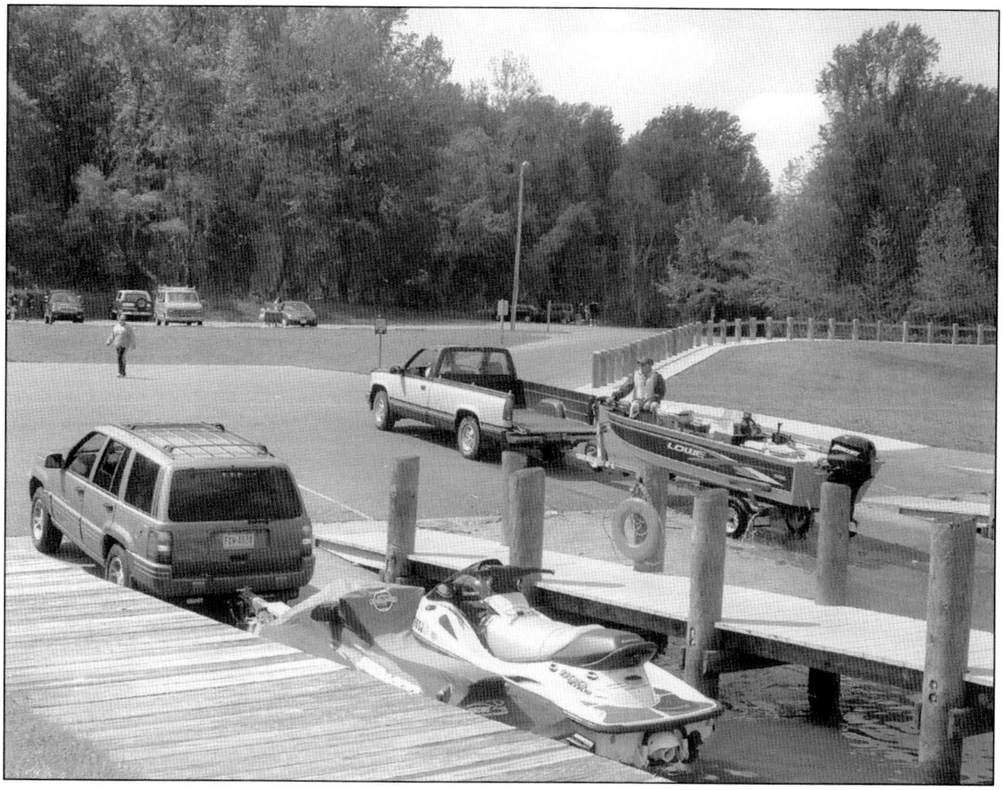

Elk Neck State Park's Rogues Harbor boating facility opened to the public on May 7, 1983. Boat ramps at the park had been open two years prior, but the pier, concession buildings, roadways, and parking area were completed in 1983. This facility sees plenty of use today for trailered boats, including Jet Skis, fishing boats, and water sports. Below, tubers enjoy a ride behind a powerboat alongside the shores of the park. (Photographs by Christopher Knauss.)

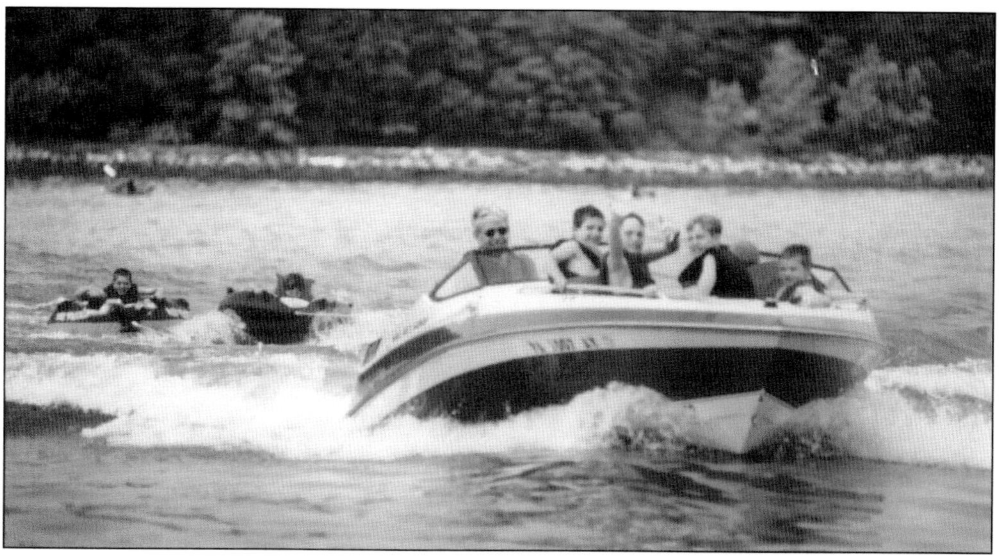

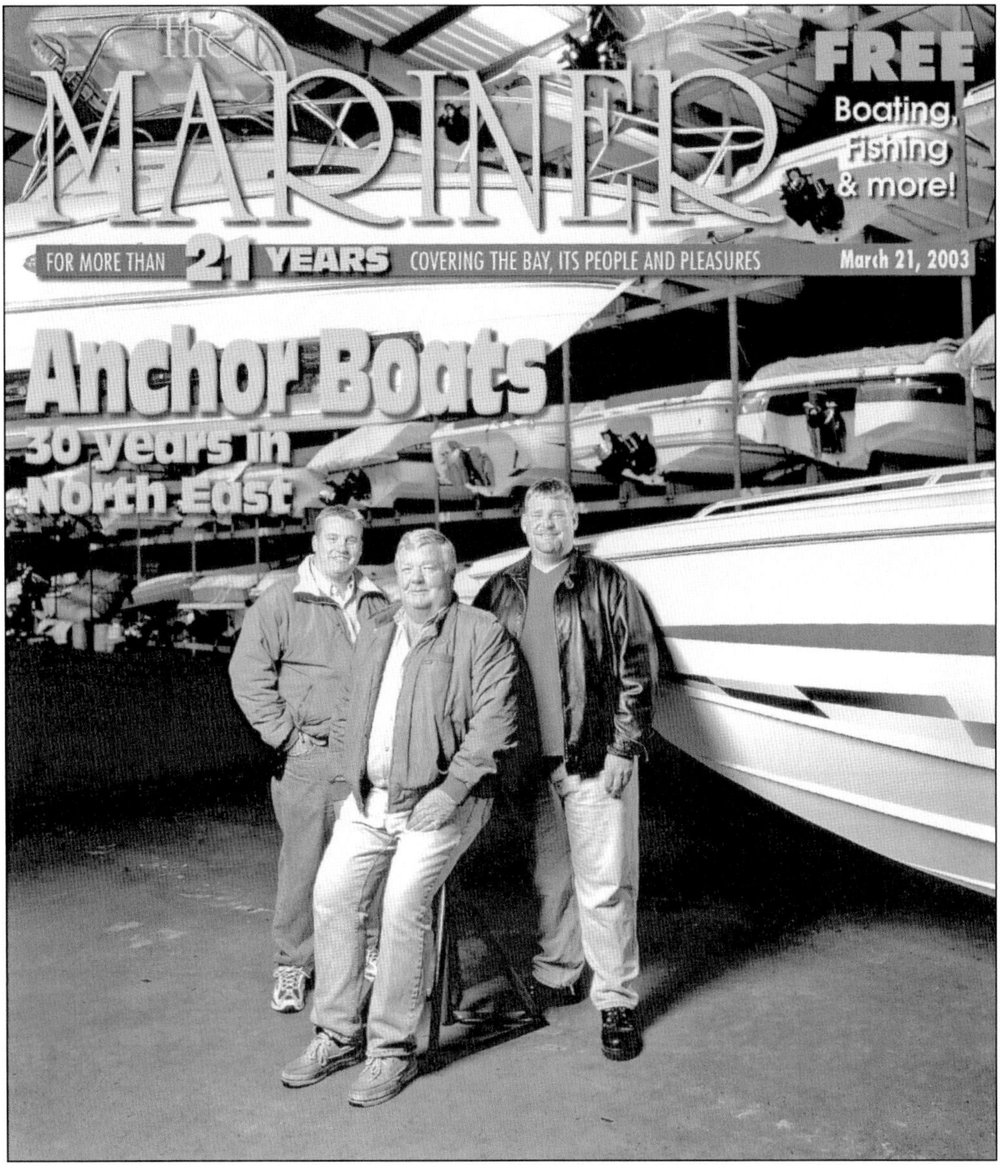

Chesapeake Publishing's *Mariner* magazine was introduced to Cecil County's boating scene on June 17, 1982. Targeting the many boaters frequenting the county's waterways, the publication was presented as a "Guide to Boating and Leisure on the Chesapeake Bay." Originally printed just five times a year, the *Mariner* has evolved into a magazine published 23 times a year and distributed to 700 locations around the bay. Featured on this cover is the Trainer family—Matt (left), Butch (center), and Ed—of Anchor Boats, at their high-and-dry facility in North East. Butch Trainer began the business as a sporting goods shop on Route 272 in the late 1960s. He closed the shop and opened Anchor Boats just down the street in 1973 and later, around 1980, opened Anchor Marina at North East harbor. Today the two businesses are thriving, with Butch's sons Matt and Ed handling daily operations. (Courtesy of *Mariner* magazine.)

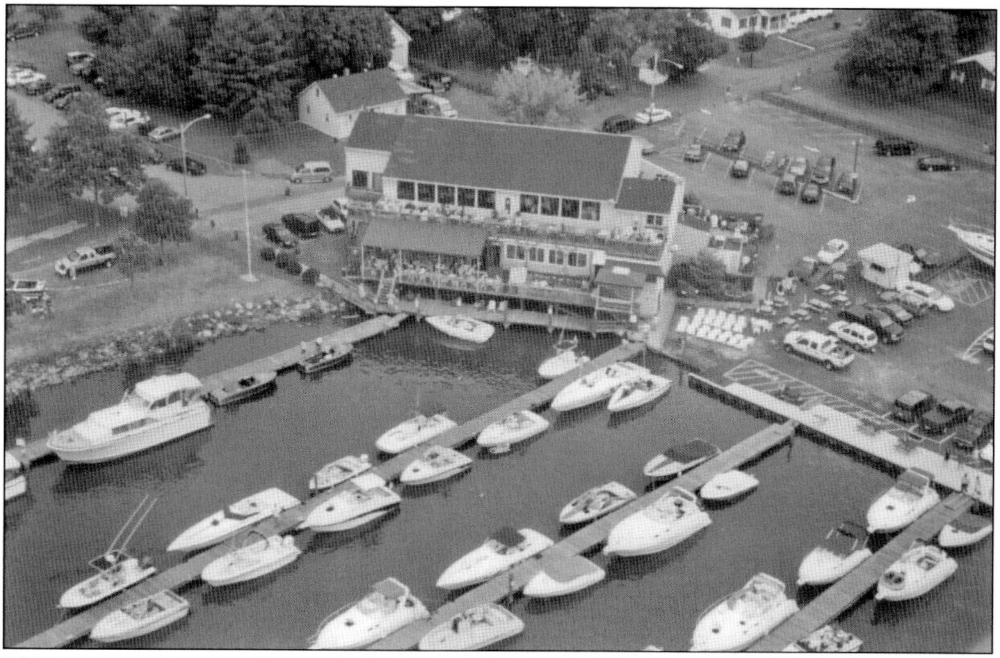

This is an aerial view of boats docked at Anchor Marina in North East and the Nauti-Goose Saloon. This site hosts poker run tournaments, fishing tournaments, and the annual Upper Bay Boat Show, the largest gathering of new and used boats on the upper Chesapeake Bay, held the first weekend in May. (Courtesy of *Mariner* magazine.)

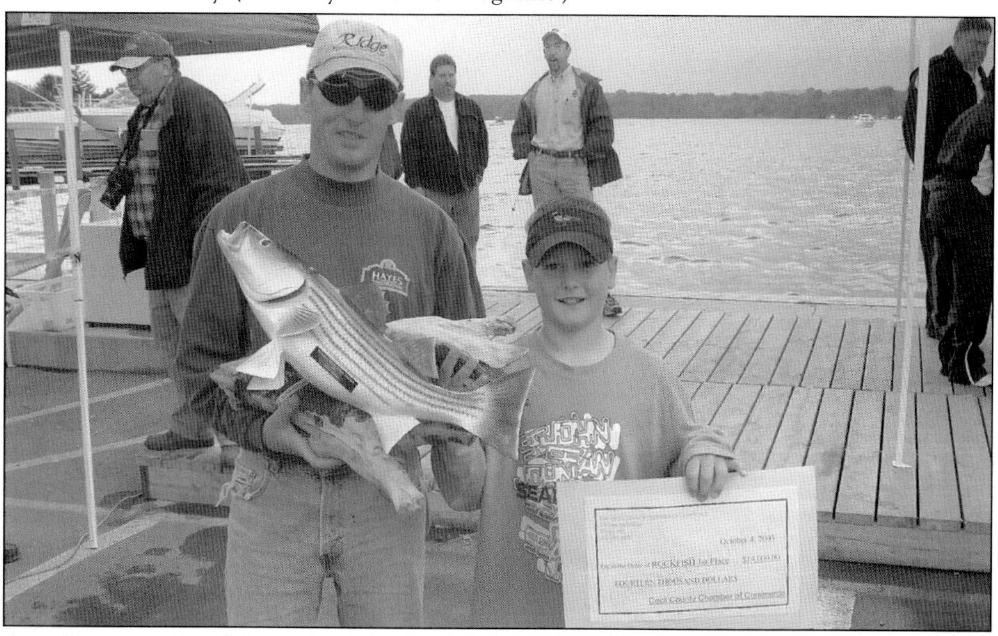

Ryan Popp, age 10, of Kingsville, Maryland, fishing aboard his dad Jeff's 23-foot Sea Ox, reeled in an 8-pound, 8-ounce striped bass to win the 10th annual Upper Bay Rockfish Tournament on October 4, 2003. Ryan received a check for $14,000 and a Larry Ikner striped bass trophy. The event was sponsored by the Cecil County Chamber of Commerce with weigh-in at Anchor Marina. More than 400 anglers competed in the event. (Courtesy of *Mariner* magazine.)

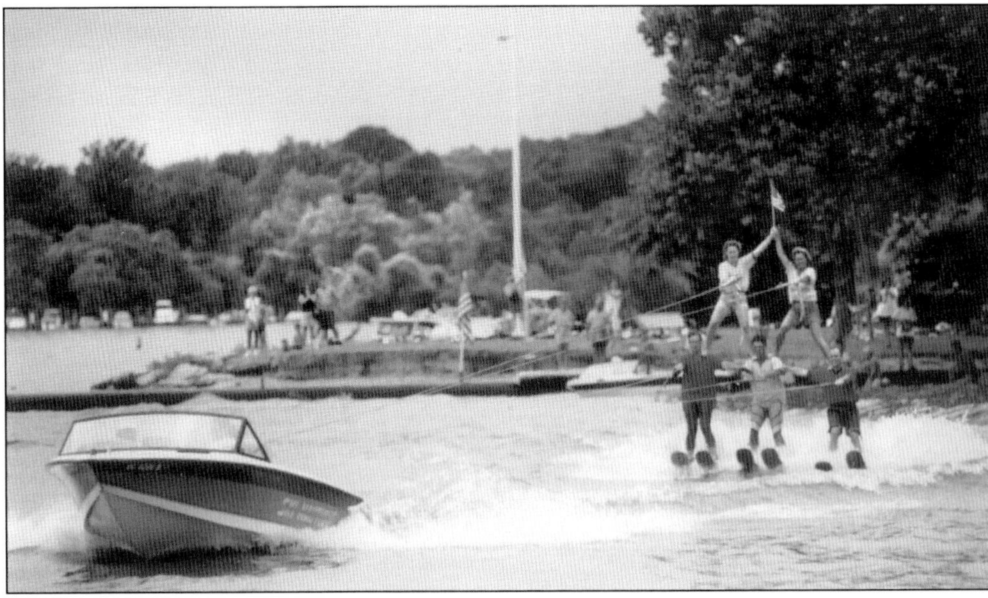

Members of the Upper Chesapeake Ski Club put on a show at the North East Waterfest. The annual event at Town Park began in 1967. Each year, thousands of families flock to the shores of the Northeast River to celebrate the culture of the upper bay. Festival features include water-oriented demonstrations, arts and crafts, new and antique boats, nautical and local history displays, watermen displays, boatbuilding demonstrations, children's activities, live music, food, and fireworks. (Courtesy of *Mariner* magazine.)

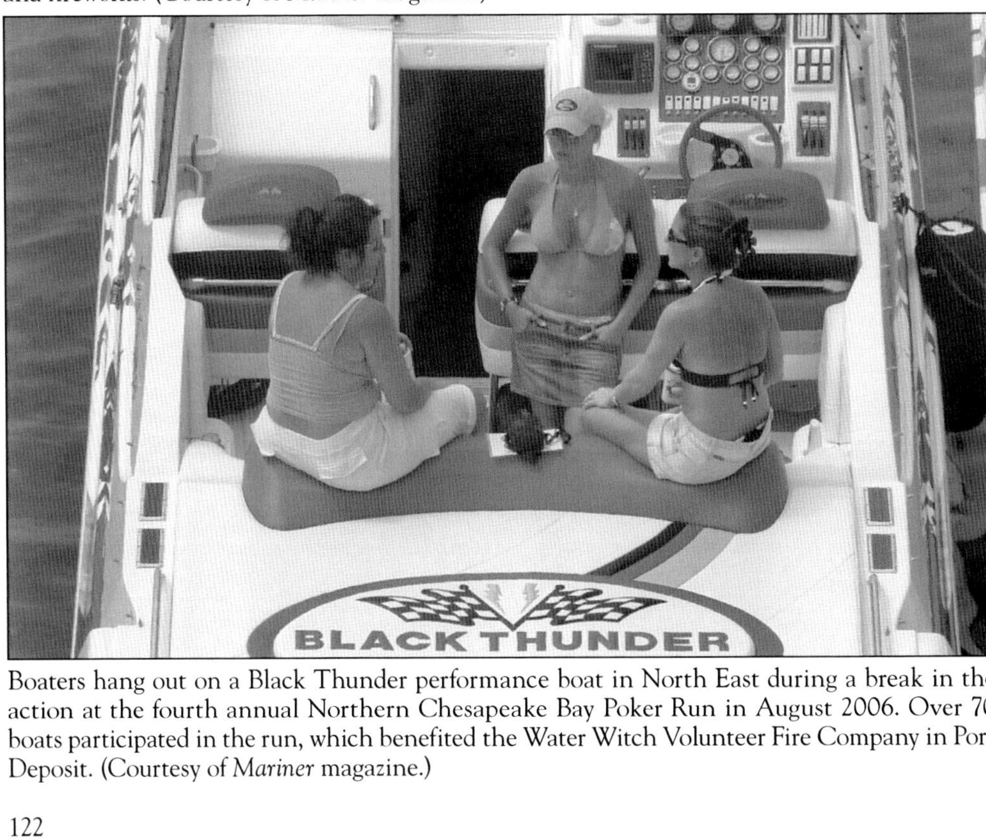

Boaters hang out on a Black Thunder performance boat in North East during a break in the action at the fourth annual Northern Chesapeake Bay Poker Run in August 2006. Over 70 boats participated in the run, which benefited the Water Witch Volunteer Fire Company in Port Deposit. (Courtesy of *Mariner* magazine.)

Here is an aerial view of Charlestown Marina, one of over 35 privately owned marinas in Cecil County providing services for boaters on the upper Chesapeake. Slip holders travel from Pennsylvania, New Jersey, Delaware, and Maryland to enjoy the waterways of the county and to take advantage of a convenient home port with easy access to the bay. (Courtesy of *Mariner* magazine.)

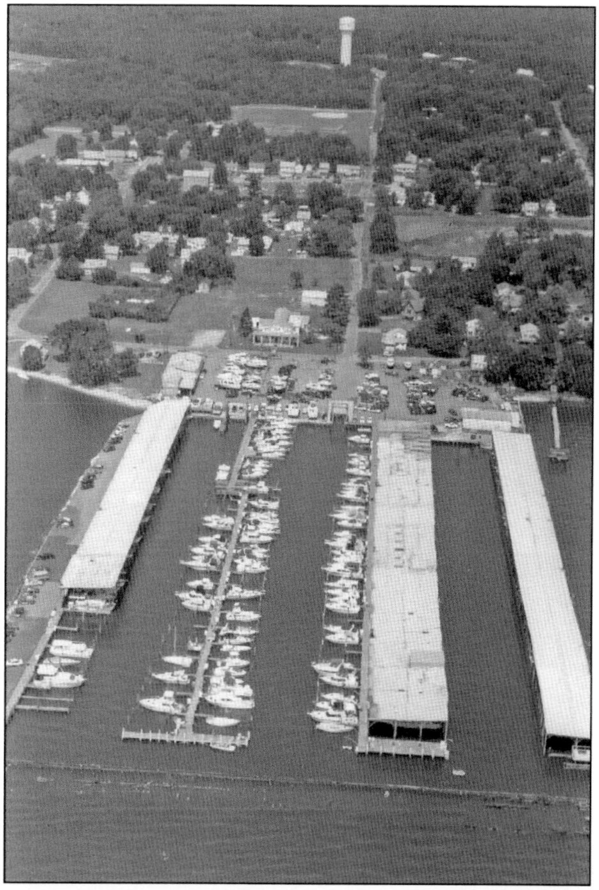

The Metz family acquired the Wellwood in Charlestown in 1958 and has restored the property to its historic charm. The Wellwood's restaurant and bar draw boaters from throughout the Chesapeake region. In 2006, the Wellwood Marina reopened, offering 51 slips and amenities, including individually metered power, cable television service, a gated dock with keypad entry, water and electricity, air-conditioned restrooms with showers facilities, and pump-out capabilities from each slip. (Photograph by Christopher Knauss.)

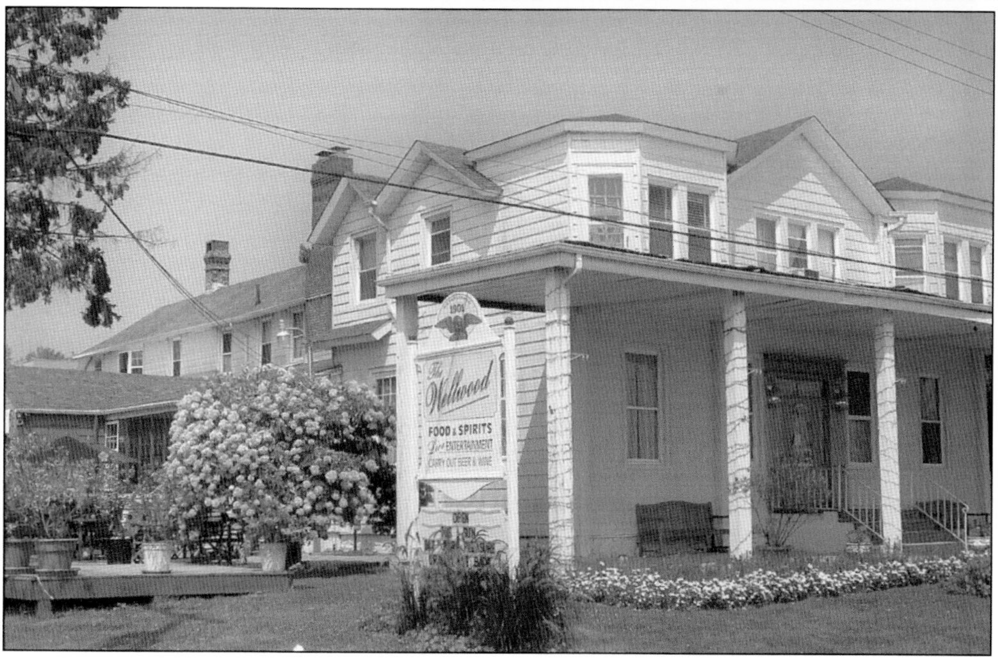

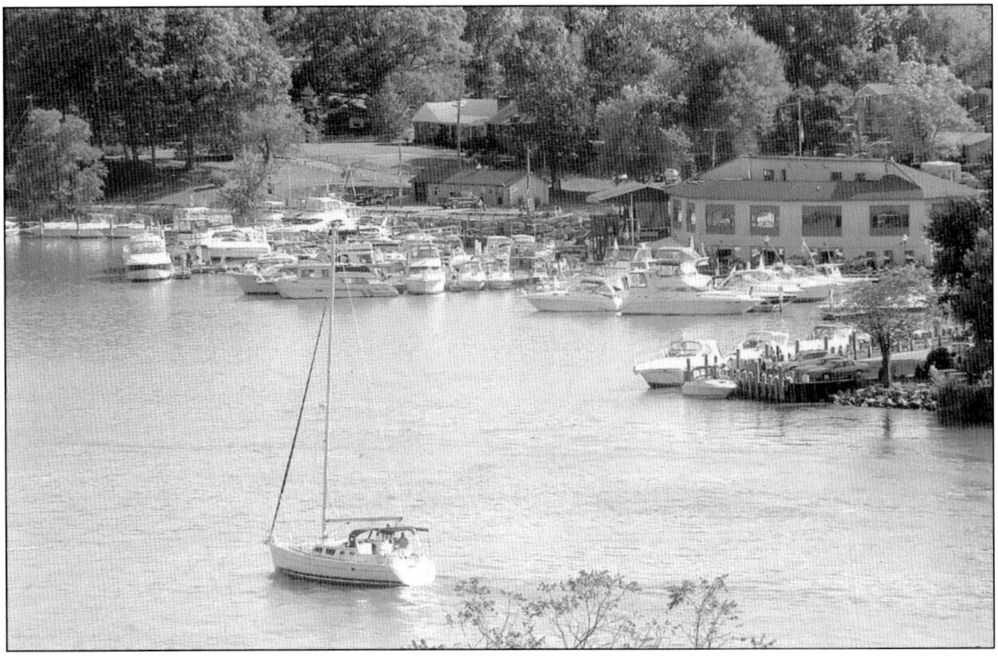

A sailboat motors east on the C&D Canal in this 2004 photograph taken from the highway bridge. In the background is Back Creek Basin and the Chesapeake Inn Restaurant and Marina, a favorite destination of Chesapeake Bay boaters and cruisers traveling intercoastal waterways in the United States. (Photograph by Christopher Knauss.)

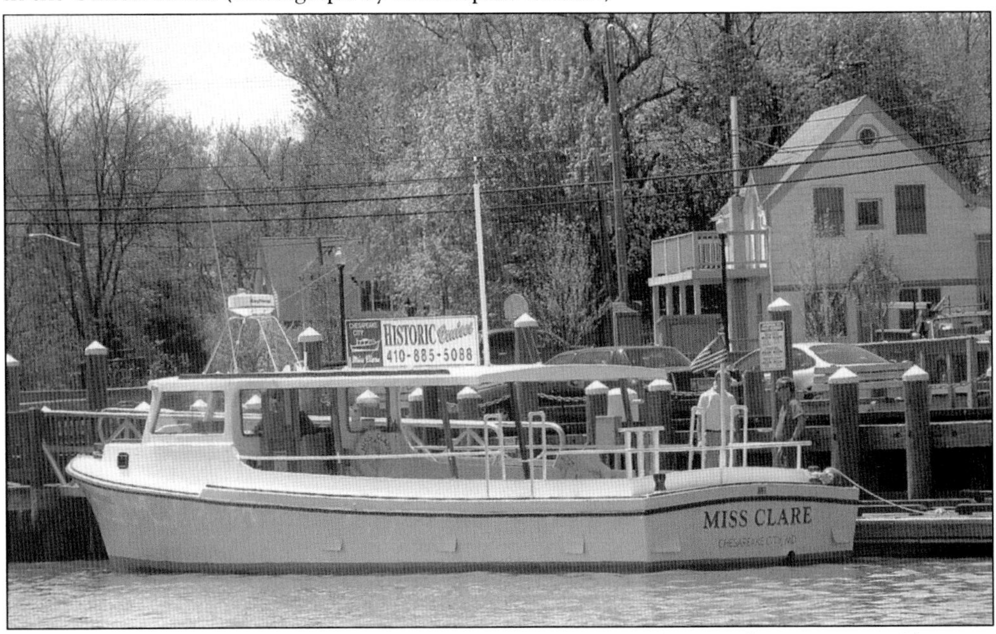

Capt. Ralph Hazel operates Miss Clare Tours out of South Chesapeake City. *Miss Clare* is a Chesapeake Bay workboat built in Cambridge, Maryland, in 1979. During excursions, Captain Hazel, a direct descendant of a mid-19th-century steamboat captain, talks about the culture of Chesapeake City and the history of the C&D Canal and the upper Chesapeake Bay. (Photograph by Christopher Knauss.)

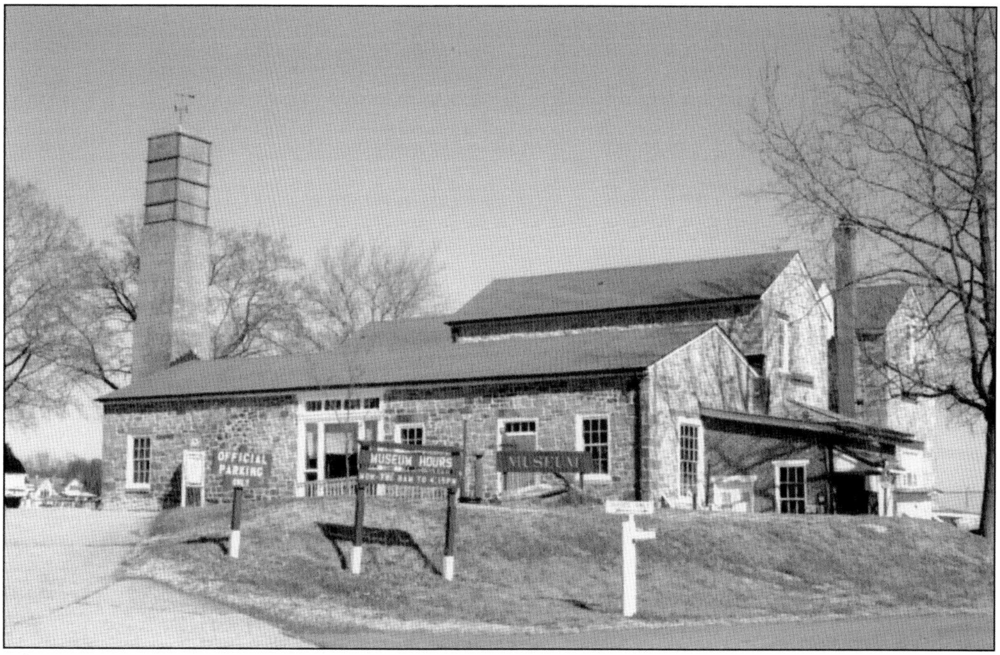

The U.S. Army Corps of Engineers' Canal Museum at Chesapeake City provides visitors with a glimpse of the canal's early days. The waterwheel and pumping engines remain in the original pump house, which is now the museum. The steam engines are the oldest of their type in America still on their original foundations. (Photograph by Christopher Knauss.)

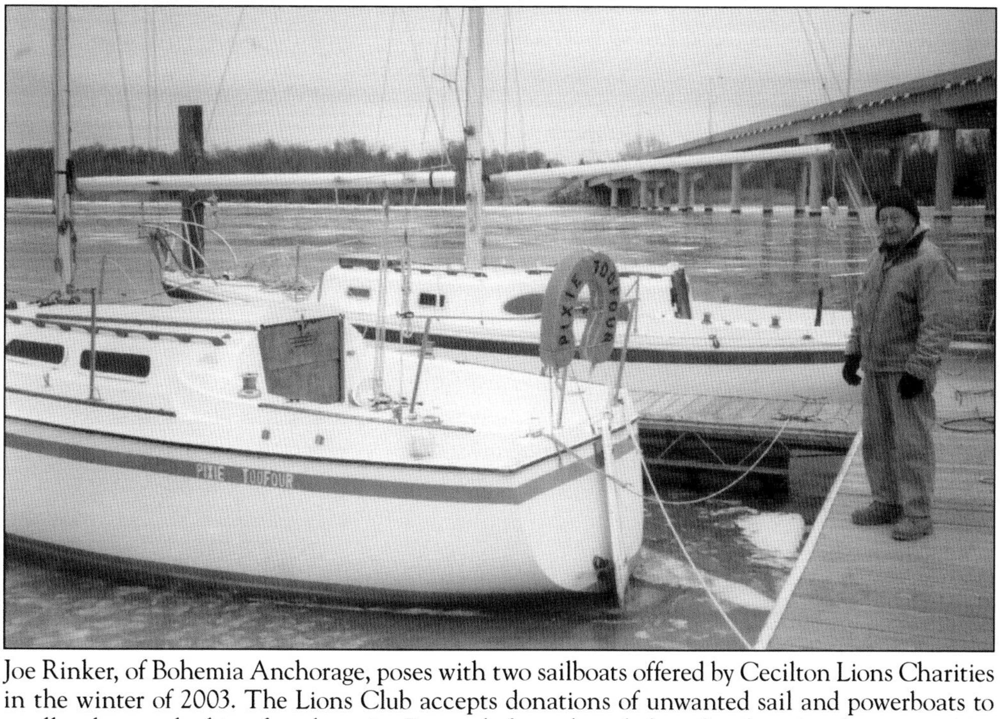

Joe Rinker, of Bohemia Anchorage, poses with two sailboats offered by Cecilton Lions Charities in the winter of 2003. The Lions Club accepts donations of unwanted sail and powerboats to resell to boaters looking for a bargain. Proceeds from the sale benefit educational opportunities and vision care for Cecil County students. (Courtesy of *Mariner* magazine.)

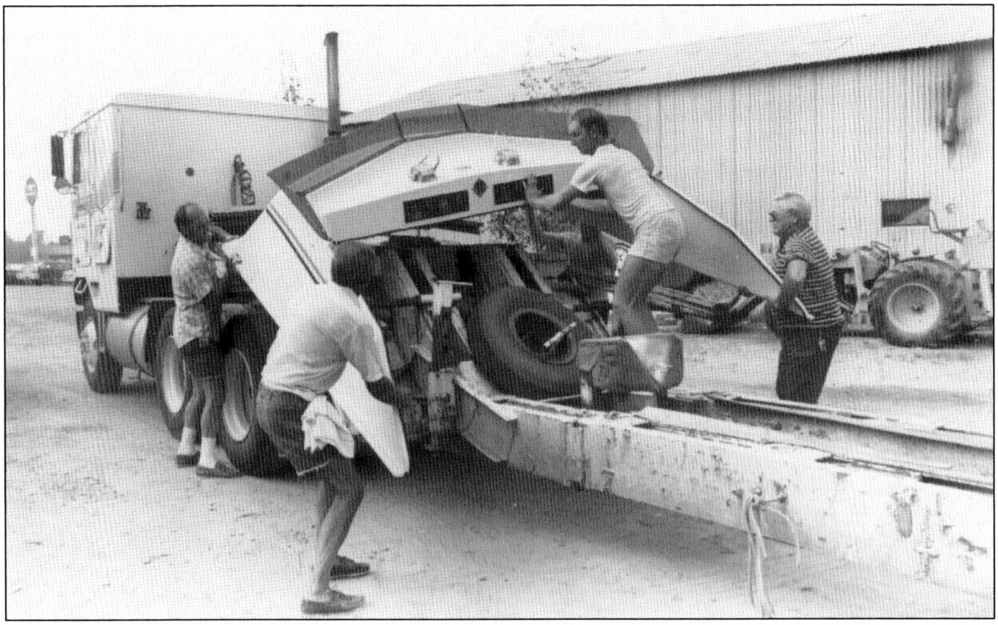

Phil Martin, left, and unidentified workers unload the bridge on a Holiday Mansion houseboat. People with normal land-based careers, Phil and Shirley Martin started the first Holiday Mansion dealership on the East Coast in the early 1980s after seeing the boat at the Annapolis Power Boat Show. They quickly grew their business at Harbour North Marina in Chesapeake City into the top Holiday Mansion dealership in the world. (Courtesy of Phil and Shirley Martin.)

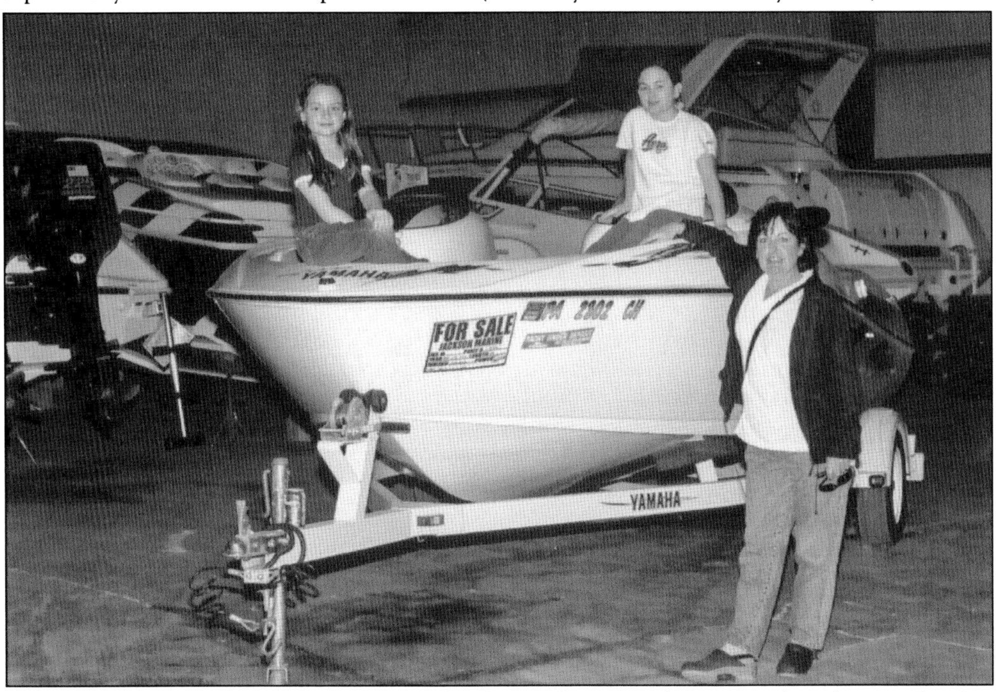

Holly Emmons of Newark, Delaware, with daughters Christie and Amy, purchased a Yamaha 270-horsepower jet boat at Jackson Marine's St. Patrick's Day Boat Show in March 2002. (Courtesy of *Mariner* magazine.)

BIBLIOGRAPHY

Brewington, M. V. *Chesapeake Bay: A Pictorial Maritime History*. 2nd ed. Centerville, MD: Bonanza Books, 1956.
Hazel, Robert. *Riding the Ferry and Other Adventures*. Chesapeake City, MD: Rare Harmony Publishing Company, 2001.
Healy, David. *1812: Rediscovering Chesapeake Bay's Forgotten War*. Rock Hill, SC: Bella Rosa Books, 2005.
Johnston, George. *History of Cecil County, Maryland*. Elkton, MD: Genealogical Publishing Company, Inc., 1881.
Jones, Carleton. *Maryland: A Picture History, 1632–1976*. Baltimore: Bodine and Associates, Inc., 1976.
Miller, Alice E. *Cecil County, Maryland: A Study in Local History*. Elkton, MD: C and L Printon Company, 1949.
Mills, Eric. *Chesapeake Bay in the Civil War*. Centerville, MD: Tidewater Publishers, 1996. Morgan, Karen T., and Kevin J. Titter. *Chesapeake City: The Canal Town Through the Years*. Chesapeake City, MD: Briscoe Hill Publishers, 2000.
Shannahan, John H. K. *Steamboat'n' Days and the Hammond Lot*. Baltimore, MD: The Olympic Press, 1930.
Shomette, Donald G. *Lost Towns of Tidewater Maryland*. Centerville, MD: Tidewater Publishers, 2000.
www.archives.gov
www.cchistory.org
www.cecilbusiness.org
www.charlestownmd.org
www.chesapeakecity.com
www.fleeco.net/Published/Schaefers/Schaefer/Schaefer%20History.htm
www.loc.gov
www.msa.md.gov/msa/homepage/html/homepage.html
www.northeastchamber.org
www.perryvillemd.org
www.portdeposit.com
www.seececil.org